Israel and the Quest for Permanence

Israel and the Quest for Permanence

DAN PERRY
with ALFRED IRONSIDE

McFarland & Company, Inc., Publishers
Jefferson, North Carolina, and London

For Maya

All photographs except the first (page 15) were provided by the Israeli Government Press Office photograph archive. The poem "On the Mouth of the Volcano" by Dan Almagor is reproduced by permission of Dan Almagor.

> The present work is a reprint of the softcover edition of Israel and the Quest for Permanence, first published in 1999 by McFarland.

LIBRARY OF CONGRESS CATALOGUING-IN-PUBLICATION DATA

Perry, Dan, 1963–
    Israel and the quest for permanence / by Dan Perry with Alfred Ironside.
        p. cm.
    Includes bibliographical references (p.) and index.

    ISBN 978-0-7864-7401-1
    softcover : acid free paper ∞

    1. National characteristics, Israeli. 2. Jews — Israel — Identity. 3. Israel — History — 1967–1993. 4. Israel — History — 1993– 5. Arab-Israeli conflict. 6. Israel — Ethnic relations. 7. Israel — Social conditions. 8. Judaism — Israel. I. Ironside, Alfred. II. Title.
DS113.3.P47   2012
956.9405 — dc21   99-22620

BRITISH LIBRARY CATALOGUING DATA ARE AVAILABLE

© 1999 Dan Perry and Alfred Ironside. All rights reserved

No part of this book may be reproduced or transmitted in any form or by any means, electronic or mechanical, including photocopying or recording, or by any information storage and retrieval system, without permission in writing from the publisher.

Manufactured in the United States of America

McFarland & Company, Inc., Publishers
  Box 611, Jefferson, North Carolina 28640
    www.mcfarlandpub.com

Acknowledgments

It is impossible to list all the people who helped with the creation of this book, knowingly and unknowingly, over the decades that my life has been intertwined with Israel's. Nevertheless, I will never forget the many Israelis—Jews and Arabs—who opened their minds and hearts and whose words and stories are related in these pages. In particular, I'd like to thank Yossi Beilin, Amos Oz, Haim Yavin, and a number of professors and scholars who gave very generously of their time.

Some material in the historical passages is gleaned from other books mentioned in the bibliography, and the relating of more current events has been aided by reports on the pages of Israel's major dailies, *Ha'aretz*, *Yediot Aharonot*, *Maariv*, and the *Jerusalem Post*. In many cases I was a witness to historical events myself, as so many Israelis so frequently are.

The manuscript, in various forms, benefited greatly from the critical comments of Marco Greenberg, Chris Riback, Richard Brecher, Andy Goldberg, my parents, my wife, and others.

Last but not least, my profound gratitude to Nick Tatro, whose advice and understanding beyond the call of duty were critical to the project.

—Dan Perry

Contents

Acknowledgments   v
Preface   1
Introduction: Nation   3

Part I. Emergence

1. Victory   15
2. Settlement   23
3. Disillusion   41
4. Light   57
5. Darkness   77
6. Emergence   93

Part II. Beyond

7. Citizens   117
8. Siblings   135
9. God   157
10. Beyond   179

Bibliography   203
Index   205

Preface

This book was co-authored by my friend and colleague Alfred Ironside. I have known Alfred for over 20 years, and our paths have crossed more than a few times since our days as high school journalists together. When he visited Israel in 1996 and made a decision to move to Tel Aviv later that year, he approached me with an idea for a book. This is the outgrowth of that conversation.

In time, we realized that the story would be better and more powerful if told in the first person. But while the story follows my own experiences — both personal and professional — the finished work truly owes as much to Alfred's contributions as to mine. Based on our first conversations, I cobbled together an early draft. From that point forward, we labored together. We prepared a proposal and pitched it to agents and publishers together, wrote and reorganized text late into the night at each other's homes, and over a period of months redrafted and expanded the manuscript to more than double its original size. We conducted many of the interviews in tandem, traveled throughout the country together, and made every important decision about the book as a team.

Parts of the manuscript originally drafted by Alfred and parts originally drafted by me blend together throughout the book. In a few spots in the story Alfred appears along with me. In many others at which he was present the reader will find no note of him. His presence is noted here.

Without Alfred, there would simply have been no book.

—Dan Perry

When you read in the papers about a volcano eruption in Sicily
About the burying of two whole villages in Chile or India,
You ask yourself "Why? Why do the farmers return to the slopes that betrayed them?
Why don't they flee to a safer place?"…
And then sometimes you meet a tourist, and he asks
"Tell me, why do you insist on living on the mouth of the volcano?
Why not move to a safer place where you can live in peace once and for all?"…
And then you understand the farmer on the Chimborazo
And the mother on the Fujisan, and the child on the Vesuvius.
Certainly they also know the world has calmer places.
They are waiting for the day when the volcano grows silent.

— *"On the Mouth of the Volcano" by Dan Almagor,
translated from the Hebrew by Dan Perry*

Introduction: Nation

What ties someone to a certain piece of earth?
What makes people "a people," and why does the notion of being a people obsess them so?
On June 7, 1998, just a few weeks after the formal celebration of the fiftieth anniversary of the State of Israel, a special public meeting of the New Israeli Opera was held in an auditorium in Tel Aviv.
For all of the opera's short life, and for all the life of the state, the live, public performance of works by German composer Richard Wagner had, by general consent, been prohibited in Israel. The public hearing was convened to consider whether that taboo should finally be lifted.
Wagner had been an anti–Semite, it was well known. But more importantly, his music was closely associated with the Nazi regime of Adolf Hitler. Thousands of survivors of the Holocaust could never forget the sound of Wagner's music being played on loudspeakers as other Jews were being sent to their deaths in the camps.
The meeting was rancorous. The chairman of the New Israeli Opera, Zalman Shoval, was against the NIO breaking the taboo. The institution's musical director, Asher Fisch, supported by most members of the board, was an advocate.
When Shoval tried to say that there was no place for Wagner in an Israeli opera house, he was shouted down. And there was sustained applause when Fisch suggested that the Wagner prohibition was an anachronism, a leftover from a bygone era, and that the time had come to move on. It seemed that perhaps the tide was finally turning against a sentimental deference to the dwindling Holocaust generation.
But when, midway through the meeting, Fisch prepared to perform a brief piano-baritone duet from Wagner's *The Flying Dutchman*— unannounced in the promotional mailing for the gathering— there was an uproar. According to news-

paper accounts, dozens of people stormed out of the hall in protest, some shouting, "Rape!" and "This is unthinkable!"

The show of emotion made its mark. There would be no live performance of Wagner in Israel that night. The old order of things — the old consensus — had won out one more time.

Throughout Israel's fiftieth year the signs were many that the old order had been supplanted. The unified resolve that the world had come to see in Israel's external military successes seemed to be dissolving into increasingly divisive internal battles.

Perhaps no event captured this divisiveness as strikingly as the official fiftieth anniversary celebration itself. On the very night that Israel was throwing its gala Jubilee bash in Jerusalem, televised live across the nation, ultra-Orthodox leaders were still working to get the internationally acclaimed Bat-Sheva Dance Company to stage its performance in long shirts and pants rather than the modern dance tights that were standard for this particular dance. After days of heavy political lobbying, the religious said they would boycott the national celebration that night unless the dancers covered up.

The controversy continued right up until broadcast time for the event, which was to be attended by American vice president Al Gore and other visiting dignitaries. Rather than be coerced, however, the Bat-Sheva company felt it had no choice but to pull out of the program at the last minute, leaving unapologetic religious leaders satisfied — but multitudes of secular Israelis enraged. In the following days there were public demonstrations, angry recriminations, and the sudden formation of a new "centrist" political party that claimed it would make religious coercion its main issue.

But divisions over religion were just one aspect of the domestic discord that was gradually changing Israel. The Bat-Sheva episode merely symbolized a broader disharmony gripping the nation.

Looking around Israel as it entered its sixth decade, I wondered if the confusion enveloping its people was not, to a certain extent, natural to a nation in the years beyond its fiftieth anniversary.

Any young nation, after half a century, will have lost most of its founders — the men and women who were there at the beginning, who took the words and ideas of independence and transformed them into physical existence and deeds. Entering its second half century of existence, such a nation might have some founders still in its midst, but not many and not for long. When the last of them slips away, the powerful moral authority with which they governed slips away, too, and the vision of the nation that they established must struggle to live on without them.

When the United States was fifty, two of the men most responsible for the nation's independence died on the very same day. They were John Adams and Thomas Jefferson, the second and third United States presidents. They died on July 4, 1826 — exactly fifty years from the day that their extraordinary document, the Declaration of Independence, was signed. Their deaths marked a turning point.

America's founding generation gave the nation its first five presidents. The fifth, James Monroe, was the final founder to live and serve in the White House. When his second term ended in 1825, America's forty-ninth year, it was also the end of a string of consecutive two-term presidencies that has yet to be equaled in American history.

Like Israel today, America beyond fifty was a nation in change, a nation where territorial issues were the main concern and where divisions in the political and social fabric were beginning to take hold. In the three decades that followed that fiftieth year, only one president served a second term: Andrew Jackson, hero of the War of 1812. In his footsteps came an unprecedented series of one-term leaders, none of whom seemed capable of grasping and holding the reins of a growing, diversifying, rambunctious people.

Down the road, the Civil War was waiting.

As Israel enters its second half century, many of its people say they expect their own civil war, most likely between secular and religious Jews, or between nationalists and peaceniks. There are even great rifts between European-descended Ashkenazim and the Sephardim who hail from the Middle East.

They worry with good reason. For all its courage in staking out its place in the world and overcoming extreme external threats, Israel has not yet had the courage to face the deeply divisive threats that are tearing at it from within.

I was born in Israel in 1963. It could have been Belgium or Baltimore. My parents, who had survived the Holocaust and were looking for a fresh place to start, chose Israel. But it didn't last. Ten years after I was born in Tel Aviv we left for the United States, and in fifth grade I found myself becoming American, with the fortunes of the Philadelphia Phillies my primary concern, the antics of Bugs Bunny my chief entertainment.

Yet even as my parents were living comfortably in a placid suburb of Philadelphia, driving a Ford LTD and filling me with Twinkies, they were essentially unhappy. Their abandonment of Israel left them profoundly discontented. They discovered they had left behind a part of themselves — an invaluable part, something they could not duplicate in America. And even though I quickly adapted to my new country, in the back of my mind I knew that an essential part of me remained in Israel, too.

During those years Israel was not producing international rock stars or doing much else to entice an adolescent from across the Atlantic to come back home. There was the flowering of peace with Egypt, but a few years later Israel invaded Lebanon, bringing on a tailspin of international isolation, domestic disillusion, and economic troubles.

Yet, when I finished graduate school in New York and stood looking out on the world from that city's broad palisade of opportunity and stability, I made a choice I seemed destined to make: I decided to return to the country of my early childhood, a country of irresistible magnetism but vast uncertainty, a country periodically at war, always in the breach, ever in peril.

The land of Israel grabs the imagination for fundamental reasons. For the adherents of three major religions, it is simply "the land of God." For neutral onlookers, it is the land where the adherents of three major religions collide. But for the Jews who choose to live here, there is something else: Israel is a personal project. This is the bond that holds them, this is what keeps them coming back, this is the feeling they can't find anywhere else. More than faith and more than strife, it is the everyday participation in the project of building that has defined the Israeli experience.

For fifty years, as Israelis each played a small part in the building and maintenance of a state, they felt a growing, intoxicating sense of common effort and, sometimes, the perception of shared values. It's like the famous photograph of American troops — anonymous, silhouetted — planting the Stars and Stripes at Iwo Jima. A world away, on a different hill, under a different banner, Israelis scrambled to lay their hands on the flagpole — planting it, steadying it, guarding it, enriching its surroundings.

This was especially true for the solemn, purposeful Jews who came to Israel in the wake of the Holocaust. In the back of their minds, in the sanctuary of their hearts, those early Israelis were unyieldingly conscious of the mothers, fathers, friends, siblings, and many others who had not made it here, to whose memory the new state was, in a very personal way, dedicated. Every acre irrigated, every new stone laid, every tree planted, every hostile incursion repelled was part of an unspoken memorial. No Jew could live and die in Israel without this feeling of involvement and possession. Almost everyone felt a part of the project — normal people, not fanatics or saints.

Of all the follies in which people indulge, nationalism has to rank as one of the greatest. What impulse has caused more pointless destruction in the last 200 years?

When I was a foreign correspondent in Eastern Europe in the early 1990s, I heard hundreds of people in newly liberated countries throughout the region and the Soviet Union explaining why their particular group was special, why some competing nationality was despicable, and why they would fight, kill, and die for their nation in a squabble over a few miserable acres. I often didn't bother masking my outrage or amusement as I scribbled down the diatribes.

Only later did I ask myself whether I make allowances for my own nation, too. Don't I think the Jews are somehow special? Don't I think they are worth preserving, even worth fighting for? Perhaps I do.

This occurred to me one day during a drive from Tel Aviv to Jerusalem with my friend and colleague Alfred Ironside. It's an affecting experience, that hour-long ascension from the coast to the capital.

The founders of Tel Aviv gazed at little but sand dunes in 1909. The city they built seems to be constructed of sand, too — its concrete facades eroded by the sea breeze, seemingly about to crumble before the next hale wind. Likewise, its spirit rests on shifting sands. It is a city of change and adaptation, of modernity and moderation.

Jerusalem, only an hour's drive away, is its physical and spiritual opposite. Most of the buildings there, by tradition and fiat, are faced with white limestone from the surrounding Jerusalem hills. Even the newest structures, with their sober stone facades, look as if they have existed forever.

I thought of the two cities, so contradictory in the visions of Israel they represent, as we left the scattered skyline of Tel Aviv. Ten lanes of traffic dropped to four as we passed from inner to outer suburban developments, the rolling grass and farmland of the coastal plain beginning to emerge. All that lay between us and a relaxing, scenic drive were a few industrial sites, Ben-Gurion airport, and the last outpost of the seaside metropolis, a huge industrial plant of twisted piping and metal towers that looks like a giant car motor dropped on its end from the sky. Then we would pass through fields of flowers and small crops, the rolling countryside building into the bulging Jerusalem hills, green at first with pines and other conifers, then drier and more bare, the road climbing, twisting through the rock. The hulks of tanks and armored cars that blazed the trail to Jerusalem in 1948 are still visible, along with crumbling stone walls, small Arab villages, and finally, the ancient city of stone in the distance. No matter how many times you pass this way, it always has the power to stoke your imagination.

Alfred and I drove for a while in silence, watching history roll by, framed in the windows.

"If you could pick someone from the past to bring into our present time," he suddenly asked, "and be that person's guide, who would you choose?"

"Well," I ventured, "the real question is, is there any reason to choose someone specific whose name we know? Maybe bringing over an anonymous person would be more interesting."

But Alfred had someone specific in mind already, and I knew who it was. It was someone he'd been thinking about for years, someone who in his day was connected to the same piece of earth as Alfred is.

Alfred has lived on three continents and traveled from Osaka to Anchorage to East Berlin. He now lives in Tel Aviv. But there is only one place, I'm sure, that he could ever truly call home, and that is Philadelphia, where he was born and raised. Alfred, then, would extend his invitation to Benjamin Franklin.

"Did you know that in Franklin's day almost all the roads he traveled were unpaved?" he asked. "I wonder what he would make of this restrictive maze of concrete and asphalt we've layered over the earth to move about and live upon." He went on to remark that it would surely be the low-tech things, like concrete, that we take for granted, that would first capture Franklin's attention.

"So who would you pick?" Alfred asked again.

When he had first asked it, I considered the question one to joke about. But as I thought more about what Alfred's answer revealed about who, fundamentally, he is, I realized that my answer would reveal as much about me.

"I'd have to go with Theodor Herzl," I finally replied.

I, who scorned nationalism, had chosen the first great Jewish nationalist of modern times.

I thought back to the rabble-rousing Romanian mayor I once met. This man advised me in all seriousness that the Hungarians, whom he believed his rivals for control of the territory of Transylvania, were "a barbarian, migratory people who still have barbarian genes." His expression reflecting a sorrowful calm, he explained that the Hungarians were engaged in a secret mission to infiltrate and genetically overtake the world's elites through "the greatest export of women in history" to important Western universities, where they were programmed to wreak sexual havoc upon the local men, especially future world leaders.

Theodor Herzl, a Viennese-born Jewish journalist with a long black beard, was not such a xenophobe. But he was a serious and stunningly effective nationalist.

In 1896, Herzl published a pamphlet called *Der Judenstaat* ("The Jewish State") in which he outlined his seemingly impossible vision for a Jewish state reborn in the land of the ancient Hebrews. Herzl asserted that the position of the Jews in the countries of their Diaspora was becoming "daily more intolerable" because of systematic societal, economic, and physical oppression. He considered it undesirable for the Jews to address the problem by assimilating into their host nations, for "our national character is too famous and, in spite of every degradation, too fine to make its annihilation desirable." Hence, he concluded, the only answer was "the restoration of the Jewish state."

"Let the sovereignty be granted us over a portion of the globe large enough to satisfy the rightful requirements of a nation; the rest we shall manage for ourselves," he wrote in his treatise. Although he considered alternatives like part of Argentina, which already had a Jewish immigrant population, he eventually preferred Palestine, "our ever-memorable historic home."

The notion of a return to "Zion"—the biblical name for Jerusalem—had existed ever since the Jews were expelled from Israel by the Romans soon after their disastrously unsuccessful rebellions in the first century A.D. Hundreds of years later, the notion persisted; in the mid-nineteenth century, Rabbi Hirsch Kalischer argued that the return of Jews to their ancestral homeland was of tremendous religious consequence, a precondition for the coming of the messiah.

The nationalist version of Zionism developed gradually, without a name, in the eighteenth and nineteenth centuries against a backdrop of anti-Semitism and the emergence of nation-states in Europe.

Moshe Hess, a German Jewish socialist, advocated the establishment of a Jewish state as a means of "normalizing" the Jews in his 1862 book *Rome and Jerusalem*—one of the first references to the idea that the Jewish Diaspora, an array of minorities scattered throughout scores of countries, was somehow unnatural.

A movement called Hovevei Zion—Hebrew for "Lovers of Zion"—sprang up in various East European communities to encourage the settlement of Jews in agricultural communities in Palestine. Leo Pinsker, a Polish doctor acclaimed for his work fighting cholera, joined Hovevei Zion after publishing the 1882 pamphlet *Auto-Emancipation*, in which he argued that the return to their historic homeland was the Jews' only possible salvation from anti-Semitism.

All these men now have streets named for them in Israel. Herzl, who was a high-minded intellectual, would probably not be too pleased with his own street in Tel Aviv, which is known mainly for hosting the greatest concentration of secondhand furniture stores in the country. To "go to Herzl" means to look for a good deal on a used love seat.

As a young cosmopolitan in 1880s Vienna, Herzl became fascinated with what he viewed as the universal enmity toward the Jews, at one point toying with the idea that simply baptizing all Jewish children might solve the problem. His views changed in 1895 when, as a correspondent for Neue Freie Presse, he covered the trial of Alfred Dreyfus, a Jewish officer in the French army falsely accused of treason. The Dreyfus Affair, he wrote, "embodies the desire of the vast majority of the French to condemn a Jew, and to condemn all Jews in this one Jew."

After publishing *Der Judenstaat* a year later, Herzl became famous in some circles and notorious among Jewish conservatives who did not wish to rock the boat just as Jews were becoming more accepted in Western Europe. He met with world leaders and philanthropists and traveled to various Jewish communities to lobby for his ideas.

On August 29, 1897, he presided over the First Zionist Congress in Basel, Switzerland, where an impressive array of Jewish activists adopted his program to secure for the Jewish people "a publicly recognized, legally secured home in Palestine." In his diary, Herzl was prophetic: "If I were to sum up the Basel Congress in a single phrase I would say: In Basel I created the Jewish state. Were I to say this aloud, I would be greeted by universal laughter. But in perhaps five years, in any case, certainly in 50 years, everyone will perceive it."

Five years after the congress, Herzl died at 44. Fifty years after the congress, the United Nations General Assembly adopted a historic resolution ending the British Mandate in Palestine and approving the partition of the land between Jews and Arabs and the establishment of an independent Jewish state.

In Tel Aviv, where I write these words, the Jews felt the chill of a coming storm. But on that night they were dancing in the streets.

Herzl appears to be one of history's more remarkable visionaries. Not only did he foresee the establishment of Israel, he also predicted the disarray it would suffer if it did not follow his exact vision. In this sense he was a prophet not only of Israel, but also of its possible doom.

In a piece he wrote two years before *Der Judenstaat*, Herzl had fretted over the cultural estrangement of Jews from so many different nations: "And if the Jews really 'returned home' one day, they would discover on the next that they do not belong together. For centuries they have been rooted in diverse [nations]; they differ from each other, group by group." He didn't know how accurate this would turn out to be.

Regarding government, he argued in *Der Judenstaat* for a "council of State jurists" that would formulate "the most modern constitution." But at the same time he believed that "a democratic monarchy or an aristocratic republic are the finest forms of a State."

Worriedly, he observed that a democracy without a sovereign's useful counterpoise is extreme in its appreciation and condemnation; tends to idle in discussion in Parliaments; and "produces an objectionable class of men — professional politicians." He was also distrustful of "the masses," whom he saw as "prone ... to be swayed by vigorous ranting."

Adopting exactly the system Herzl warned against, Israel became a pure parliamentary republic, filled to the brim with the vigorous ranting of professional politicians. A constitution, meanwhile, has been put off indefinitely by the objections of the religious minority who see the Bible as their constitution and who systematically object to the kind of ideas Herzl might have considered "the most modern" — like separation of religion and state.

On the matter of religion, in fact, Herzl was most emphatic, and his fears proved well founded: "Faith unites us, knowledge gives us freedom. We shall therefore prevent any theocratic tendencies from coming to the fore on the part of our priesthood. We shall keep our priests within the confines of their temples.... They must not interfere in the administration of the State which confers distinction upon them, else they will conjure up difficulties without and within."

A century after the Basel Congress, the Zionist cause appears to be a major success story. A state for the Jews has been established; it is militarily strong and able to defend itself; and as a nation it has prospered. With a little more time, it will likely even be home to the majority of the world's Jews.

Yet its people are not really celebrating, as was clear in the downbeat festivities marking Israel's fiftieth anniversary. Herzl, I'm sure, would quickly see why: The moderate, secular, and national ethos that Herzl laid out, which guided Israel through its first half century, is under attack.

The ultra–Orthodox religious, a minority who were initially opposed to the founding of the state, now claim to be the sole keepers of the Jewish flame, and many of them attempt, where possible, to foist their ways on the rest of the nation. The idea of the Jews as one people has been undermined by the arrival en masse of groups that were simply too different to fit under one umbrella. Herzl would cringe at the growth of political parties in the Knesset representing "the Russians" and "the Moroccans," which sometimes openly mock his national Jewish idea. And the project of populating the land, shaping it, laying stones, and planting trees has been largely usurped by controversial right-wing movements leading the drive to settle the disputed territory of the West Bank and agitating against compromise with the Arabs.

My kind of nationalism took the primary form of quiet pride in national achievement, tempered by my international upbringing and the skepticism inherent in my trade. But the actions of today's extremists make clear that any kind of nationalism rests upon dangerously unstable ground; they illustrate how easily even apparently benign nationalism can slide toward jingoism, parochialism, and even racism. This is because the underlying argument of nationalism — we are unique, exceptional — can be employed to justify practically anything, any kind of action, any set of principles. In Israel, it has already been used to justify the shooting of Arab mayors, the massacre of Muslim worshippers, the assassination of a peacemaking prime minister.

At times Israeli society, so deliberately cobbled together through years of nation-building, seems to be shattering into its component parts, leaving the Zionist enterprise in disarray.

For a half century Israelis fought against hostile Arab neighbors. The external challenge galvanized them, enabling them to overcome or simply put aside their own considerable differences as they struggled to become one nation. This struggle was in part successful: The children and grandchildren of yesterday's immigrants have much more in common than their ancestors did.

But Israel is performing an about-face. Its people increasingly choose to put emphasis on those cultural and religious differences that remain. Ironically, it is the peace process with the Arabs that has unleashed this emerging dynamic of division; it is disagreement over peace itself.

Indeed, the electorate has long been divided right down the middle on the question of giving the Arabs land for peace, infusing political conversation in Israel with a particular brand of anger and urgency. It is often felt that the single vote of any given fellow citizen could be the one to shatter your own dreams and aspirations.

And this political divide runs deep, corresponding to a dangerous degree with personal background and socioeconomic status. Ashkenazi Jews of European background, the secular, the educated, and the well-off tend strongly to the dovish left. Sephardi Jews who hail from the Middle East, the religious, the undereducated, and the poor lean to the nationalist right.

Sometimes the tension can be felt in the street as a secular Jew passes a black-hatted, ultra–Orthodox Jew. The opposing world view of the two is so obvious in their appearance, their gait, their body language.

Sometimes you see it as an Ashkenazi winces at the blare of Arab-sounding Sephardi music in a taxi, or as a secular Sephardi couple defiantly explain under the unblinking stare of a TV camera why they are sending their children to a Sephardi-run religious school that both stokes ethnic divisions within the country and educates their children not to appreciate the amazing achievements of the secular state.

And if you look closely, you will see the tension in the careful segregation of Israel's Arab population, whose quietly enforced status as second-class citizens seems ever more glaring and egregious in a time of rapprochement with the Palestinians and other Arabs outside Israel.

Prosperous though Israel has become, some kind of existential conflict divides virtually every random group of Israelis you can assemble. And some people are starting to feel hate, a kind of hate they never thought they would feel.

How did this happen? Herzl did not envision Israel this way. David Ben-Gurion, the country's first prime minister, did not lead Israel in this direction. For a considerable time Israel was not this way at all. But as the country heads into its second half century, the sense of common purpose that has characterized it is slowly but dramatically being undermined and replaced by fractious disagreement about the future, angry revisionist thinking about the past, and extremism in everyday public discourse.

This book is not simply a story of these emerging divisions, however. It is the story of how the past is shaping the future.

Part I, "Emergence," traces the historical events that gave birth to Israel's internal divisions, exploring the ways in which a nation of extraordinary, unifying purpose became a place of such deep schisms. It begins with the Six Day War of 1967, an unprecedented and still unmatched moment in Israeli history. The six chapters of Part I chronicle the cascading impact of the war, from the settler movement of the early 1970s, to the 1982 invasion of Lebanon, to the era of "land for peace" in the early '90s. It is the ironic conclusion of this part of the book that while peace with the external world was finally dawning across Israel under Yitzhak Rabin and Shimon Peres — the last of the founders — long-suppressed internal issues were simultaneously emerging into the daylight. These emerging issues — citizenship, race, and religion — have the potential to challenge Israel more deeply and in more fundamental ways than the external threats ever did. And now the founders are gone.

Part II, "Beyond," explores the divisions in depth, taking the reader on startling visits into the very soul of a conflicted Israel and exploring how, in its second half century, Israel must finally come to terms with some enormous questions of nationhood.

I don't know whether Israel will answer its national questions in a way that I can be proud of. It may emerge completely transformed in ways that will shut me out.

Part I
Emergence

Victory

Dan Perry's proud father perches his son on a captured Egyptian tank (photographer unknown).

I was on the verge of four years old when everything changed for Israel, but I remember those days well.

It was a simple country then, especially for children. There was no TV and only one radio station, run from the prime minister's office. There were no mass-produced toys imported from Taiwan.

Most of the population consisted of recent immigrants who had streamed into the country from all over Europe and the Middle East after the founding of the state in 1948. My parents, who had come from Romania, labored to adjust to the new society, even as the society was creating itself and adjusting to them. The societal problems, conflicts, and imperfections were so obvious that they were hardly even noticed. Few people asked questions. Most worked hard just to scrape together a meager living.

Yet my mother, who worked as a chemical engineer at the Weizmann Institute of Science south of Tel Aviv, recalls the 1960s as the happiest time of her life. She pines for what she remembers as a healthy and content country very different from the materialistic and divided one that she sees growing around her today. I think that what she really misses most is her youth, and the indescribable joy she felt at the birth of her first child. Like many new immigrants, she never felt fully Israeli until she had children there, whose Israeliness carried no asterisk. I keep a fading black-and-white photograph of the two of us: a radiant blonde woman clutching her little bald baby, whom she proudly considered a dead ringer for the Soviet leader Nikita Khrushchev.

My father worked as a civil engineer for the state water planning authority. He's still proud of his role as a designer of the National Water Carrier, a huge pipeline built in the 1960s to transport water from the Sea of Galilee to the rest of Israel, guaranteeing both urban apartment dwellers and desert farmers a steady water supply for the first time. He rose quickly, and we became one of the first families on our street, in the Tel Aviv suburb of Ramat Gan, to own a car: a little white Ford Anglia, which today would be just about big enough to comfortably carry one weight-lifting, well-fed American male. My mother used to needle her husband about being so vain as to insist on such a glorious automobile.

My own existence was carefree. Each morning I was taken to the kindergarten down the street, which was operated by a fearsome, blue-haired woman from Poland named Yona. Yona's idea of a good time for the children was to bring in, once a week, an accordionist to belt out old Russian folk songs with Hebrew lyrics. My idea of a good time was to sneak out into the yard whenever possible and climb into a barrel placed horizontally on metal supports, where I would hide and imagine I was driving a farm tractor.

About once a month, my father came home from work with a special treat: a small can of industrial-style hummus, the Arab paste made from chick-peas that, almost by default, became the Israeli national dish. In the heat of our little kitchen, he would take off his shirt, leaving only a white sleeveless undershirt, crack open the can, and meticulously improve the hummus by mixing in various spices and oils. We'd then sit down at the kitchen table, the two of us, and happily consume the odorous delicacy. I imagine this tradition was part of my father's own process of becoming Israeli.

And so it went, until I was three years and ten months old.

Perhaps my father didn't bring the hummus that month. Or maybe it was something else. But I could sense the adults were different — they were upset. For weeks their anxiety grew until I knew something was very wrong. Eventually, while sitting with my parents in the living room one evening, I asked for an explanation.

My father got up and motioned for me to follow. We went to my room — basically a storage closet adjacent to the living room — where he sat me down at my rough wooden table, on a stool he had built for my birthday. This meant a serious talk would follow, in which key information would be passed from father to son.

I sat upright, prepared to listen.

My father told me that there existed a very bad man named Nasser, who hated us with a tremendous passion. This Nasser had been making boastful threats for several weeks now. "But we're not scared," he reassured me, "because there are also good men," like a certain Rabin, who would protect us. This corresponded to a hit song from the time, which I now know was attempting to raise sagging spirits with the chorus: "Nasser is waiting for Rabin, ay, ay, ay!" In any case, I felt better now that I was informed, and hopeful that everything would work out. The alternative was literally unimaginable to me.

A few days later, I was awakened by air raid sirens.

Gripped by excitement, I rushed out of bed and dashed across the living room to the terrace, where I leaned over the railing and craned my neck up at the sky, breathing in the warm air of early Mediterranean summer. Alas, there seemed to be nothing out of the ordinary except for the shrill noise of the siren. I remember disappointment. All the hype about Nasser and Rabin had come to this?

Then my mother arrived, dragged me away from the terrace, and delivered the great news that there would be no going to Yona's today. I cheered. Instead, she told me, we would have a fun day in the underground shelter that our apartment building, like most in Israel, was equipped with. My mother is not always the calmest of women but, as I recall the moment, she was stoically heroic as she whisked me down to the shelter.

This was June 5, 1967, the day everything changed for Israel.

As we huddled in the shelter to wait for air raids that never came, Israeli warplanes headed southwest. They followed a course out over the Mediterranean toward 11 Egyptian air force bases from the Sinai Peninsula to the Nile. The squadrons took off in a staggered pattern so that they would all arrive at their targets at the same time, precisely 7:45 a.m.

Israeli intelligence knew exactly where and when the Egyptians were in practice flights, when the pilots took coffee breaks, what frequencies they used to communicate — and the execution was perfect. In a crippling preemptive strike that lasted just under three hours from take-off to return, 90 percent of Egypt's 340 combat planes were turned into smoldering wrecks, the majority of them on the ground. Israeli air force chief Motti Hod later admitted that he was stunned by the effectiveness of his operation.

No longer threatened from the skies, Israeli infantry and armor swept into action.

Word filtered down into the shelter. Within a day or so we were allowed out, and the sirens stopped. Well before the guns fell silent there was already relief and celebration in the air.

The Israeli attack ended a nerve-wracking three weeks now known as the *hamtana*— the "waiting" — begun when Egyptian President Gamal Abdel Nasser expelled the United Nations peacekeepers from the Gaza Strip and the southern tip of the Sinai Peninsula, blockaded the nearby Straits of Tiran to Israeli ships, and deployed his massive army along the Israeli border. To meet the threat, much smaller Israel had mobilized all its reserves, a drastic measure that — had it dragged on — would have devastated the infant economy. Bus transportation was halted. Vehicles were commandeered for military uses. Many men of military age were called up for reserve army duty, replaced in their jobs by high school students. Normal life came to a near standstill.

Any map that shows the pre–1967 border (and most maps not published by the Israeli government do) reveals why my parents were so unsettled and why the government reacted with such an all-encompassing military deployment. Israel at its narrowest point was a meager 12 miles wide, a precarious situation for a nation surrounded and badly outnumbered by bona fide enemies with mortal grievances. Jordanian troops, stationed in what is now called the West Bank, could practically have occupied Jerusalem or Tel Aviv by jumping the wrong way during morning calisthenics. From the Golan Heights looming just above Israel's northern border, Syrian soldiers easily looked down upon the slender shoulders of the Jewish state and the Mediterranean Sea beyond. From the Gaza Strip, a sliver of Palestinian-populated territory sitting on Israel's coast like a razor blade, the Egyptian army was within easy firing range of Israeli population centers and an hour's leisurely drive from Tel Aviv.

Israelis had watched as the threat became terrifyingly real. By the end of May Egypt had reached pacts with Jordan, Iraq, and other nations to fight Israel. Iraqi President Abd al-Salaam Aref on June 3 told his men of the approaching battle to avenge the Arab humiliation of 1948. "We shall, God willing, meet in Tel Aviv and Haifa," he said.

Prime Minister Levi Eshkol had taken over from Israel's legendary founder, David Ben-Gurion, only a few years before. He was a seasoned politician, capable bureaucrat, and highly amiable man — but woefully miscast when it came to soothing the nerves of a citizenry facing a mortal threat. The spectacularly eloquent foreign minister, Abba Eban, also came up empty in his efforts to win world backing for Israel.

After weeks of building tension, Eshkol gave in to a national clamor and appointed retired war hero Moshe Dayan as his defense minister. A few days later, the decision was made: the military, led by Dayan and Chief of Staff Yitzhak Rabin, would address the problem directly. With the jaws of the enemy military closing in, Israel would end the hamtana on its own.

At that time the army disseminated major decisions to the troops with flyers offering a brief motivational statement. On June 5, the flyer circulated to soldiers read: "The word has been given. Today we crush the hand that has reached out to strangle us…. We did not want this war—the enemy did. And he shall have it."

The air force raid began just before dawn.

Hours later, Israeli tanks plowed into Arab territory, seizing strategic high ground and establishing, where possible, territorial buffers between the enemy armies and Israel's population centers. It captured the Golan Heights from Syria, the West Bank from Jordan, the Gaza Strip and Sinai Peninsula from Egypt. In six days, Israel quadrupled its territory and crushed the forces of Egypt, Syria, and Jordan. Even more damaging, the small Jewish nation had crushed their pride.

In Israel, the outcome of this very short war was considered to be nothing less than a replaying of the biblical story of David defeating Goliath. But for the victor as for the vanquished, the greatest impact would be on the soul: ultimately, it transformed David into Goliath.

In the West, few seemed un-awed by the spectacle of the Six Day War. At the United Nations Security Council, only four delegations supported the Soviet proposal to condemn Israel.

In Israel there was elation. Israelis never expected to go from the hand-wringing of hamtana to complete victory in the space of a week. It was akin to winning the lottery just as the bills are piling up on the desk and there is simply no money to pay. For Israel, hamtana was like that uncomfortable pile of bills; the enemy armies amassing on the borders were a pack of collectors at the door. Suddenly the nation was rich—in relief, in repose, in newfound faith, in territory. And, like a lottery jackpot, it made the winners giddy with joy.

But the Six Day War was no random roll of the dice. Israel's victory was the reward of hard work, careful stewardship of scarce resources, good planning, a universal sense of purpose, and relentless—almost fastidious—worrying. The victory was justifiably something to take pride in.

A few days after the war ended, my parents bundled me into the back of the Anglia and we drove to a desolate sandlot in central Tel Aviv that today is an open plaza encircled by select European boutiques. Then, it was circled by a phalanx of tanks and other weaponry seized during the war. I happily climbed onto a Soviet-made tank, with its exciting Arabic numerals—exciting because they were so foreign and mysterious—and posed for a picture under the turret. Braver kids climbed all the way up and swung like monkeys from the cannon.

The generals who ran the Six Day War—especially Dayan, with his trademark eyepatch—were feted as heroes who could do no wrong. Albums commemorating their escapades were considered tasteful gift items. The inaugural broadcast of Israel TV, a black-and-white outfit operated by the government, was a military parade. The newspapers were filled with pictures of desert sands littered with the shoes of fleeing Egyptian troops. Arab cowardice was also the dominant theme in newsreels played in movie theaters.

Israelis were not simply proud of their victory. Gradually, powerfully, they contracted a Goliath-sized hubris.

For 19 years, Israel had been something of a child nation, bringing in immigrants, housing them, building institutions, expanding the economy. The Six Day War was a certificate of national adulthood, like a degree that read: "You are hereby declared a state that is here to stay, a state that must be reckoned with—and there's nothing the Arabs can do about it."

But reality proved much more complicated.

The primary spoil of the war—occupation of the Arab territories—was to force Israel into a reckoning of its own, one that would completely shift the country's political course. Over the years, the question of what to do with the territories came to overwhelm everything else in Israeli politics, challenging Israel's democracy, its decency, and its people's notions about what kind of country theirs was really meant to be.

More than three decades after the war, Israelis still struggle with this fundamental conundrum, although this struggle may be coming to an end.

In recent years a strong current of revisionism has arisen about the war itself. It holds that Israel did much to provoke the war in the years leading up to 1967; that the Arab armies, with their poor equipment, meager training, and weak motivation, never really stood a chance despite their numerical advantage; that during the war Israel conducted expulsion of Palestinians and destroyed West Bank villages even in cases where there was no military justification; and that, as Dayan admitted in an interview published posthumously in 1997 by the Yediot Aharonot newspaper, Israel attacked Syria and seized the Golan unprovoked, primarily because it desired the territory. "It was unnecessary," Dayan said. "You don't hit the enemy because he's evil; you hit him because he threatens you. And the Syrians, on the fourth day of the war, were not threatening us."

No such doubts were evident in the immediate aftermath of the war, as the citizens rejoiced in their new expanses. Before the war Israel had been no larger than New Jersey. For the first time in nearly 20 years of statehood, Israel was not sleeping standing up; there was room to spread out a little, to get comfortable. With the Sinai Desert in the south, the Golan Heights in the north, and the West Bank in the east, Israel now controlled large buffer zones between its population and the guns of neighboring Egypt, Syria, and Jordan.

The economy expanded, too. Cheap labor—Palestinian workers from the newly occupied territories—was integrated into the Israeli economy, helping to generate a boom. Israel put much of its new wealth into huge infrastructure projects like the highways that my father would help design, which would soon criss-cross the nation.

A more subtle economic shift began taking place, too, family by family. In the nation's first two decades it was considered almost shameful to seek wealth for its own sake; the nation had, after all, been founded on the ideology of socialism and reared on the necessity of austerity. But the growing economic opportunities, the rapid progress in national development, and the hubris that sprang from the swift victory all combined to change how individuals perceived their place in the bigger national picture.

No longer was it so urgently necessary to think of the state first. To judge by the news, the state was doing quite well: it had respect from the world, a seemingly invincible military, a sense of security, a booming economy. People absorbed the steady stream of good news in the postwar years and, feeling that the state could survive with something less than 100 percent of their devotion, began to indulge themselves. Interests and priorities took on a more individualistic nature.

My own family reflected the shift. Having arrived in Israel in the wake of the Holocaust, thankful to be alive and grateful to have a place reserved for them in the new Jewish homeland, they toiled with Zionist ideals and a real sense of purpose. But a few years after the Six Day War, my parents left for the United States. Their plan was to earn big, spend carefully, and save enough in a short time for a speedy and comfortable return to Israel.

They never imagined it at the time, but they would not return for 20 years.

The shift in values was touching every community and every family, leaving an impression that was comparable to that of World War II on America.

But the circumstances were different, and so was the result. Victorious America occupied whole nations devastated by war and decided that it was in its best interests to help rebuild them. America never developed a taste for staying on as a permanent occupier.

Israel, on the other hand, did not occupy faraway lands but, in the case of the Sinai and the Golan, parts of angry neighboring states. And with the West Bank and Gaza, Israel stumbled into an even greater quagmire: the large Arab population there started to insist on its rights as a distinct nation — the Palestinians — even as a movement in Israel was growing to hold onto the territories forever.

Israeli philosopher Yeshayahu Leibowitz was probably the first to identify what the new state of mind — and the occupation of a large population of Palestinians — would do to Israeli society. He warned that there was no such thing as a "benign occupation" of a foreign people, and that Israelis would have to give up the new territories before the twisted norms of military occupation seeped into Israel itself and destroyed its tenuous democracy.

The Eshkol government at first seemed ready to forsake the new acquisitions. On June 19, only days after the end of the war, it offered the Arabs most of their territories back in exchange for peace — the first offer of "land for peace."

Today, this basic principle, and this precise exchange, is the core policy of the Arab mainstream. Beginning in the early 1980s it became apparent that the leaderships of most Arab nations — now only Iraq and Libya are holdouts — are willing to grudgingly accept Israel and grant it some form of peace in exchange for the return of the territories lost in 1967.

It was the Six Day War that forced them to stop viewing Israel as a temporary phenomenon and accept it as a fact of life. But in the months after the war, when Israel was actually agreeable to a sweeping land-for-peace deal, the Arabs, shell-shocked and humiliated, did not respond to the Eshkol government's offer. A few months later, the offer was rescinded.

The Eshkol government, which was headed by Mapai, the forerunner to today's Labor party, was considered "pragmatic" compared to the hawkish Herut party led by former underground radical Menachem Begin. For Begin, the war opened up a golden opportunity to establish Jewish sovereignty over Eretz Yisrael — the entire "Land of Israel" ruled by the ancient Jews.

On this point Eshkol was ambivalent. But some ministers in his government — notably Dayan — began to view the West Bank and Gaza as part of Israel. In a speech on August 3, Dayan said, "We have returned ... to the cradle of our nation's history.... We have returned to Hebron, to Shechem [Nablus], to Bethlehem.... We know that to give life to Jerusalem, we must station the soldiers and armor in the Shechem mountains and on the bridges over the Jordan River."

And so, hesitantly, the door was opened to settlement of the new territories.

In the years ahead, among a small but potent minority of Jews, nationalism and religion would fuse, gradually shifting Zionism away from its workaday path. A new messianic Israeli would begin to believe that control of the territories was the nation's manifest destiny, that the finger of God was directing his comings and goings.

The fusion of nationalism and religion would make for a tinderbox of conflict between Israel and its neighbors — and within Israel itself.

Settlement

Moshe Levinger and followers celebrate after a government capitulation (photograph by Moshe Milner).

One afternoon, I decided to see just how long it would take. I got into my car in the center of Tel Aviv. I made one turn onto a major boulevard heading east, away from the beach. I checked my watch when my car passed under the 300-foot communications tower of the Defense Ministry. Taking a ramp down onto the central highway, called the Ayalon, I drove north. At Glilot junction, about five miles out of town, I checked my watch again. Seven minutes had passed. I exited the highway and turned east, inland. I went by the not-so-secret cadet school of the Mossad intelligence agency. In 14 more minutes, including one stoplight, I had reached it: The West Bank.

As far as international law is concerned, once you pass the dotted line on the map, you have left the State of Israel. From the car, the border seems even less substantial than the dotted line. A few Jersey barriers encroach from the dirt shoulder of the road, narrowing the pavement momentarily as you drive past a few bored-looking soldiers. Then you are in occupied territory.

I drove a short distance on the main road, then turned left up a winding blacktop. In another minute I was on a hill overlooking the Arab town of Qalqiliya sitting just inside the dotted line of the West Bank. In all, my trip from home took 23 minutes. Twenty-three minutes in light traffic to get from downtown Tel Aviv to a good-sized Arab town in the West Bank. From the hilltop I could clearly see the city to the south. The shining blue of the Mediterranean occupied the horizon in the west. To the north, I could make out the hills that guard Haifa, Israel's main port. Within the sweep of that view nearly half the population of Israel lives, work, plays, and sleeps. A few miles and 23 minutes from the disputed territory of the West Bank.

It is the fact that those miles and minutes are so meager that gives Israelis pause every time their government considers returning the West Bank to Arab control. It is the thought of enemy rockets sitting up on that nearby hill that so very greatly complicates the resolution of the Arab-Israeli conflict. And this is why many of the people of Israel, led by a series of uncertain governments, at first tolerated and later supported the idea of Jews settling in the West Bank.

It began with a trickle. On April 4, 1968, less than a year after the war, a group of ten Jewish families led by a gangly, bald rabbi named Moshe Levinger arrived in Hebron, a dense rubble pile of a town in the southern West Bank.

The group entered masquerading as Swiss tourists, then registered at the Park Hotel near the center of town. The next day Levinger announced that he and his group were actually Israelis, and that they came to Hebron with the intention of staying and reestablishing the town's ancient Jewish presence, the last vestiges of which had been wiped out in a massacre by local Arabs in 1929.

Levinger had a simple explanation for all this: God had given the land to the Jews.

According to the Old Testament Book of Genesis, the episodes upon which the Jewish people were forged almost all took place in and around the West Bank of the Jordan River. This is where Abraham — patriarch of both the Jews and the

Arabs—made his first covenant with God, where he almost sacrificed his son Isaac to prove his faith, and where he built an altar and established a burial site for himself and his family. After Abraham's death it is where Isaac dwelt and where his son Jacob was born, where Jacob sired his twelve sons, and where these sons had the first conflicts with their neighbors. Finally, this is where Jacob was anointed as the father of a great people, where God changed Jacob's name to "Israel" and reaffirmed his promise that this land would belong to "the children of Israel."

All these events, fundamental to the creation of the Jewish people and subsequently to religious Judaism, are described in Genesis. Although, according to the Bible, Jewish history unfolds sometimes in other places throughout the region, always do the Jews strive to return to this land, the holy land of Abraham and Isaac and Israel. For the devout Jew, there is no other land.

This is certainly how the first settlers saw it.

Herzl chose Palestine as the goal of the Zionist movement only when he concluded that this was the destination most likely to galvanize a sufficient number of Jews, and thus it was the only choice that made practical sense. He was not particularly interested in God's promises. Herzl was content with the historical fact that the Jews had come from here, and therefore logically this is where they would be most motivated to build an independent homeland.

The early leaders, mostly socialists, who turned his dream into reality—men like David Ben-Gurion—were much the same. Ben-Gurion lionized the Bible, but he used it as a historical document to prove the validity of the Jewish claim to the land. He was not a stickler about religious sites when it came to the various partition plans that were proposed for Palestine during the pre-state years. To be sure, Zionism did create a sort of land cult—after all, land was the thing the Jews were after. But as long as the land they got was in historic Israel, in close proximity to Bible country, mainstream Zionism was more or less content. The main goal was turning pale Jewish merchants, intellectuals, and layabouts into hardy farmers whom no Cossack would oppress again. For this, almost any land would do—in fact, the fertile coastal plain might do better than the rocky hills around Hebron.

Up through 1967, most Zionist leaders saw themselves as straight shooters with little time for political extremism and even less for religion. Even the main religious political grouping, the National Religious party, did not agitate for conquering the rest of biblical Israel. Until 1967, Israel was a poor, small country that considered itself lucky to have gained independence and was trying hard just to provide over a million immigrants with hummus.

With the Six Day War having wiped out this humility, Levinger's gambit lit a dormant spark of religious and nationalist zealotry that caught the Eshkol government off balance. Instead of confronting the settlers in Hebron and evicting them, the government moved them to an army compound in the town. Later, it allowed them to establish an independent Jewish settlement called Kiryat Arba on the outskirts of the town.

The strategy of non-confrontation failed miserably. At a time when the government was uncertain just what its policy should be, the compromise established a precedent for Jewish settlements in the West Bank and legitimized the idea of reclaiming it. Levinger's original plan to move Jews into Hebron itself was achieved in 1980, by which time Kiryat Arba was a bustling town of several thousand residents.

One of them was David Ramati.

Ramati doesn't look like the biggest risk-taker in the world. He seems more like the kind of man any small town in America would be happy to have as its Santa Claus. His white beard is thick and well-groomed, his face is open and a little pink, his eyes are blue and dancing, and his mop of white hair is windswept and tossed. His thickset carriage, with a pillow around the middle perhaps, would nicely fill out a big red suit.

If Ramati had come of age in any other decade but the '60s, if he had not served in the U.S. army in Vietnam, if his world view had been shaped by milder experiences, he might still be in Wisconsin. But as things turned out, Ramati ended up moving to a kibbutz on the Golan Heights early in the 1970s, when it had been Israeli-occupied territory for only a few years. The kibbutz soon collapsed, and Ramati poked his way around the West Bank for a while, finally ending up in Kiryat Arba. He liked the other young people he met there. They seemed much like himself: idealistic but pragmatic, willing to break convention, hard-working. He decided to stay.

Ramati insists the decision to join the Jewish settlement on the outskirts of Arab Hebron was not ideological. He was just keeping in mind the good advice of a commander in Vietnam: "Keep moving. Take chances. Don't sit still or stagnate." It was advice he followed in the jungle, and when it brought him safely home he decided to keep following it — straight to the front lines of Israel.

"We were a bunch of young people in our twenties with a spirit of adventure, of frontiering," he says, with a glow in his eyes. "We moved there not as a statement, but as a continuation of the pioneering spirit. It was love of the land."

Ramati seems almost oblivious to the political implications of his act and bristles at the suggestion that the early settlers were radicals. "The process was not to take away anything from anybody — it was to establish something!"

Establish what?

"We talked about it a lot, the meaning of our being here. We talked about all those generations of Jews over 2,000 years, about the dreams and aspirations they had of returning to this land, and our coming here when we did was a statement of solidarity with all the Jews that had gone before us but never made it here. We felt we had to fulfill the dreams of all those generations — to keep the promises they made to themselves. It was almost a racial obligation. So when the opportunity arrived, it had to be seized."

For all of Levinger's powerful ideology, and the romantic notions of people like Ramati, through the early '70s the settler movement remained a small blip on the national radar. Israel was still bursting with pride over the Six Day

War. The military was still considered as pure as a bottle of cold Maccabee beer. The Labor party was still holding tight to the reigns of government. And, incredibly, Israel was turning a cold shoulder to some peace overtures from Egypt.

After the death of Nasser in 1970, his successor, Anwar Sadat, sent out repeated signals that he was ready for peace in exchange for the return of the Sinai Peninsula. But Israel had offered this right after the war and had been rejected. Now it was enjoying its power to say no. Moshe Dayan went so far as to declare that it was better for Israel to have Sharm-el-Sheikh, the tiny town on the southern tip of the Sinai, without peace, than to have peace without Sharm-el-Sheikh. The peeved Sadat countered that he was ready to sacrifice "a million men" to reclaim the Sinai. The high-minded new prime minister, Golda Meir, was not impressed. Rubbing Dead Sea salt into Egyptian wounds, she once declared that her people would never forgive the Arabs for forcing them to kill in self-defense.

As a young boy I remember reading bits and pieces of all this in the Israeli newspapers. But in the summer of 1973 my family packed up and made its move to the United States. We would miss one of the darker hours in Israeli history.

All through the end of that summer, the CIA and Israel's Mossad provided a regular stream of intelligence information warning that Egypt and Syria were planning an attack. But Meir and her cabinet did not take it seriously. They couldn't imagine that just six years after the thorough trouncing Israel had administered the Arabs would actually try again.

The nation entered the fall of 1973 supremely unafraid. Through September, people enjoyed what was left of the warm days of summer and looked forward to the end of the month and the Jewish high holidays — Rosh Hashana (the Jewish New Year) and Yom Kippur (the Day of Atonement).

On October 6 — Yom Kippur — Egypt and Syria staged a mammoth surprise attack on the brooding, fasting Israelis. Egypt burst across the Suez Canal into the Sinai while Syria swept across the Golan Heights. Despite the intelligence warnings, Meir had not mobilized the reserves and Israel's defenses were totally unprepared. Many soldiers were on leave and communications and logistics sites were staffed at a minimum. Israel's positions along the Suez Canal and the Golan Heights were overrun.

In the first days, Israel suffered heavy casualties. Some officials even spoke as if they expected a complete collapse. The U.S. and the Soviet Union went on nuclear alert for fear that a desperate Israel would resort to atomic bombs. Initially ambivalent, U.S. President Richard Nixon eventually decided to support the Israeli war effort after heavy lobbying by the Israeli government. The United States staged a massive airlift of weapons and critically needed spare parts.

After ten days of losses Israel turned the tide of the war and gained the upper hand. It won back most of the early gains of its foes and was preparing to inflict severe pain before the fighting was halted under superpower pressure. The war had lasted three weeks — during which Israel lost some 2,500 soldiers, about four times its losses in 1967. At the time it meant that of every 1,000 Jewish citizens, one was killed. If America, which then had roughly 200 million people, lost an equivalent proportion of its population, the number of dead would have been 200,000 — four times the losses of the entire decade-long Vietnam War. Israel, though it had emerged semi-victorious, was crushed.

In April 1974, with the reality of the failure sinking in, Meir and her discredited cabinet resigned. Yitzhak Rabin was anointed as her successor in the Labor party and formed a new government. He was warmly received as the first native-born Israeli prime minister. His goal: to heal the wounds of the war and help Israel recover a sense of faith in its government.

That summer, a newly established group called Gush Emunim — "The Bloc of the Faithful" — set up an encampment on the ruins of ancient Sebastia near Nablus, the largest town in the West Bank and a hotbed of Palestinian nationalism. Rabin's government ordered the group to evacuate. They ignored him. Soon thousands of supporters joined their cause.

A split emerged in the government over what to do. (Ironically, Defense Minister Shimon Peres, who in later years became chief spokesman for relinquishing the occupied lands, at that time gave the settlers a measure of support.) For months the cabinet dithered and debated. Months became a year. One year became two. Rabin turned to more pressing problems, and when a scandal over an illegal U.S. bank account held by his wife exploded in 1977, he immediately resigned. By then, Gush Emunim settlers had established five communities throughout the northern West Bank. And they were just getting started.

The 1977 elections looked to be the first in Israeli history where the outcome was not predetermined. The disaster of the Yom Kippur War and the resignation of Meir and then of Rabin created a strong sense in Israeli society that the Labor party was losing touch. On top of that, opposition leader Menachem Begin successfully portrayed Labor as elitist. His Likud party, he claimed, would create a government of the people, and would tear down the socialist economic structures that were hindering individual advancement. Labor's reelection chances were further undermined by the creation of a new party, the Democratic Movement for Change, even though this party was dominated by former Laborites who did not necessarily intend to bring Begin to power.

When the vote was counted, Labor was crushed. In the 120-seat Knesset it had earned only 31 seats. Eighteen seats went to the DMC. Likud won a stunning 47 seats.

In the aftermath of this shocking outcome, Begin was joined by the religious parties and several other groups, including the DMC. He formed a new government with a significant Knesset majority.

The election was a huge coup for the settlers. Although they had been almost irrelevant in the campaign and in the political math that had summed up to Begin's landslide, there were few special interests that would benefit more greatly. Begin became arguably the greatest friend the settler movement would ever have.

Among the settlers, a core group of ideologues was growing to believe that the question of the land was essential to Jewish redemption. They worshipped the land promised by God to the Jews. Even though they rarely put it in these terms exactly, for some the very idea of peace was somehow undesirable — inasmuch as a state of isolation and conflict might better ensure the Jews remain "a people who dwell apart."

Many in secular Israel overlooked the more disturbing traits of Gush Emunim settlers because they saw them as an incarnation of the early Zionist pioneers. The group, however, was poised to challenge much that secular Zionism had stood for.

During the ten years since the Six Day War and the acquisition of the West Bank and Gaza Strip, the Labor party had never been able to produce a cogent policy regarding these lands. Its instinctive reaction — genetically coded into Israel's Labor movement — was compromise, in this case "territorial compromise." One of Labor's eminent leaders, pre-state military hero Yigal Allon, had proposed keeping some parts of the West Bank — the Jerusalem area and the Jordan River Valley, primarily — and offering the rest back to Jordan in exchange for peace. But King Hussein wasn't buying, and Labor didn't actively pursue the matter further.

For most of those years, Begin had been a firebrand opposition spokesman, furiously denouncing Labor's hesitation to claim the new territories. For him, it was as if Israel's ship had come in and no one was tying it to the dock.

Begin was not a man to hide his true feelings. When he would rise before the Knesset and speak of the biblical land of Israel, it was not just rhetoric intended to win votes with the religious. He believed in it. And although he was not very religious, he did seem to have a spiritual connection to the land, part of a grand purpose encoded deep in his brain that motivated him through 29 years of electoral failure to continue grasping for leadership.

A Zionist activist from his youth in Poland, Begin became leader of the Betar youth movement, which sought the establishment of a Jewish state in Palestine, by the time he was 25. By the time he was 30, in 1943, he was a commander in the militant Irgun Zva'i Leumi, one of the pre-state fighting units that carved out a place for Jews in a hostile Palestine. (Unlike the mainstream Hagana, the Irgun actively fought against British Mandate authorities, even sowing death and destruction by blowing up the British headquarters in the King David Hotel in Jerusalem.) When the state was founded in 1948, Begin became the instant leader of the right-wing political opposition.

From the dais above the Knesset floor, Begin spent most of the next 30 years agitating for stronger, more decisive military action by Israel. There were few government actions he did not furiously attack, from Ben-Gurion's tortured but pragmatic decision to accept German war reparations in the early 1950s to Rabin's plan more than two decades later to give back a sliver of the Sinai to Egypt. These and many other difficult government decisions he seemed to snatch from the air and throttle in his bare hands behind the Knesset rostrum. For the international press, which so often seemed to depict him without any subtlety of character, he was a caricature come to life and running amok.

But Begin was also a pragmatic and highly patriotic man. Three sometimes contradictory principles guided him: a heartfelt reverence for the sanctity of Jewish life, amplified by the Holocaust, which traumatized and obsessed him; a belief in the principles and practice of democracy; and a transcendent faith that modern Israel was meant to include the biblical lands of Judea and Samaria — the West Bank.

When Begin was finally elected, many feared his beliefs and his history of extremism would yield a warmonger. So most of the world and many Israelis were genuinely surprised a few months later, in October 1977, when Begin quickly and decisively responded to Sadat's renewed overtures by inviting the Egyptian to visit Jerusalem.

In hindsight, I see Begin's peacemaking with Egypt as an inevitable and essential part of his larger master plan: to keep the West Bank as a permanent part of Israel. After all, the Sinai Peninsula, large and strategically significant territory though it was, was not a part of biblical Israel, and thus remained outside the bounds of Begin's central agenda. It was something Begin could part with, a concession he could make, expressly because it might strengthen Israel's position with respect to the other territories.

History would bear this out: with Israel's strongest enemy declawed by a peace treaty, and with the aura of a Nobel Prize–winning peacemaker about him, Begin was much better placed to launch a major drive to settle the West Bank. And this he did.

Trying to make it easy for people to move into the disputed territory, the Begin government built a series of bedroom communities just barely inside the West Bank, advertised as being just five minutes away from "Israel proper." Even many moderate Israelis accepted this type of settlement, because it suggested not a desire to ultimately annex the whole territory but rather a clever scheme to eat around the edges of it and improve upon Israel's skimpy pre–1967 borders.

Begin's commuter towns just inside the West Bank were a minor hit. Within a few years the overall number of settlers grew from several hundred to several thousand. And they created a new type of settler, attracted not by the Torah or even by Ramati-like "love of the land," but by tax breaks, government-subsidized housing, and love of suburbia. Over the next 20 years their numbers steadily grew — along with those of firebrands peopling smaller settlements deep inside the West Bank.

The political shift that was heralded by Begin's first victory had a lasting quality: the debate over whether or not to keep and settle the land has dominated Israeli politics ever since. The land Israel won in 1967 gripped the nation first with pride, then with indecision, then with rancorous debate and divisiveness. For more than three decades this issue has seized center stage, leaving many others to fester unresolved.

There is a great moment in the movie *All the President's Men* when *Washington Post* editor Ben Bradlee is talking to Bob Woodward and Carl Bernstein on his lawn in the middle of the night. The next day they are going to run the story that says that the Watergate break-in and cover-up were carefully orchestrated from the White House. Bradlee wants to reassure his nervous young reporters. "There's nothing much riding on this," he tells them. "Nothing but the Constitution, the fate of the nation, and possibly the future of democracy in this country."

In Israel, every prime minister since Begin has probably looked out from his residence in Jerusalem with the same overpowering feeling of responsibility. "Nothing much riding on what we do with the West Bank," each might have thought on sleepless nights. "Just national security, the fate of our democracy, relations with the Arabs, and perhaps Jewish destiny."

Here's the abridged argument for continued Israeli settlement and control of the territories:

It's true that Israel didn't rule the West Bank from 1948 to 1967, but that was an unfortunate accident of history. In the fullness of time, let's say in 200 years, it will seem hardly relevant which parts of the land were liberated during the war that established the Jewish state and which were liberated a mere 19 years later.

That's because there's no moral difference between our "occupation" of the West Bank and our more widely recognized claim on "Israel proper." Both are lands the Arabs never wanted to give us, both are part of biblical Israel. Yet we have won the coastal plain, the hilly Galilee region of the north, and the Negev Desert in the south because we have stood firm in those areas since 1948. If we stand firm in the West Bank and Gaza, we can have them, too.

Besides, if we give up the West Bank, how will we ever be secure? The Israel of 1948 is simply too narrow and vulnerable for a country surrounded by real and potential enemies. To give the expanses of the territories back – in exchange for an illusory peace — is to tempt our enemies to try to take the rest.

Anyway, the proposition that it is immoral for us to occupy another people, namely the Palestinians of the territories, is absurd. Such a proposition undermines our presence everywhere in Israel. We do not look upon our 1 million Arab co-citizens within Israel proper as an "occupied people."

By making these new territories part of Greater Israel, we are doing nothing we haven't already done. We are merely finishing what we started in 1948, what our grandparents started at the turn of the century, what our ancient ancestors always dreamed of.

These are potent arguments in Israel. But there are powerful counter-arguments, too. They go like this:

This is not about compromise. Giving up the West Bank and Gaza is in Israel's interest. There are too many Arabs living in these lands for Israel to keep them and call itself "Jewish," demographically. For a country of 5 million Jews, a million Israeli Arabs are tough, but tolerable. Add another 2.5 million Arabs in the West Bank and Gaza, and we are no longer a Jewish state. Given their higher birthrate, the Arabs will eventually be the majority. This suggests they may either rule our democracy, or that we must do away with democracy and rule as a Jewish minority.

Almost as bad as annexation is the idea of keeping the territories as some sort of occupied or Israeli-administered entity. The Palestinians have tired of our domination. And we no longer have the stomach for forcing their acquiescence, either. How long do we want our young soldiers chasing around after young Arabs throwing stones at them? Is this the Israel we want?

Peace should be what we're after. A deal that removes incentives for reasonable Palestinians to attack Israel and which installs lots of guarantees of our security, guarantees that we enforce ourselves. It may be hard, but giving back most of the West Bank is the keystone.

In one form or another, these arguments have been played and replayed in front of a deadlocked Israeli electorate, with ever-increasing stridency, for three decades.

The West Bank is a land of hills. Not the verdant hills of Appalachia, not the rolling hills of Iowa, not the scattered hills of Rome or Athens. The hills of the West Bank are something different — memorable, mysterious, enchanted. They are muscular hills, rising among each other like competing biceps, crowding each other out, giving way to one another, falling away to the lonely road, where, in your car, they surround you, four or five hills crowded tightly in from every direction. Only the ubiquitous olive trees — in elaborately terraced but unkempt groves — break the hardness of the landscape. The rocky hills, dominated by stripes of silt and sediment piled heavily from base to peak, are softened only by the dancing, waving limbs and leaves.

Most of the Jewish settlements in the West Bank are situated on top of the hills, looking down and around in all directions, less for scenery than security. Where it was possible, the communities were centered right on the peaks of their hilltops, with a central public plaza at the zenith and the homes clustered tightly around it in concentric circles down the slopes. In the larger settlements, you can walk down among the houses along one of the staircases that traverse the hillsides. Dropping quickly away from the summit you find yourself standing in a quiet, breezy path lined with gardens and homes. In one moment you are among the trees, in the next standing before a small bungalow with lawn chairs under a trellis. In the distance, the rising and falling of other hills is obscured in the constantly moving mixture of their shadows upon one another.

You stop for a minute and hold your breath. The gentle brush of the wind through pine trees brings with it an aroma of vines and blooms and thistles, along with the quiet sight of white Arab villages on distant hills, each marked by the tower of a mosque. The land between them and you stands empty, empty of all but the sediment of ages and the olive groves tended by invisible hands. It is then that you notice, standing there, what had stirred your eyes from the road but had not quite become a thought: the Arab villages and the Jewish settlements are totally distinct.

The Arab villages wander about their hillsides, with no apparent plan in the overall lay of streets and buildings. They've existed for several hundred years where they stand, unguided by a single design.

The settlements are quite different. Most are tightly structured to revolve around a central common, the main road drawn in a circle, the homes built in neat symmetry around the pivot. And the most distinctive feature of the settlements dawns on you only gradually, as you arrive at your second or third community: almost all the homes have red clay tiles for roofing.

No first-time visitor, armed with this much information, could wrongly identify a Jewish town as Arab, or vice versa. They are as distinct in appearance as they are in character, the Arab places melting colorlessly into the shaded hillside, the Jewish places standing out in bold, gaudy, self-conscious defiance.

One afternoon in July 1997, Alfred and I decided to take a random drive through the West Bank to talk with people about the choices they and their governments have made over the years. Rather than get lost on the unfamiliar roads of West Bank Arab towns, we hired an Arab driver for the day. It was a small expense, we thought, for, as advertised by the taxi companies, a guided, air-conditioned ride in a car with shatterproof plastic windows.

We drove from Tel Aviv to Jerusalem in my own car, turned off the main road at the western entrance to the city, and headed into the Arab section of the city's eastern side via a circuitous route to the north. At a dusty patch of road across from a gas station and a row of crumbling shops, we met our driver, Moussa.

His boss, the owner of the taxi service with whom I had made the arrangements by phone, was not around. I asked Moussa if the car we were taking was protected, as the boss had promised.

"Yes, protected," Moussa affirmed. "When you are with me nothing will happen."

This, indeed, would be our only protection, for we found ourselves bumping around the back seat of an old, not air-conditioned, perfectly standard Subaru sedan.

Into the West Bank we went.

On our way north from Jerusalem to the settlements we first passed through the Palestinian town of Ramallah. The entrance to the city was marked by a set of concrete barriers narrowing the traffic flow to one lane. Once we passed through the barriers we were suddenly on Arab streets crowded with shops and people, and the yellow license plates of Israel all but vanished, replaced by the blue of the Palestinians. Driving in the West Bank in an Israeli vehicle you are profoundly aware of the yellow badge on your car, just as in Israel proper your eyes are trained to keep track of the occasional blue badge in traffic around you.

For a moment I had the funny feeling that I was in a different country, as, in a sense, I was: Ramallah was now an island belonging to the new Palestinian "autonomy." But the feeling vanished the moment we drove out the northern exit of Ramallah. Looming there, just a hundred yards out of town, was a fortress of stone walls and razor wire, a fat outpost of the Israel Defense Forces, watching over all.

In a few moments we were free of both the city and its shadow, and less than five minutes north we were the only car on the road, a winding blacktop descending to the bottom of a ravine and into the hills beyond. The hot, dry wind whipped in through the open windows, the sun beat down on my arm perched on the sill, and I felt an unmistakable sense of freedom as the olive trees bowed at our passage, a ripple of adventure in this land of so many adventures.

Ariel sits on a hill 45 minutes north of Jerusalem. Built in the early 1980s, it has grown to be one of the West Bank's largest settlements, with about 5,000 residents living mostly in single-family homes around the hilltop. A single main road rises up the hill and through a set of imposing gates, then makes one circle around the conical dome of the hill, crowded both above and below by houses and the narrow walkways between them. A surprising variety of bushes, flowers, and small trees grows thickly among the homes, obscuring them from view. In the center of town, situated at the highest point on the hill, is a little plaza of shops. Here we got out of the car and walked around.

There was a bakery where the only worker present, a Russian immigrant, did not know the cost of the strudels and begged us to wait for the owner. We left what we thought was a sufficient payment on the counter and departed with a few pastries. There was a little bridal shop, closed in the afternoon. Also a grocery store, a pharmacy, a falafel stand.

We sat down at an unassuming open-air restaurant where we had some tangy lamb on pita bread, served up by an efficient young roughneck who turned out to be the owner. As we were his only customers at three in the afternoon, he accepted our invitation to sit down and talk.

He introduced himself as Raz Cohen, age 25, owner of two small restaurants and a pleasant home in Ariel. "I'm lucky," he said with disarming openness but without a smile. "In Israel this is not so easy."

He looked at me intently from under his bushy eyebrows and deep-set brown eyes. His large shoulders and beefy arms leaned forward on the table earnestly. I asked him what he was doing here, and he paused thoughtfully before offering his reply.

Raz was only 21 when he moved to Ariel, fresh out of the army. "I served in a special unit," he said, giving no further explanation. "I saw a lot of people die. A lot of friends."

Moving to the West Bank, he said, helping Israel maintain larger, more secure boundaries, was his way of ensuring that his friends had not died in vain.

"I came for ideological reasons, I guess. But now, sometimes, I am a little unsure. I get wrapped up in everyday life, my business, my family, and I stop thinking about where I am or why I'm here. And when I stop thinking about it for a long time, then it doesn't feel the same when I think about it later. So I'm not sure why I stay. It's confusing, and sometimes it's difficult."

Although he can't quite put his finger on it, Raz knows that his choice to live in a West Bank settlement is part of an elaborate and seemingly interminable conundrum for Israel. He thinks that in some ways being here helps Israel, but he's noticing that in other ways it doesn't. In particular, he knows that his presence will never advance peace with the Palestinians — and yet he wants peace.

"I want quiet with the Arabs," he said with a sigh. "But I want someone else to decide. If it's war, OK — we go fight and end it. If it's peace, OK — sign the damned contract and end it. But now we are like in the middle."

I asked him if he would shut down his nice little restaurant here, pack up his family, and move back to Israel proper if that's what the government decided was necessary.

"Would I leave?" he echoed, thinking it over. "For me, it's no longer only my heart that drives me. I have a son now. I have to think about what's good for him. Considering that, I'd probably leave."

"Did you have some idea when you moved to the West Bank what you thought Israel's future policy should be? Annexation? Endless military occupation?"

"I don't think I was thinking about politics," he said.

I presented Raz with a theory I call "Israel's Impossible Triangle."

"The way I see it, Jewish Israelis have a triangle of national goals," I told him. "One, that Israel should be a true democracy. Two, that Israel remain a 'Jewish state.' And three, that the land be kept 'whole,' meaning retaining the West Bank as part of a larger Israel."

Raz agreed that all three were important national desires.

"Trouble is, one must go," I said. "The three cannot exist together."

He leaned more deeply across the table, interested.

I detailed the three options:

1. Abandon democracy. Israel keeps the West Bank and Gaza but does not extend citizenship to the Arabs. The voting population remains overwhelmingly Jewish. Israel has a virtual apartheid with a huge and permanently disenfranchised population.

2. Abandon the idea of Israel as a Jewish state. Israel keeps the West Bank and extends citizenship to the Arabs. With Arabs making up almost half the population, Israel is no longer a Jewish state. With time, Arabs dominate parliament, change the name of the country to Palestine, and add to the school curriculum courses on Ben-Gurion as a war criminal. Herzl rolls over in his grave.

3. Abandon the territories. Divide the country; renounce most of the West Bank and Gaza. The Palestinians get a state, or link up with other countries. Israel remains a democratic and Jewish state, but smaller and arguably less defensible.

You might think the Impossible Triangle is obvious, but Raz, like most Israelis I've talked to about it, admitted that he had "never heard it put in those terms before."

"You've got a very good point," he added after a pause. "But you know what? Maybe there's just no solution at all."

He turned to Alfred, who had been living in Israel for only a few months, and earnestly offered a piece of advice in English: "You should just take your girlfriend and get the hell out of this place — while you can!"

About an hour later, as we were finishing lunch and preparing to leave Ariel, I told Raz that I suspected that were he pressed for an answer on the Impossible Triangle, he would reluctantly choose to divide the land before abandoning democracy or the idea of a Jewish state.

"I think you're right," he said quietly. "I think most people in Ariel are this way. We just put off the decision, hoping someone will make it for us."

About ten miles east of Ariel, on one of the tallest hills in the area, sits a very different kind of settlement with the benign-sounding name of Kfar Tappuah — "Apple Village." The name is misleading, for Kfar Tappuah, located in the heart of the northern West Bank, is home to some of the most ideological settlers, including the leaders of the officially banned Kach and Kahane Hai movements, which advocate the expulsion of all Arabs from the Land of Israel.

Unlike Raz Cohen, Rivka Shifren has no doubts whatsoever about why she lives in the West Bank — or about staying put.

I met her on the front steps of her small house, more or less by accident. Moussa had dropped us off in the dry, dusty community of some 40 homes so I could look around a bit. I thought I could meet a few people casually, and get some idea about their lives in this remote outpost.

As it turned out, few were willing to talk to a stranger. I saw several women duck away from windows as I walked past, and a few men in yards stole suspicious sideways glances at me through long curls of hair hanging down from their foreheads in the manner of ultra–Orthodox Jews.

I felt like a gunslinger walking out onto Main Street in an old western town, the townsfolk already alerted to something uneasy in the air and disappearing into shadows behind water barrels and saloon doors. It was high noon. My hand fidgeted lightly on the reporter's notebook sticking out of my pocket. I strained to hear a sound beyond the wind whipping past my ears and the crunch of gravel under my feet. I stood in the middle of the road. Suddenly I heard approaching footsteps from a driveway to my side. Slowly I turned.

"You a reporter?" a man whispered loudly at me from the sidewalk. He would come no closer.

I told him I was.

"Maybe the Rabbi Shifren will talk to you. Middle house down the road, where that white van is parked."

I tried to ask a question, but he had turned back to his yard. I went in search of the Rabbi Shifren.

When I found him, I was suddenly transported from an old western town to the back seat of a 1960s VW bus on its way back from Woodstock.

"Flower power!" exclaimed Nahum Shifren as he cleared a vase of daisies and some boxes of fruit from his kitchen table. "Have a seat!"

The rabbi welcomed us into his home immediately. It turned out he was "the only surfing rabbi in the world," according to his own hype and the pile of newspaper clippings he shoved at me as soon as I sat down. A former Hare Krishna from California, Shifren returned to his Jewish roots and adopted strict Orthodoxy in the mid–'80s, but he never gave up surfing. Even from his base in the middle of biblical Israel, he makes weekly pilgrimages to the Mediterranean to preach surfing and Jewish mysticism to an awestruck group of young Israelis that have become his hangers-on.

Despite all this, in a one-hour conversation I succeeded in learning nothing of his motives for living in the West Bank other than a preference for "being away from the crowd." I pressed and pressed, but he receded easily into his "peace, man" persona and evaded anything resembling conflict or commitment. The only thing he was interested in revealing was a long line of chatter about spiritualism and surfing and the revelations available to one in the waves off any beach.

I was fairly convinced, however, that his hippie exterior was only skin deep, especially after watching him burst through the storm door into the front yard several times to holler loudly at his small children and their friends. On two occasions he threw a plastic toy ten feet into the air while speaking to the kids about the need to play more serenely.

Through an open window I saw Shifren's little girl dancing around a small tree while saying to a friend; "OK, let's sing Torah together and…"

Then the rabbi barged out onto the porch and hollered that the friend had trampled the sapling. "Get outta here!" he shouted in English. "And don't come back! I don't wanna see your face!"

When he returned to the kitchen he was docile again.

"Could I hitch a ride to Jerusalem with you, man?"

We went up the street to find Moussa and the car, and signaled for him to meet us in front of the house. We waited for Shifren out on the hot, gravel road. Suddenly a middle-aged woman in a flowered dress appeared. It was my first sight of his wife, Rivka.

"Can I offer you a cold drink?" she asked deferentially. Moussa, Alfred, and I took them readily.

To my surprise, Rivka was of a completely different type than her husband: direct, assertive, and happy to explain the exact nature of her powerful devotion to the West Bank.

"The spiritual aspect of Israel is what's important to me," she said with a smile. "It's clear, and I think the Arabs know it: this land belongs to the Jews. It's very clear in the Torah, and I don't think it can be questioned."

"Maybe it's not so much about Israel's right to be here," I probed, "but about whether it's in Israel's interest to be here."

"Why wouldn't it be in our interest?" she snapped, the smile fading.

I suggested that it might make it harder for Israel to reach peace with the Palestinians.

She held me with a gaze that verged on pity. "You think you're gonna get peace with the Palestinians?" she asked. "Giving the land back to the Palestinians is a sign of weakness! If we give them the West Bank, then what will they want next, the Galilee? When will they stop wanting more, and when will we stop giving in?

"The Arabs are welcome to live here, if they follow the rules," she continued, warming to the subject. "But they have to understand that it is a state of Judaism. They have lots of Muslim and Arab states that they can call their own. We only have this one little place. Why should we take our little slice of pie and keep shaving off pieces to give to them, when they have the whole rest of the pie!"

So Rivka Shifren was different from Raz Cohen. He would give up the land; she wouldn't. But if not the land, which part of the Impossible Triangle would she give up? Democracy or a "Jewish" state?

"If you won't give up the land," I postulated, "and Israel incorporates territories that add more than 2 million Arabs to its population, it won't be long before your state isn't so Jewish anymore."

"But if you give up the West Bank, give up the land God gave the Jews, what will make our state Jewish? The fact that it's mostly Jews who live there? Look," she continued, and I realized we were coming to the crux of the matter, "a state made up primarily of Jewish people is not a Jewish state. Judaism is what matters. Why should the Jews even have a state if not for Judaism? You can live in America, have all your freedoms, send your kids to Hebrew school, and be a so-called Jew. You don't have to have a state to do that. You can do that in America. A true Jewish state is a state of Judaism."

I asked if her plan was to keep the West Bank but deny its Arab residents political rights, like voting for the Knesset. "That's not a democracy," I noted.

"I'm not concerned about Israel's democracy. Judaism is not a democracy. Judaism is a theocracy. Democracy has nothing to do with it. And if the Arabs don't like it," she added, smiling again, "they have other choices. For example, they don't have to stay."

As Rivka said this by the open doors of the car, I could only think of Moussa sitting silently in the shade of the driver's seat, sipping the water she had doled out so benevolently.

Today, the movement that began with Moshe Levinger and his small group in Hebron has grown to more than 150,000 settlers and more than 300,000 if you count the Jews in annexed but still-disputed East Jerusalem. Most of them live only a few minutes from the border of Israel proper, in line with the "just pushing the border back a bit" idea. But tens of thousands live much deeper in the territory. Their communities are connected directly to Israeli land by new bypass roads that Israel began building in the early 1990s to keep settlers from having to make the increasingly dangerous, provocative drive through Arab villages. Reaching like a mass of life-sustaining veins from Israeli territory, these roads now complicate the prospects for convincing the settlers to leave under any future land-for-peace arrangement with the Palestinians.

The Israeli and Palestinian creators of such arrangements clearly must reckon with different kinds of settlers. There are those, like Raz Cohen, who are living in the West Bank for somewhat indeterminate or not particularly compelling reasons. They might be persuaded to leave if their communities end up in — or surrounded by — a future Palestine. And there are those, like Rivka Shifren, who cling to the land with religious devotion and faith. They are politically active and not likely to relinquish their vision.

I'm not exactly sure where to classify David Ramati, who insists he is in neither group. He loves the land to the point of endangering himself over it, yet he rejects the pathos of some of the extremists and honestly sees his actions as benign. He places himself above politics, absurd though this may seem. He says there are many like him, and he has coined a term for them: the "hard-core" settler.

"Your hard-core settler leaves home early in the morning and comes back in the evening. He has six to ten kids; he's making relatively little money; he gets shot at, but doesn't shoot back, generally. He's not an 'activist'; he doesn't spend every weekend at a rally. He wouldn't have the strength, after a day at work, to throw a rock. But he does his army reserve duty. He prays three times a day. He doesn't spend the day thinking about much more than getting through it. He's a grit-your-teeth kind of guy, and he has to be, because building a Jewish presence in the land of Israel is hard damn work."

He painstakingly distinguishes his fellow hard-core settlers in Kiryat Arba from the several hundred more fanatical Jews who followed Levinger into the heart of Hebron, where they now live in a few well-protected enclaves in a tempest of mutual hatred with 130,000 Palestinians.

It is a distinction that perhaps was lost on David's daughter Elisheva, who married a young firebrand and moved into Levinger's community of messianics.

Blonde, blue-eyed, and very pretty, Elisheva is now the mother of several children whom she cares for on her own while her husband, Noam Federman, a devoted activist, often spends several months a year in detention of one sort or another. I heard her on the radio condemning a decision by the Israeli army to equip the school bus used by the Hebron children with armor plates; her argument was that knowledge of this would draw Arab fire.

Undoubtedly Elisheva got her independent streak from her father, so he can hardly condemn her choices. "I prefer to live in a place that requires less confrontation," he demurs. "But if they have the energy for that kind of sport in the evening, well, that's their choice."

His face souring, he goes on to belittle the values of her community. "Most of the people who live in Hebron exist off the government. They have jobs in the state-sponsored school, in the local settlement administration, and so on, or they have the benefit of outside gifts, outside money, political money from American Jews and all kinds of organizations.

"They've become politicized and radicalized.... I think it's absolutely counterproductive. I think people like me will be around a lot longer than the other type, after everyone else has gone home, after they've worn themselves out with shouting."

Levinger himself is still around, a stooped, bearded figure skulking through the alleyways of Hebron with a pistol holstered at his side. Never satisfied with the settlers' treatment, he often engages in shouting matches with Israeli officers and officials who arrive in the town. Over the years he has served several brief stints in jail, including one for killing an Arab merchant while firing his pistol into the air to scare off a hostile crowd during the Palestinian uprising.

I met him in the ragged old Jewish cemetery in Hebron, at a memorial for the Jews killed in the 1929 massacre. He was lingering about the hillside graves, watching over the proceedings distractedly, content to let others, professional politicians mostly, make speeches, while he looked on like a prophet of doom.

I asked him what he thought the future held.

"Nothing very good," he murmured with resignation, staring at the Arab homes on the hillside. "There will be more bloodshed, more fighting, more unhappiness, until we start to act like the masters here. Until we make the Arabs understand."

Disillusion

A broken Menachem Begin, a few weeks before his resignation (photograph by Herman Chananya).

Borders between countries are amazing places, the fault lines where societies, ideologies, and economies rub up against each other in grinding disharmony, where you can stand and look out upon freedom, despotism, abundance, starvation, the future, the past — depending on the border and on which side of it you stand. Unlike rivers and mountain ranges, they are artificial boundaries, created out of a conscious effort to distinguish one place from another, an almost random delineation that arises out of an equilibrium of opposing forces. Many are not friendly; most are serious business and are patrolled with grim rigor. People who have crossed an international border tend to experience an odd discomfort, as if something in the soul tugs at the mind, placing it on alert. And in that fleeting moment of heightened sensitivity, you realize what troubles you about borders — they stand as monuments both to internal confinement and to external dangers, and they make you want to get away from both with haste.

It was, therefore, one of the more defiant acts of Zionism that Israelis went out of their way to build homes and communities virtually on top of international borders. The border communities were seen by some as a first line of defense, but mainly they served to tell the world: "This land is ours."

Nowhere is this settlement philosophy more apparent than on Israel's northern border. Where rolling hills rise to mountains, and wind sweeps down from Lebanon in regular gales, where the soil is ragged and its most prevalent fruit is rock, early Zionists built their homes using the barbed-wire border fence to mark their backyards. In dozens of places on the Israeli side — the commons of a kibbutz, the main street of a town, the backyards of homes — daily life bumps up against the line of demarcation. Yet on the Lebanese side there is no such claim. There is generally not a home or town within a half mile.

It is a different place, Lebanon — just as the border was established to suggest, just as the barbed-wire fence insists, just as your eye, traveling up the wide valleys not to be followed by your feet, confirms. From Israel, Lebanon looks like a mysterious, troubled, mixed-up land. There is no neighbor across the barbed wire to reach out to, to get to know up close, to understand. From the Israeli side of the border, Lebanon is not Lebanon, but simply the void where Israel ends.

When this border was established, few imagined that the land across it would play a major role in Israel's internal and external battles, or come to have a pivotal impact on its psyche.

Beirut, to the north, has been conquered by many successive invaders and empires, but never truly owned by any. The Phoenicians, the Greeks, the Romans, the Crusaders, the Byzantines, the Ottomans, and others came and went.

Dwarfed in ancient times by Tyre and Sidon, Beirut eventually surpassed those settlements and developed as a free port, a trading post, a resting place for caravans that traveled from Marrakech to Bombay and beyond. Much later, a disunited Arab world adopted it as its principal commercial and financial center.

It seemed to be everyone's little prize on the eastern shore of the Mediterranean, a pearl thrown up from the sea.

The last non-Arab power to have dominion over Beirut and its mountain environs was France. Handed over to French authority from the rubble of the Ottoman Empire after World War I, Beirut adapted quickly to the mentality of the French Riviera and earned itself the nickname "Paris of the Middle East."

When World War II brought a temporary end to France's own independence, Lebanon gained its. That was in 1943. Yet Lebanon was perhaps never meant to be independent.

For roughly 25 years, the new state made its way under a power-sharing agreement between the thin majority Maronite Christians, who had been around since the first centuries after Christ, and the minority Sunni and Shi'ite Muslims, who took hold in the seventh and eighth centuries. But it was a tentative agreement, for the differences in religion, class, and culture that had developed among the three groups over the centuries were just reaching their fullest flower, and, as the Muslim population gradually overtook the Christian, Muslim groups began agitating for revisions. This set up an internal power struggle that, had the country had more experience running its own affairs, might have been resolved. But Lebanon, on its own for only a generation, was extremely vulnerable to outside forces.

"I would describe Beirut like a whore," said Walid Chamoun one afternoon over beer. "She let everybody come in and out — from every race, every region, every kind of ruling empire. And I have no shame in saying it. The Lebanese are very commercially oriented people. If there's a benefit, a deal, a market share, a power share, some sort of gain, then Lebanon welcomes the outsider."

Walid should know. His great-uncle Camille Chamoun was Lebanon's first president. His cousin Danny was thought to be a leading presidential contender until he was murdered in 1991 by unknown parties.

"That is the struggle of my country," he went on. "While we share a certain cultural affinity — our adaptability, our rich history, our difficult personalities, our resourcefulness and success as a people around the world — no one has yet figured out how to make unity out of us. We just don't care about a national idea. We are shortsighted. We think about our family, our immediate family, but nobody thinks about the whole country, all 10,452 square kilometers of it."

Walid was born in Beirut in 1966, just in time to grow up as witness to the ultimate unraveling of his country's brief period of independence. He did that growing up — nine years of exciting activity and exuberance, as he remembers it — right next door to one of Beirut's large refugee camps for Palestinians. Running past it on his way to school, he could not have known how important that camp — and others like it throughout the southern countryside — would become for his country.

By admitting Palestinian refugees from Israel in 1948, just five years after gaining its independence, Lebanon had unwittingly opened its doors once again to an outside force that would tear it asunder.

In 1959, Yasser Arafat—born in Jerusalem, educated in Cairo, a one-time businessman and self-taught guerrilla—founded the liberation movement Al Fatah. At the time, the fate of the Palestinians was still in the hands of various Arab governments, primarily those of Egypt, Syria, Jordan, Lebanon, Iraq, and Saudi Arabia. The willingness of those Arab governments to fight Israel and their effectiveness in the fight were all the Palestinian refugees, festering in camps throughout the region, had going for them.

Al Fatah sought to change that. Its declared mission was to make the struggle against Israel first and foremost a Palestinian affair. It made the liberation of Palestine a philosophical prerequisite to pan-Arab unity, rather than the other way around. It saw armed guerrilla warfare as the only path to success. And, following the revolutionary path already trodden by Che Guevara, Fidel Castro, Ho Chi Minh, and others, Arafat sought the creation of a "people's army."

For years, Arafat built that army. Then, in the middle of the decade, in 1964, the PLO was founded, not as a competing organization but as an umbrella group to coordinate and support the activities of a wide array of Palestinian groups. It was not long before the PLO became synonymous with guerrilla warfare and terror campaigns against Israel.

Arafat became PLO chairman in 1969, two years after the loss of the West Bank and Gaza to Israel, and quickly made his first major decision: the PLO could no longer operate effectively from its base in Egypt. It needed to be closer to the territory it sought to liberate. The first move was to Jordan, just across the river from the newly expanded Zionist state and home to a large population of Palestinians.

King Hussein, aware that the Palestinian group might inspire revolutionary elements within his own country, quickly made the PLO unwelcome. It was a critical moment for Hussein, whose rule was based on the loyalty of Bedouins. As a result of the Six Day War, hundreds of thousands of new Palestinian refugees had flooded into Jordan, and they constituted a potential power base for Arafat. A proud, careful man, Hussein was determined to preserve his kingdom and its small advances toward prosperity. He would not back down to Arafat; by 1970, open conflict had broken out between Arafat's forces and the Jordanian army. In a bloody ten-day battle Palestinians remember as "Black September," Hussein chased the PLO out of his country.

Having abandoned Egypt and been thrown out of Jordan, Arafat turned to his last, best alternative. Possessing a long, shadowy border with Israel, home to a large population of Palestinian refugees, and too disorganized to resist, Lebanon became his host. Arafat's army, mostly Muslim, soon played a major role in sparking a bloody civil war among Lebanon's factions, destroying Walid's Beirut and leaving more than 100,000 people dead.

By the time Menachem Begin came to power in Israel in 1977, Lebanon was in pieces. The full-scale war that erupted in 1975 had, by late 1976, reached a formal cease-fire, but it was tenuous and gave way regularly to outbursts of fighting among Christians, Muslims, the PLO, and others. The Syrian army and a multinational UN force attempted to enforce the truce, yet even in times of relative quiet Lebanon continued its precipitous slide into disarray. But as Israel's new prime minister assumed the reigns of government he had other things on his mind.

Some people look back on Begin with a wistful respect. "He was the first to trade land for peace," they say.

And he was. But the honorific casts Begin's greatest moment in a deceptive light, revealing only part of the picture.

After Anwar Sadat's historic visit to Jerusalem and his speech to the Israeli Knesset on November 19, 1977, the peacemaking between Israel and Egypt unfolded quickly, at least by the laggard standards of future endeavors. Using eager U.S. President Jimmy Carter as chaperon, the two nations — with so much history between them — went through a 16-month courtship. It culminated in a March 1979 ceremony on the South Lawn of the White House with the two parties signing an agreement under which Israel would give back all of the Sinai Desert, Egypt would declare peace with the Jewish state, and the countries would commence a normal neighborly relationship.

It was a daring deal for both Sadat and Begin. For the former, it brought a hail of condemnation from the rest of the Arab world, isolating Egypt for several years. It also ultimately led to Sadat's assassination at the hands of Islamic fundamentalists in October 1981. For Begin, the agreement required quelling dissent from the more extreme corners of his own party and coalition and, worse still, forcibly displacing Sinai settlers from their homes.

Sadat did this for the welfare of his people. After three decades and three military defeats — although its honor was repaired by a credible showing in the 1973 war — Egypt needed to move forward, open itself to the developed world, and build some prospects for a brighter future. Put more simply, Sadat needed — and got — massive U.S. aid.

Begin held up his end, too, even in the painful and unsightly task of dislodging his fellow believers from the Sinai, the land the ancient Jews, led by Moses, had crossed on their trek from Egypt to the Promised Land. Many Israelis watched in disbelief as Israeli TV beamed back from the Sinai indisputable evidence that Begin was clearing the settlers and giving the land away.

It was a clear example of "land for peace." But peace itself may not have been Begin's ultimate goal. His later decisions, including stalling any discussions concerning the West Bank and Gaza, suggest that Begin sought, through the Sinai deal, to secure Israel's border with Egypt so as to leave the other territories in Israel's firm control. Egypt, with more people than the rest of Israel's neighbors combined, was scratched off Israel's "mortal enemy" list, and Begin, instead of seriously negotiating on the West Bank and Gaza, as he had promised Sadat, embarked on his plan for large-scale settlement of those territories.

Even though he had predicted this abandonment of the Palestinian cause by the Arab states years before, Arafat, watching from Lebanon, was furious.

He had not been wasting his time. He had built up the PLO into a more structured army, had obtained Soviet-built missiles from Syria, and had carried out a campaign of terror in northern Israel, including a series of deadly infiltrations that culminated in concerted rocket fire on Israeli settlements in the summer of 1981.

With his reelection campaign just ahead, Begin turned his attention to the menace from the north. His first move was straightforward, aimed at knocking out Syrian and Palestinian rocket positions in Lebanon. In the early summer of 1981, Begin authorized tactical air strikes, which were a military success.

Then, alerted by Israeli intelligence that Iraq was secretly planning a nuclear weapons plant at its Osirak nuclear facility near Baghdad, Begin made a bold move that brought immediate worldwide condemnation but that, behind closed doors, was probably welcomed by many countries, especially in the light of later events.

In an overnight raid in June, Israeli jets streaked over hostile territory into Iraqi air space, bombed the uncompleted nuclear facility into rubble, and returned safely home.

"Never again!" thundered Begin, would Jews go like lambs to the slaughter.

Opposition leader Shimon Peres condemned the operation as a transparent election ploy, a position that was woefully out of sync with that of the public. Among the Israeli people, the operation achieved the dual purpose of wiping out what Begin had successfully presented as an imminent mortal threat and proving yet again that Israel — however outnumbered — had the qualitative edge over the Arabs. Israelis could sleep soundly in their beds with an air force so fine, and with leaders so daring.

The Osirak bombing — and Peres's poor political judgment in criticizing it — were crucial in turning the tide of what initially had seemed to be a hopeless election campaign for Likud. Begin and his bloc of nationalist and religious parties defeated Peres's Labor-led coalition by one Knesset seat in the June 1981 election.

With Begin reelected, Israeli air attacks on Palestinian bases in southern Lebanon and in Beirut continued through that summer and fall, amid a growing debate within Begin's cabinet about how to proceed with the PLO in Lebanon. Extreme hawks, such as defense minister Ariel Sharon, urged Begin to finish them off. Others counseled restraint. Begin, satisfied with his strategic military decisions to date, was not eager to get ahead of the game. But always his mind turned back to the occupied territories: to Jerusalem, Hebron, and the new settlements that he had encouraged. With the PLO still on the loose, they would always face a challenge.

On June 6, 1982, fifteen years and a day after launching one of history's classic preemptive strikes in the Six Day War, Israel initiated war again. Three Israeli divisions rumbled across the Lebanese border, through a strip of territory controlled by a friendly Lebanese militia — the South Lebanon army, run by a renegade Lebanese army officer, Major Saad Hadad — and headed due north toward PLO positions.

The pretext was the near-fatal shooting of the Israeli ambassador to Britain, Shlomo Argov, by a young Palestinian two days before. But everybody knew that this was an effort by Israel's government to complete unfinished business. Having secured peace with Egypt, it was determined to eliminate the PLO's state-within-a-state in Lebanon. Not only had Lebanon become a convenient and effective launching pad for terrorist attacks against Israel — by both land and sea — but it also placed the PLO uncomfortably close to the territories that it sought to claim: the West Bank and Gaza and, if at all possible, Israel itself.

Begin and Sharon had promised the government and the people that the goal was to move the PLO forces 40 kilometers north of the border — out of rocket range — and they promised a swift, clean victory. And Israel had no shortage of allies in Lebanon. There was Hadad's militia. There were the Christians in the north led by the Phalange forces of the Jemayel family, and there was the Tiger militia run by Walid's Chamoun clan. Many of the Shi'ite villagers in South Lebanon welcomed the Israelis too. There was little love there for the heavy-handed and foreign PLO.

Israel achieved the stated aims within days. The PLO was expelled from the coastal towns of Tyre and Sidon and from the main inland villages in South Lebanon. The Israeli army seized tons of materiel — tanks, rockets, antitank weapons, artillery pieces. The Syrian air force, from its own positions in the north and east of the country, unwisely took on Israel and was virtually wiped out.

But the cost in Israeli lives was higher than expected. The PLO resistance was considerable, and by June 13 Israel had about 130 dead — including Major General Yekutiel Adam, the highest ranking casualty ever — and 600 wounded.

And it was becoming apparent that Sharon's army was not stopping at 40 kilometers.

Polls had shown a majority of Israelis supported the invasion at first. Thinking of it as a short-term operation that would greatly enhance security in the north, most of the nation rallied to the cause. Even Peres, leading the opposition in the Knesset, was cautiously supportive.

Yet there was unease about the invasion as well. Even supporters wanted it over quickly; and it took several days, even a few weeks, before the nation began to come to grips with what was making it feel so uneasy: it was Israel's first prolonged war that was by no means a matter of survival, but a matter of strategic gain. The difference took some time for Israelis to swallow. When it went down, it changed Israel.

Because Israel was born of the Holocaust, Jews had come to see their country as a fundamentally righteous place. Herzl's utopian ideals, Ben-Gurion's benevolence in hardship, Eshkol's egalitarian principles, even Meir's hand-wringing morality and Begin's bluster — all of it seemed, to Israelis, to be part of a natural rightness. After the murder of 6 million mothers and fathers, brothers and sisters, daughters and sons, cousins and friends, after all that loss, the Jews might have been given leeway to do any number of things. What they chose to do was to pull themselves together, go to the desert of their ancestors, and build themselves a new future. They did it with socialist ideals; they did it with communal farm living; they did it with their own blood, their own sweat, their own tears; remarkably, they did it with a good deal of democracy. For Jews of that first immigrant generation, and for many generations after, Israel could be seen as the place that took everything that was wrong and made it right. Not perfect, not necessarily the best, but right. On this, Israelis were in agreement for 35 years: Israel, all things considered, was a place of justice.

This sense of justice deepened after each of Israel's first four wars, despite the calamities that befell the Arabs. The War of Independence, the 1956 war, the Six Day War, and the Yom Kippur War were all won in spite of the far greater numbers of Israel's enemies and amid a general feeling — however subjective — that Israel was the good guy. Almost all Israelis agreed that they were being threatened with destruction, they were defending their right to exist, they were not picking fights but being challenged by bullies, they were fighting fair, and they were doing no more than necessary to repel attack and assure victory.

Israelis even developed fancy ideas about a so-called "purity of arms" — the notion that their troops did not massacre, pillage, rape, or loot — which a critical look at history reveals as mostly but not entirely true.

All these notions became so ingrained in the national character that it was virtually inconceivable to most Israelis that their government would declare unjustified war. This was the "national consensus" that had held the young state together during times of both war and reprieve.

Until Lebanon.

Fittingly, I met Yitzhak Devash at a party being thrown by Walid Chamoun, my Lebanese friend. It was very soon after I had first met Walid, who was living in Tel Aviv, and I did not yet know him well. Standing in his apartment with a drink in my hand, I looked around a spacious room filled with people I knew nothing about. I struck up what conversations I could over the noise of the music, and in between lingered near the smorgasbord and admired the large American, Israeli, and Lebanese flags that our optimistic host had hung from the rafters. When I observed another man about my age, also apparently alone, also hovering over the food, I casually moved in his direction.

Yitzhak Devash was born in Libya in 1962. Immediately after the Six Day War, his family, like most of Libya's Jews, was kicked out of that country. After two years in Italy, they moved to Israel.

"It's interesting," he told me. "Even though I came here as a youngster, I spent years adopting my new identity as an Israeli. One thing I decided early was that I wanted to become a soldier. It was obvious that the army in Israel was the great equalizer, your ticket to Israeli society, and so for me joining was a culmination of all my efforts to become an Israeli.

"I think all of us here grow up thinking that the army is very, very clean, that it's upright, the best expression of our national aspirations, and throughout the '70s, when I was coming of age, the moral association with the army was almost inhumanly high."

Devash entered officers' training as soon as he graduated from high school. "All I wanted to do was to live up to my charge," he told me, "to be the very best soldier."

I myself was still in college in Philadelphia back then, watching Devash and others among my contemporaries—and childhood friends—fight in my place.

The invasion happened when Devash had six months remaining in officers' training. He had every reason to believe, gnashing his teeth at the unfairness of it, that the war would be long over by the time he was available for duty, what with the promises of Begin and Sharon.

But by August, two months into the operation, Israeli troops were still in Lebanon, occupying part of Beirut, well north of the 40-kilometer goal advertised. Although the PLO had been routed in the south in the first week of the invasion, evacuating north to Beirut, Sharon convinced Begin to keep in hot pursuit, to destroy them for good, and to cleanse Lebanon for a reinvigorated Lebanese government and military to maintain. The plan necessitated the conquest of the last PLO stronghold in Lebanon, West Beirut. Taking the city in street-to-street fighting would have been a very costly affair; so the decision was made to lay siege to the western half of the war-torn metropolis and force the PLO out with attrition and bombardment.

The air force had begun bombing the Lebanese capital in mid-June. The once vibrant city, already haunted by the hulks of scores of empty buildings, standing like urban tombstones to mark the civil war, was being reduced to rubble in some areas. From positions atop Shuf Mountain to the south and from gunboats at sea to the west, and with the Lebanese Christians in East Beirut as its allies, Israel's siege was thorough and effective. After two months of heavy action, capped by American mediation, the PLO agreed to leave the city. On August 21, some 14,000 Palestinian fighters and some Syrian troops supporting them began their evacuation.

A week later the Lebanese parliament elected Israel's friend, Phalange leader Bashir Jemayel, as the new president of Lebanon. Begin congratulated him warmly, anticipating that the successful war would culminate in a peace treaty with a pro–Israeli Lebanese government and a great PLO-free zone stretching from the Israeli border to Beirut and beyond. Already, Jemayel was promising to root out the several thousand PLO troops that Israel suspected remained behind in the Palestinian refugee camps.

And then, in the balmy afternoon of September 14, the whole edifice collapsed.

A massive explosion ripped through the Phalange office in East Beirut as Jemayel was addressing a public gathering. Many were killed and wounded, and Jemayel was dead before he ever took office. Within hours, Israel seized key junctions in West Beirut and decided to allow the Phalange militia into the Palestinian refugee camps. Later, Sharon claimed he had warned them against harming civilians. But in their fury, the Phalangists ran amok in the Palestinian camps of Sabra and Shatila and murdered hundreds of refugees — some say more than 1,000.

In Israel, there was shock. Hundreds of thousands gathered in a mass protest in Tel Aviv. Calls mounted for a commission of inquiry, and Begin relented. A half year later, the commission Begin had appointed vindicated the prime minister but found a number of Israeli officials indirectly responsible for the massacre and forced the ouster of Sharon from the Defense Ministry.

Unable to admit defeat, the Begin government remained in Lebanon, through useless peace talks with the government of Amin Jemayel, Bashir's brother and successor as Phalange leader. A treaty the sides eventually reached was soon canceled by Syria, which occupied the north and east of the country and was now a silent partner and power broker in Beirut.

The Likud government did not seem to know what to do. To leave Lebanon without a central government in firm control, without a peace treaty, and with Syria calling the shots, would be to admit that the whole operation had been a fiasco. So they stayed.

And young Yitzhak Devash, newly minted as an officer of the Israeli Defense Forces, got his chance to be "the very best soldier" he could be.

His first command assignment was to "clean up" three small Arab villages in southern Lebanon. This meant his unit and several others were to sit tight, keep an eye out for any PLO fighters, and report any serious developments. Almost immediately there was a report of a PLO operative on the loose, and a chase ensued.

"Within an hour there were something like 200 men chasing after a single enemy," Devash recalled. "They eventually cornered him in a cave near the village. When I got there a bunch of soldiers were firing wildly into the hillside. You know who the Hitler was that we finally captured? A scared 16-year-old kid, unarmed."

Devash recounted this episode not because it was the first thing he saw, and certainly not because it was the worst thing he saw. It was just so typical of what he saw, and at the time it made him reconsider everything he had thought about Israel's military all his life.

"At first I thought what we were doing was right, but that dissipated quickly," he said. "I began looking closely at the dead bodies of our enemies wherever I encountered them, and looking into the eyes of the prisoners we captured. I began to see them for what they were — a hopeless people caught in an endless cycle of warfare. And what disturbed me about the larger Israeli approach to this enemy was that no one was challenging the context, no one was challenging the basic assumptions, no one challenged the setting. We all played out our roles: the bad guys, the good guys, the vanquished, the victorious — the same thing we had been doing for 35 years."

Throughout Israel, however, people were beginning to challenge.

In newspaper articles, on radio talk shows, in private conversations in their homes, at sidewalk cafes, at work, Israelis began to question. As the invasion and occupation dragged on, as chaos mounted, it became harder and harder for Israelis to accept what their government was doing.

In some ways this period was for Israel comparable to the American experience with Vietnam, more compact in scope and duration but not in impact. For many people the Lebanon war ended Israel's right to claim moral superiority. It divided the nation between those who supported the operation as a patriotic necessity and those who asked difficult questions. It utterly destroyed the national consensus about what was acceptable as justification for war. It left at least half of Israel's people, probably more, dispirited about the goodness of their nation, about the rightness of their national enterprise. And it put the right-left divide into its sharpest relief yet, adding bitterness and rancor to the mix, especially from the left toward the right. From this moment on, many Israelis sensed, we will never be certain of each other again.

In the end, Begin's Lebanon adventure did more: it set a boundary between those who would justify almost anything their nation did, and those who would not.

Israeli author Amos Oz — one of those who would not — knew something was happening to his people. Famed for his poetic novels and ruminations about life in Israel, he tackled the subject of the war and the disillusionment it had created head-on.

"When the war in Lebanon began I was very angry and I wrote a number of articles criticizing the government," he explained when I met him in 1997. "At some point I had the feeling, three or four months into the war, that many Israelis out there had a point of view that I didn't understand. I decided to travel the country to find out their rationale."

The Israelis that Oz wrote about back in the early '80s are as recognizable and politically resonant today as they were then — most even more so. The ultra-religious, the West Bank settler, the Sephardic Jew in his isolated town, the Israeli Arab — they were all powerful figures in Oz's journey through the hinterlands, and the cautionary tone he sounded throughout his essays made these types of Israelis seem more than a little ominous.

When Oz's essays were assembled and published in early 1983, the war in Lebanon was still going on. The book, titled *In the Land of Israel*, focused not so much on the war and the division it revealed as on the people who populated one side of that division. As such, Oz's work seemed to institutionalize the idea of "sides" in the Israeli population.

Looking back on it fifteen years later, from the serenity of his little office at Ben-Gurion University in the desert town of Beer-Sheva, Oz said the war indeed changed Israel's ideas of itself. As a result of the invasion, he said, "Many Israelis started looking back to ask themselves, 'Maybe history could have been different if we had acted differently.' So Lebanon was an eye-opener for Israelis and a source of many radical reevaluations of the entire history of the Middle East — and in some cases of the entire Zionist project."

It certainly was so for Yitzhak Devash, who left the country soon after his discharge, looking to "rebuild." Only years later, after earning his M.B.A. from Harvard University and holding a variety of jobs in New York, London, and Tokyo, would he return.

"It was the first war we chose to fight using old excuses that no longer fit," he said of Lebanon. "I think we took the Holocaust too far as our moral rationale. The Holocaust psychology impacted everything the state did in the years before 1967, and then that war was like the total opposite of Holocaust—it was like 'war therapy.' But '73 brought the return of helplessness. It reinforced the idea that we're the weak ones, the ones on the defensive, and the right ones. It was Israel's rebirth of moral rectitude, and it was that which we rode into Lebanon."

"Are we really to see Beirut as Berlin?" wrote Professor Ze'ev Manowitz, an expert on the Holocaust, in the *Ha'aretz* newspaper, as the Israeli army hammered the Lebanese capital. "Begin has lost touch and is pursuing phantoms born of the greatest tragedy that ever befell our people. Whatever its final outcome, the epitaph to be placed upon the war in Lebanon will read: Here lies the international stature and moral integrity of a wonderful people. Died of a false analogy."

With the outcome in Lebanon souring by the day, the proud, patriotic Begin began to die, too. More than a year after the "three-week" invasion began, he seemed deflated and exhausted by the rancor and criticism. On August 28, 1983, Begin announced his resignation, saying simply, "I cannot continue."

Three days later his stunned party voted in Foreign Minister Yitzhak Shamir—once the head of Israel's most radical pre-state underground—as Begin's replacement.

Israelis—supporters and detractors both—watched in a mixture of sorrow and dismay as Begin became a recluse, unable or unwilling to answer the painful, urgent questions that emerged out of the Lebanon invasion.

After nine years of self-imposed seclusion, Begin died in 1992.

He stands out in my memory as a leader who in service to his country was dignified, impassioned, deeply flawed, and ultimately wounded. Too late he saw what a mistake the Lebanon invasion was, perhaps even what a mistake the rationale for it had been, and how he had destroyed, perhaps irrevocably, the most fundamental part of Israel's sense of righteousness.

Tens of thousands of Israelis left annually in the years during and after the Lebanon war. The economy went into a tailspin, with a stock market crash in 1983 and inflation topping 400 percent in 1984.

When Israel finally pulled out of Lebanon in June 1985—after losing more than 600 soldiers (the equivalent of approximately 25,000 in American terms)—it felt compelled to retain a narrow buffer zone to shield its northern border against the new enemies it had made during its three-year occupation. In this misnamed "security zone" Israeli soldiers still die by the dozens each year, fighting an Islamic fundamentalist militia of Lebanese called the Hezbollah, not knowing when it will end.

Thus, the Lebanon war mired Israel in what turned out to be unending disillusion. Arafat lived on in Tunis, Walid's Lebanon continued in desperate disarray, and thoughtful Israelis like Devash continued to look back with doubts and anger for years. Some left Israel and never returned. I took the opposite route. My parents may have saved my life by taking me to the United States — had they not, I would have been in my second year of mandatory army duty during the Lebanon invasion. But in January 1987, armed with a graduate degree, a few thousand dollars, and a taste for adventure, I moved back to Israel.

I shielded my ears as the machine's huge blades began spinning, generating an overwhelming noise that weighed on the air over us, a physical mass that alone seemed to keep us anchored to the ground. After a moment, though, the whole thing — the chopper, us, and the noise — slowly lifted from the helipad on the Knesset grounds, swiftly executed a 90-degree turn, and zoomed off toward the north. A minute later we were above the lightly forested, terraced hills of the West Bank.

I had been invited onto the flight in my capacity as political reporter for the *Jerusalem Post*. I looked to my left. Prime Minister Yitzhak Shamir, who like me wore a helmet to protect his ears, seemed determined not to speak. I wasn't surprised. Speaking would have been difficult now, and he was tight-lipped even when conversational conditions were ideal.

Shamir was a lonely man in the summer of 1989, saddled with three rebellions. Half of his "national unity government" were Labor party ministers opposed to his policies. Within his own party he was facing constant challenges from three top ministers who wanted to succeed him. And the Palestinians of the West Bank and Gaza were in the throes of a rebellion against the Israeli army.

From Tunisia, Yasser Arafat's PLO was pulling the strings of the uprising, which became known by the Arabic word *intifada*— a "shaking off."

Today, *intifada* has become part of the world's language. In Israel, it is bandied about as the punch line of jokes, as a youngster's threat of disobedience, as the universal notion of what happens when Arafat snaps his fingers. But in December 1987, when the Intifada — capitalized — broke out, it was not a well-known word.

At first, it seemed to be just another car accident. Perhaps it was. But because it had been an Israeli driver behind the wheel of a truck that swerved out of control, and because it had been a carload of Palestinians who were hit – four died — rumors quickly spread throughout the Jebaliya refugee camp in the Gaza Strip that the incident had been a deliberate act of violence, and it led to an outburst of rioting in the area. The riots spread almost immediately to the West Bank, and in the days and weeks that followed began to take on a life of their own.

For months, Israeli media referred to the demonstrations and stone throwing as "the disturbances." Soon they simply became a fact. The territories were burning. The occupation was finally no longer painless for Israel.

Every day Palestinian youths burned tires on the main roads, threw rocks and bottles at Israeli soldiers trying to patrol the area, and led foreign TV crews through winding, smoky alleys as if by leash. Palestinians stopped paying taxes, stopped applying for Israeli permits for every little activity, and otherwise ended their tacit cooperation with Israel's occupation authorities. Palestinian policemen working for Israel quit their jobs. Workers in the territories frequently went on strike. Universities shut down.

The joint Labor-Likud government that had resulted from the tied 1984 election could not agree on the future of the Palestinian areas. At heart, Labor wanted to vacate them, while Likud saw keeping them as the main task facing Israel. They agreed, however, on one thing: the Palestinians "will not get anything through terrorism," in the words of Yitzhak Rabin, who was now defense minister. Rabin's policy was known as "beatings, not bullets." But there were plenty of bullets too. In all, more than 1,000 Palestinians were killed by Israeli troops during the six years of the uprising.

A few months before my helicopter ride with Shamir, Arafat had made a speech ambiguously forswearing violence and declaring that his new, slimmed-down goal was the creation of a Palestinian state only in the West Bank and Gaza Strip.

The world had expected Shamir to respond somehow, to pick up the gauntlet. But how could he? First, Shamir didn't believe Arafat's claim that he had given up on retaking of all of Israel. Second, he had no inclination to relinquish such central real estate to the man his predecessor, Begin, referred to as "that two-legged animal."

Yet the ranks of Israelis who viewed the West Bank, and especially the smaller Gaza Strip, as a burden were growing by the day. Dozens were refusing army call-ups to serve in the occupied territories – something previously unheard of. At demonstrations Israelis clamored for a change. "Two states for two peoples!" was their slogan.

Such a notion was unfathomable to Shamir. How could Jews want to give away the heartland of their country? Shamir argued tirelessly that "the Arabs are still the same Arabs, and the sea is still the same sea" — that is, one into which the Arabs schemed to sweep the Jews. The way to quell the rebellion was not to give in to demands, but rather to show that "violence" against Israel could never be profitable.

To stand firm.

For this, the one-time underground leader and Mossad agent was perfectly cast. Diminutive but powerfully built, with enormously bushy eyebrows and taut features that projected stubbornness and determination to a world that towered above him, Shamir seemed like he literally could not be knocked over.

But for all his determination, Shamir mustered no solution for his major conundrum: what to do with the increasingly difficult, boisterous, and rebellious occupied population in the West Bank and Gaza. Not only did they reject Israel's occupation, but in sharing the entity called Israel they were transforming it from a Jewish state into a binational one. The simple, incontrovertible fact was that as long as Israel controlled the West Bank and Gaza, the population of the country was almost 40 percent Arab — and growing.

Shamir, I imagine, was hoping to win time, hoping for a miracle.

Our helicopter roared over Ramallah, the center of Palestinian wealth and nightlife in the West Bank. From our height of some 1500 feet it looked like a sprinkling of Lego pieces nestled in the hills. The next major Arab town was Nablus, about 25 miles north. We passed over patches of earth — sometimes green, sometimes brown, and sometimes almost yellow — punctuated by hillsides of exposed sedimentary rock. Occasionally we saw a wadi, one of the dried-up river beds known for their flash floods in winter.

Shamir said only one thing during our entire half-hour ride over the West Bank.

Pointing down and raising his eyebrows, he shouted, "See? It's empty!"

From our vantage point, it certainly did seem so. But down on the ground were more than 2 million Palestinians. People who learned about democracy from Israel but were denied a role in it. People whose lives were ruled by often unqualified and apathetic military administrators whom they did not choose.

People who were getting sick and tired of being invisible.

Thus the Lebanon invasion had a lasting impact — though not the kind that Begin had envisioned.

Instead of securing Israel's borders and helping it hold on to the territories, the invasion that divided the Jews had helped unite the Palestinians. Their drive for independence became a thorn in Israel's side, closing out a miserable decade of directionlessness and disillusion. As the 1980s ended, more and more Israelis began to feel that maybe the thing to do was to let the Palestinians have the territories and end the struggle once and for all.

Light

Yitzhak Rabin (left) and King Hussein, whose warm friendship symbolized the peace process (photograph by Yaacov Saar).

Late on the evening of June 23, 1992, as polling stations across Israel were closing, I was a world away in Bucharest, desperately panting up the steps of my apartment building.

I had been posted in the Romanian capital in 1990 as the correspondent for a wire service. From that position in the heart of the Balkans I traveled across the region during years of stupefying upheaval, witnessing history unfold before me and chronicling its effect on the bewildered people whom communism had left behind.

But even in the frozen plains of Eastern Europe, Israel was never far from my mind. One of the most important people in my life became an impish man named Virgil Ciobotaru, a local technical genius. He was an invaluable resource because, with a few simple tools and electronic devices, he could create links to almost any satellite bearing TV transmissions from one's home country.

Early in my stay I learned from Ciobotaru that Israeli television was available by satellite, too. While its signal was spotty, and much depended on the location of my apartment and the type of dish I was willing to pay for, Ciobotaru was optimistic that he could have me watching Israeli TV in no time at all.

Initially, the system he set up failed to yield an intelligible signal, and Ciobotaru spent several weeks perfecting the apparatus. His gray hair flapped in the wind as he hung out of the kitchen window, laboriously adjusting the dish. Often he shook his head sadly at the weakness of the Israeli signal, lamenting the fact that I was not from France or Italy — proud countries whose satellites were easy to locate and produced a strong and steady beacon for their expatriates. His melancholy indicated that he took my troubles to be a reflection of the Jewish condition. Like most Romanians he had a sympathy for the fellow downtrodden, and we developed a strong rapport aided by the thousands of dollars I was willing to pay for his services. Eventually his reputation proved to be well-deserved, and I was coming home each evening to watch the news from Israel.

Sadly, however, there was not much to watch — especially compared to the madcap pace of events in my new domain. I saw the overhaul of the communist system in Romania and most of the other countries of the region. I covered the collapse of the Soviet Union and watched with my own eyes as several republics became independent countries overnight. All these events were the result of a decades-long build-up of tension, like the build-up of tension between opposing tectonic plates before they finally give way in an earthquake. The tectonic plates of history were at the breaking point when I got to Eastern Europe, and the repeated earthquakes of political and social revolution seemed scripted for newswire. Some new, profound aftershock seemed to unfold every day.

In Israel, in the years before, I had spent months covering the tortuous, slow unfolding of depressing minutiae, like the Shamir government's efforts to maintain a dialogue with the United States without giving a direct response to U.S. Secretary of State James Baker's request for basic position statements on his proposals for negotiations over the West Bank and Gaza. Weeks passed with elaborate bickering over whether members of a proposed Jordanian-Palestinian negotiating team might be allowed to have a symbolic second home in Jerusalem, the city that Israel wanted to keep all for itself.

Two and a half years after I'd left Israel, Shamir was still in power, the Intifada was still simmering, peace talks launched in Madrid in October 1991 were deadlocked over similar procedural issues, and Baker's famous questions were still unanswered. The Middle East seemed doomed to wallow in endless strife accompanied by bureaucratic, half-hearted rounds of peace talks that seemed more a lip service to the Americans than a genuine effort at reconciliation between peoples.

Yet as I watched the Israeli news from Bucharest in early 1992, things seemed to be moving somewhere at last. The Labor party had finally dumped the no-luck Peres in a nationwide primary and replaced him with the former military chief, Rabin. Even though Rabin had turned in a mediocre showing as prime minister in the mid–1970s, in his advancing years sentiment had elevated him to the position of "most popular" politician in Israel. The key to this title appeared to be the appreciation of some lifelong Likud voters for Rabin's gruff manners and tough talk, even though these were markedly at odds with his dovish positions on the actual issues. In electing Rabin as party chair, Labor was betting that his aggressive-seeming and unpolished personality would attract enough right-wing voters to defeat Likud at last. Labor's plan, in effect, was to deceive key swing voters by portraying Rabin as a man who—despite dovish views—would do nothing unpredictable, like dealing directly with the hated PLO. Instead, the party played up his record as the conqueror of Jerusalem.

I had a feeling this strategy might work. And I knew that if it did, it would bring the pace of events in the Middle East in line with those in Eastern Europe.

On June 23, after a week-long trip to Yugoslavia, I arrived back in Bucharest in time to catch the results of Israel's national elections, skipping past my satellite dish that night. At exactly 10 P.M., I stormed into the apartment, banged my shoulder against the protruding coat rack, stumbled into the living room with its eight-foot Dracula-era mirror, and landed next to my Israeli wife, Iris, in front of the TV.

Live from Israel, a familiar face filled the screen.

It was Haim Yavin, Israel's Walter Cronkite. He was the news anchor back in 1968 when Israel TV first went on the air; he was there during the Yom Kippur War, when TV really came into its own in Israel; he reported on peace with Egypt; the invasion of Lebanon; the Intifada. Businesslike, dark-haired, authoritative, a little aggressive but always benign, he conveys from behind his anchor desk a very Cronkitian aura, with a dash of Ted Koppel.

Such a veteran anchor develops a unique and special role in the unfolding of his country's history, no matter how "objective" he strives to seem. One of the many moments that give Yavin that special role came in 1977, when Likud displaced the Labor party for the first time. On that occasion, with the nation wide-eyed in anticipation, Yavin turned his businesslike look to the camera and said one word: "*Mahapah.*" Literally translated, it means "reversal." It had never been used in this context before. In one instant, from the lips of Haim Yavin, the word took on a new meaning: A spectacular change in government.

Now, as Yavin turned to the camera, gazed through his glasses, and performed his practiced dramatic pause, I had the distinct sensation that the man was enjoying the fraying of my nerves in faraway Bucharest.

"This is only a projection," he said slowly, checking a page of notes, "but according to Israel TV's sample ... *Mahapah.*"

With that sentence from Yavin, about half the people of Israel felt as if a radiant, overpowering luminescence lit up the night, lit up their lives.

Under the glare of spotlights at Labor party headquarters in Tel Aviv, Rabin, true to his campaign, seemed almost angry in his victory speech, shouting red-faced over the cheers of the exuberant crowd of party activists and (no less exuberant) journalists.

"I will navigate!" Rabin bellowed, looking around as if he expected boos instead of cheers. "I see myself and the Labor party answerable to the entire people of Israel ... [but also] to our policies, which we presented to the people. And they knew what it is we are committed to."

Rabin's campaign manager, Haim Ramon, put it more directly: "We've waited 15 years for this. We will bring peace."

At Likud headquarters across town, there was a searing, stunned silence, as Shamir gave a speech more fit for the underground leader he used to be than for the outgoing prime minister he had just become.

"There are years when we succeed," he said, his lower jaw shaking and visage bitter. "And there are other times when we must withdraw before the oppression and the attacks against us.

"I know, and we all know," he continued, "that there are on this night people the world over, in the Middle East and other places, who are cheering and happy. The Likud—their dangerous enemy!—is going down. I tell them: your joy is premature. The Likud lives!"

The party leaders sat disconsolate at the head table, like brides deserted at the altar. As Labor had in 1977, it seemed the Likud simply hadn't considered losing to be an option. Its chieftains had come to believe they were destined for eternal rule—regardless of what calamities their governments had wrought.

On that strange, historic night, only one man at Likud headquarters smiled. A youngish, handsome man with receding and prematurely gray hair. He appeared wryly thoughtful, almost welcoming the developments.

He was Deputy Foreign Minister Benjamin Netanyahu.

Even the most ignorant Israelis knew that Rabin had earned his place in the country's history books during the War of Independence. As a 26-year-old officer, he commanded the Harel Brigade in its successful effort to blaze a corridor through well-trained troops of Transjordan's Arab Legion and occupy part of Jerusalem, connecting it to the coastal plain and to the rest of the country.

Later, as military chief in 1967, Rabin was widely credited—along with

Defense Minister Moshe Dayan — for Israel's victory. In that war, Rabin oversaw the conquest of the territories whose fate would come to dominate Israel's political discourse for 25 years.

In 1982, when Begin's forces were surrounding Beirut during Israel's invasion, Rabin's criticism was muted, and he even made waves by advising the government on TV to "tighten! tighten!" the siege of the Lebanese capital if they wanted to see real results in the campaign to expel the PLO from Lebanon.

Still later, as defense minister during the Labor-Likud unity governments of the mid-1980s, Rabin gained a reputation for toughness in suppressing the Palestinian uprising in the West Bank and Gaza. He became particularly famous for declaring that "the Palestinians must be taught that through terrorism they will gain nothing," a patently false but popular phrase that, in the finest tradition of Israeli officialese, stretched the definition of terrorism to the limit. He also became associated with an alleged command to troops to "break the bones" of rioters, a statement he denied but which stuck to him nonetheless and served him well with the centrist swing voters.

These would, of course, be excellent credentials for a hawk. But beyond matters of style, Rabin was always an absolute pragmatist. He was a secular man not terribly impressed with the biblical significance of the West Bank. He was horrified by the idea of an Israel teeming with hostile Arabs. And, even during the Intifada, at party meetings I often heard him utter, "I am not afraid of returning territories." Those who knew him and actually listened to what he said were therefore hardly surprised by his actions as prime minister.

Ever since Israel had conquered the West Bank and Gaza, Rabin believed Israel's strategy should be to return those territories in exchange for the recognition and peace the Arabs had hitherto withheld. Immediately after the Six Day War he advised the Eshkol government to establish a Palestinian state. But Israel hesitated, the Arabs gathered in Khartoum and rejected peace outright, and by the time they changed their minds around 1980 Israel was ruled by the right-wing Likud.

Rabin, as he tried to convey in his 1992 victory speech, felt he now had a mandate to end the occupation. Not because he was idealistic about peace with the Arabs, but because he was a big believer in having Israel be "democratic and Jewish."

Although he never discussed the Impossible Triangle in the terms I used with Raz Cohen, Rabin understood it instinctively and made his calculation. Governing more than 2 million Palestinians in the territories, restive to varying degrees, was anathema to the hopes for a democratic and Jewish Israel, Rabin felt. Annexing the areas and making the Palestinians Israeli citizens meant transforming the country into a binational state. On the other hand, an Israel that kept a third of its residents under military occupation could not call itself a democracy. Therefore the only option was to relinquish the territories in the context of a peace deal engineered so as to minimize the security risks to a smaller Israel.

Like his predecessors, Rabin at first refused to deal directly with Yasser Arafat's Palestine Liberation Organization. He employed the same argument: it was a terrorist outfit bent on destroying Israel. But his heart didn't seem in it. It wasn't a position a pragmatist can be proud of. First, because Arafat's means were hardly a reason for Israel to avoid doing what was in its own self-interest. Second, because Arafat made plain as early as 1988 that he was willing to seek a two-state solution and live in peace alongside Israel — and even if the Palestinian leader did not inspire Israeli trust, it did seem to be worth checking out.

As the talks dragged on, with the delegation of local West Bank leaders periodically calling Tunis for instructions from the supposedly uninvolved Arafat, the avoidance of the PLO became increasingly a farce. Rabin, the straight-shooter, hated farce. So in January 1993, his Labor party led a Knesset motion abolishing the law that forbade Israeli contact with the PLO.

Soon after that, Deputy Foreign Minister Yossi Beilin launched secret contacts with the PLO in Oslo, Norway. At first, the contacts were led by two academics associated with him, but within weeks they were joined by Uri Savir, the foreign ministry director-general. The Palestinian side was led by Ahmed Qureia, a pleasant, bald man known by the misleadingly ominous-sounding nickname "Abu Ala."

The peace talks had some real momentum from the beginning. For one thing, the 1991 Persian Gulf War gravely weakened the PLO while simultaneously allowing Israel to demonstrate remarkable self-restraint. The war had been precipitated by the Iraqi military invasion of Kuwait. U.S. President George Bush and his cabinet immediately assembled an international military force that took up positions in Saudi Arabia and ordered Iraq to retreat from Kuwait. In the showdown that followed, Arafat made the miscalculation of siding with Iraqi President Saddam Hussein. When the American-led force entered Kuwait in early 1991 to forcibly liberate it, Hussein's forces were quickly humbled and staged an ignominious retreat. But for a few weeks in the heart of the war Iraq launched a series of random missile strikes at Israel; 39 SCUD missile landings killed two people and caused scattered damage, particularly to the national ego. At American urging, Israel did not retaliate, avoiding enabling Iraq to cast the war in an Arab-Israeli context and thus possibly enfeeble the Arab-Western coalition against it. When it was all over, Kuwait was restored as an independent state, Iraq was defeated and isolated, Israel was toasted for good behavior, and the PLO was left hanging out to dry.

Thus, Arafat was hungry for progress. And on the other side of the table, Rabin's government was clearly the most dovish administration Israel was likely to produce. As a result, it soon became apparent that the PLO was willing to settle for an initial, temporary arrangement in which the Palestinians would get "autonomy"; later they could hope to upgrade it to independence. Arafat needed a foothold in Palestine and was willing to compromise to get it.

By the spring of '93, the Oslo talks — which continued in parallel to the fruitless official talks in Washington — were being supervised by Peres, now foreign minister. But Rabin was still hiding the negotiations from the public; as late as July, he told an Israel TV interviewer to "forget it" when asked if he would ever meet with Arafat.

In Oslo, the negotiators were well on their way to reaching an agreement on "Gaza First," a nickname denoting that the "test phase" of autonomy would be in the crowded, tiny Gaza Strip. It made sense from Israel's point of view: if ever there was a piece of undesirable real estate for Israel, it was Gaza, a strategically marginal and historically unremarkable slice of shore that housed about a million Palestinians, half of them refugees. In relinquishing Gaza, Israel was reducing the Palestinian population it administered almost by half. Compared to the 1.5 million Palestinians in the West Bank, the Gazan population was poorer, more inclined to fundamentalist Islam, more hostile to Israel. Many Israelis wished it would just float out to sea.

Dumping Gaza first was so attractive a prospect for Israel that the Palestinians suspected the whole peace negotiation was a ploy for relinquishing Gaza only. It was then Peres's idea to add a confidence-building foothold in the West Bank as well. Thus was born the "Gaza and Jericho First" plan: in addition to autonomy for Gaza, Israel would throw in the Jericho region as well, a pleasant oasis in which 30,000 Palestinians lived close to the Jordanian border. Jericho was the calmest of all the Palestinian towns during the uprising, so it was unlikely to become a hotbed of hostile activity once autonomous. Jericho, Peres reasoned, would serve to prove Israel's good intentions. Rabin agreed. So did Arafat. Savir and Qureia secretly signed "Gaza and Jericho First" at the Oslo Plaza Hotel on August 20, 1993. A few days later the news broke.

Three weeks later, Arafat and Rabin met for the first time in Washington, D.C., for a formal signing ceremony on the White House lawn. The scene was witnessed by one of the largest viewing audiences in Israeli history. They watched with the fascination of soap opera junkies: would Rabin shake Arafat's hand? After all, it was under orders from Arafat that terrorists had come out of the shadows to hijack Israeli buses, shoot up tourist hotels, plant bombs in family cinemas. No matter how much some Israelis may have wanted an end to the occupation of the West Bank and Gaza, the vast majority of them still saw the ever-unshaven Arafat, with his trademark *keffiyeh* headdress arranged in the shape of a map of all Palestine, as the personification of evil.

Rabin, too, still had qualms about sharing a stage with Arafat. "I have butterflies in my stomach," he told his aides, who dutifully leaked the sentiment to the media.

Every move made on the red-carpeted podium on the South Lawn was studied intensely by all of Israel as Peres and Arafat's deputy, Mahmoud Abbas, signed the document. Rabin and Arafat, flanking President Bill Clinton, gazed at the silently moving hands of their designees. Then the documents were finished.

With his arms spread wide like the wings of a condor, Clinton, through elaborate stage gesture, gently propelled Arafat and Rabin together. The

Palestinian was ebullient, savoring a moment he'd clearly anticipated for decades. Rabin, hesitant and sheepish, his face locked in his famously stiff smile of embarrassment, limply held Arafat's hand. It seemed that the great Israeli leader was not yet fully cognizant of what the moment signified.

The fine print of the accord involved much more than Gaza and Jericho. It committed Israel to a second phase of pullouts that would extend Palestinian autonomy to include all of the West Bank except Jewish settlements, army bases, and undefined "security areas." Furthermore, after five years of autonomy, the sides promised to establish an unspecified "permanent settlement." The Palestinians expected to receive — in one form or another, perhaps with some restrictions — their own independent state.

Peres wrote a breathlessly optimistic book called *The New Middle East*, in which he foresaw a future of harmony and cooperation in the region on a par with the European Union. His vision was widely ridiculed as premature and superficial, ignoring, for example, the fact that unlike the countries of Western Europe, Israel and the Arabs were worlds apart both in culture and economics. But the reality of the Gaza and Jericho treaty offered a dazzling temptation to believe, and every day seemed to bring word of new breakthroughs.

In addition, the day after Rabin and Arafat shook hands, Israel and Jordan signed a less-ballyhooed agreement to strive to reach a peace deal as well. A day after that, Rabin, Peres, and their entourage were welcomed in Morocco. Soon Israelis were also allowed to go to Tunisia, Oman, and other Gulf states.

Day after day, the news seemed very bright, indeed.

The next month marked my return to Israel, where I took up the job of Tel Aviv correspondent for my wire agency. Iris and I moved into an apartment in central Tel Aviv just across from City Hall and Kings of Israel Square. At last, we could watch Haim Yavin without the annoying satellite-produced blips flying across the screen, and without need of help from the sympathetic but expensive Ciobotaru.

Interestingly, the man who was the bearer of the good news took it all with a grain of salt. Relaxing in his pre-broadcast garb of dockers and a rumpled shirt, Yavin was reluctant to cast a golden glow over the Rabin years when I talked to him in 1997, even though he acknowledged that the sudden peace was awe-inspiring.

"Rabin promised a deal with the Palestinians within nine months, and after eleven months suddenly you got this 'Oslo'! Everyone was overwhelmed, of course. We didn't believe this was happening — Arafat, at last, shaking hands with Rabin.

"But the Middle East is really a very pessimistic place," he said, speaking with a newscaster's taste for short, dramatic statements. "The problem is very, very deep, and I think in a way we are cynical about these happy events because we know how complicated and unsolvable the situation really is. If you strike an accord with the Palestinians about dividing the land, half the people aren't going to be happy, and terrorism is going to emerge from somewhere."

If you have never been inside a TV studio during a news broadcast then you might not imagine that the most revealing moments of an anchorman's life happen when the camera is off, when there is live or taped footage coming in from a news scene, and he is watching it along with the rest of the audience — in solitude, in silence. Americans are used to seeing Peter Jennings let his gaze linger on the monitor following such segments, looking up only after a brief sigh and a pause that conveys somehow that he, too, is just a fellow citizen, no more or better informed than the rest of us, equally moved by the news of the day.

Watching the handshakes and peace deals from his quiet studio, looking down at a monitor built into the surface of the news desk, Yavin too seemed moved and pensive. Yet what he never let on was that his mind was racing ahead to the potential negative consequences with the clarity of a man who knows that, after the good news is over, it will be his job to once again spread the bad.

The bad news was that the peace plan was born with two sworn enemies.

On the one hand was Israel's population of nationalist and religious extremists, whose dream of incorporating the West Bank into Israel was being shattered. At the forefront of this camp were some of the settlers that lived in the 144 Jewish settlements scattered through the territories.

On the other were the Palestinian opposition movements Hamas and Islamic Jihad. As Islamic fundamentalists, they saw Israel as a state of infidels that could not be permitted to control Muslim holy places such as Hebron and Jerusalem. As political extremists, they believed that the Palestinian people, as the authentic natives, had absolute rights to all of Palestine — not just the pieces negotiated for by the compromising Arafat.

Moreover, like extremist groups everywhere, the goal of Hamas and Jihad was not necessarily to ever reach a goal, but to always have a goal. Like their ultra-Orthodox Jewish counterparts, who are unlikely to ever agree that the messiah has arrived, the Palestinian extremists may have difficulty accepting the notion that their goal of a righteous Palestinian homeland is at hand.

Finally, as fervently observant Muslims, the opposition to Arafat and his supporters was partly based on the belief that any Palestinian state must be religious, not a secular place that tolerates non-Islamic social norms. In this regard, they need only look at the half-baked religious compromises in Israel itself to see that religion must be in the driver's seat from the beginning, else it be caught in a perpetual uphill struggle against the encroachments of modern thinking.

Incredibly, the Oslo timetable mandated that Israel would have to go through another national election before it was completely implemented. That amounted to a referendum on the process while it was still only half in place — a precarious state of affairs, since it invited extremists within the Palestinian community to try to scuttle the deal with terrorist attacks. It was well known that parts of the Israeli electorate react to terrorism by shifting to the right — and the Rabin coalition's one-seat majority meant that even a slight shift would return Likud to power. Rabin had practically invited his fellow citizens to do that by announcing that he himself would judge the agreement based on its impact on "security."

Here was a recipe for mayhem.

On the very day the agreement was being signed in Washington, Hamas killed eight Israeli soldiers on patrol in Gaza. Through the fall dozens more Israelis were killed in shooting attacks throughout the country.

In December 1993, a Jewish settler named Mordechai Lapid and one of his children were gunned down near Hebron. As they died, they were cradled by a neighbor, Brooklyn-born physician Baruch Goldstein, a deeply observant Jew.

Two months after, unable to manage his anger, Goldstein visited Hebron's revered Tomb of the Patriarchs, the reputed burial place of Abraham, where Jews and Moslems pray in different halls. Seeking consolation with a submachine gun, he walked into the mosque inside the castle-like structure and began firing at the worshipers, killing 29. Dozens more soon died at the hands of Israeli troops in riots that erupted in the territories.

Hamas issued an ominous warning that it would avenge the massacre with spectacular attacks in Israel. The first came in April 1994, when a car exploded near a bus in the northern Israeli town of Afula, killing eight Israelis. It established a grisly precedent: some 200 Israelis were killed over the next two years in similar attacks, mostly suicide bombings of the sort in which the assailant, strapped with explosives, walks onto a crowded bus and pushes a button.

The peace process, instead of bringing Israelis the security they had long sought, left them with a new definition of hell: never knowing who—the man passing them on the street, that one getting on the bus with a nervous look, the darkish one sitting two seats up?—might blow them up.

And the man who led the charge to Jerusalem in '48 grimly pressed on, vowing to "continue the peace process as if there is no terror, and fight terror as if there is no peace process."

In the summer of 1994, Rabin had been in office for two years. His first year had been quiet, with most of the peace deal being worked out in secret meetings in Scandinavia. His second year had been tumultuous: Gaza and Jericho went to Arafat, terrorism raged, Israeli nationalists fumed.

Rabin needed more to back up his vision of a more peaceful Middle East. He needed more than just Arafat to come to terms with Israel—more openness, more trade for his country's reviving economy, more proof that his path was the right one. He needed another Arab state to follow where Egypt, and now the PLO, had led.

In the high heat of July, King Hussein of Jordan stepped forward.

Appearing one evening on Jordanian television in one of his magnificently tailored suits, King Hussein announced to his people—and to Israeli viewers who could catch Jordanian TV on cable—that the time had come for a bold move. He would meet Rabin in Washington in a few days.

The king's announcement, while not triggering the tornado of emotion that the Arafat peace deal had, still caused a stir in Israel. As people heard the news — sitting in the parlor, relaxing with neighbors around a lone newsstand in the center of town, taking an evening drive under the stars — they could almost feel the air stir around them in a pleasant and caressing way.

It was a cool breeze from the desert.

Israelis had always had reason to have a soft spot for King Hussein, who seemed somehow less hostile than the other Arab leaders and comfortably Western-seeming to boot. He was just 15 when he watched his grandfather, King Abdullah, be shot to death by a Palestinian man enraged with his soft line on Israel. That was in 1950. Two years later Hussein became king, and while he took part in the 1967 war against Israel, the Jewish state was never the main issue on his long-term agenda. He wanted to build his country, his kingdom.

Jordan was another country created from the collapse of the Ottoman Empire in the wake of World War I. The British, whose mandate over Palestine included what is now Jordan, had etched out a country on the east side of the Jordan River and installed their friend Abdullah, a Bedouin Arab of Saudi descent, as king. At the time, in 1921, Transjordan, as it was then called, was populated mostly by Bedouins; but with Israeli independence in '48 came the first of two waves of Palestinian refugees who eventually constituted a majority in Jordan. Many who arrived in 1948 established new lives there; fewer of the '67 arrivals did so. Of the roughly 1.8 million Palestinians in Jordan's population of 3.5 million, some could be said to be true Jordanians while others remained clearly Palestinian at heart.

This delicate mixture of subjects with varying loyalties required Hussein to sometimes lead, sometimes be led. Surrounded by bigger, richer, and more powerful nations, he had ample need for cleverness and restraint. That Hussein managed to maneuver his nation through 40 years of extraordinary upheaval and tension in the Middle East and still arrive in the 1990s more or less intact was a testament to his enormous personal determination, political skill, and plain good luck.

Most Israelis understood King Hussein and his tough situation. It was, indeed, an open secret that Hussein had met privately with most of Israel's prime ministers through the years, reputedly even walking the streets of Tel Aviv in disguise on one occasion. But an open relationship was a different matter entirely. It would send a clear message not just to Jordanians but to millions of Arabs elsewhere that the efforts toward Israeli-Palestinian peace heralded far broader regional reconciliation too.

Even so, few expected the king's foray into Middle East peacemaking to be as swift as it was. For when Hussein emerged with Rabin from the ceremonial south doors of the White House, as he had promised just days earlier, it seemed that he had never been an enemy at all.

Standing before Congress, his eyes glistening, he simply said, "The state of war between Israel and Jordan is over."

Rabin, the man who had beaten him in the Six Day War, who had taken

East Jerusalem and the West Bank from his Jordanian army, was now to be his counterpart in peace.

"Although we have labored for so long under conditions of hostility, I am certain that we can see these conditions for what they are: emblems of an unnatural and sinister state. We have all known the portents of this state — the fear of death, the silence of isolation — and we have all felt the fear that has mesmerized us, preventing us from moving forward to create together a bright future for the coming generations."

Rabin, with Hussein by his side, echoed those sentiments in his clumsy but touching fashion.

"I, military I.D. number 30743, retired general of the Israel Defense Forces, consider myself to be a soldier in the army of peace today. I, who served my country for 27 years as a soldier, I say to you, to Your Majesty, the King of Jordan, I say to you, our American friends, today we are embarking on a battle which has no dead and no wounded, no blood and no anguish. This is the only battle which is a pleasure to wage: the battle for peace."

In a beautiful twist of fate, Rabin and Hussein developed a close, deeply personal, and rare friendship.

Three months later, in November, I was on a bus carrying the first group of Israeli visitors into Jordan, a country I had known only from a distance all my life. My first glimpse of its forbidden mountains had been in the early '70s when my parents took me on a drive through Israel's Negev Desert.

On the 200-mile drive from the town of Beer-Sheva, the "gateway to the Negev," to the southernmost Israeli town of Eilat, on the Gulf of Aqaba, you almost never lose sight of Jordan's Edom Mountains rising in the east, paralleling your passage toward the gulf. All that separates you from those mountains, their red clay glowing in the desert sun, is the flat Arava Valley.

The Arava is actually just one appearance of the major geological depression that runs from the Sea of Galilee in the north of Israel, down the Jordan River to the Dead Sea, on through the desert to the Gulf of Aqaba, and finally into the depths of the Red Sea alongside Africa. These are all evidence of the major tectonic fault line dividing the Asian and African continents.

In my mind, this Great Rift was not merely geological but spiritual, too. It separated Israelis from the great mass of Arabia to the east, a land inhabited by Arabs who represented not only a very real enemy but a frighteningly different society.

In Eilat, Israelis gazed with curiosity at the Jordanian port of Aqaba across the water. The buildings at the edges of the two towns were separated by a distance of only a half mile — but they may as well have been on different planets. Mysterious, forbidding Aqaba was in Arabia. It was profoundly off limits. I never thought I'd see it up close.

On this improbable November day my taxi took me out of Eilat a short distance, made a turn off the Arava highway, and dropped me at the Israeli-Jordanian border, where brand new terminals had been built in only a few weeks.

After the "tour group" assembled — most appeared to be reporters, quasi-VIPs, and cronies of the imposing tour director, Moshe Hananel — the Israeli border guards checked our passports, opened the gates, and let our tour bus out of the country. Within seconds the bus rambled past a sign that said, in English and Arabic, "Welcome to Jordan." We went a short distance on a fresh blacktop that seemed to have been scrubbed by hand, then stopped. Abdullah Jaber, a Jordanian tour guide, hopped on and greeted us.

"Welcome to Jordan," he proclaimed. "Now we have peace and can visit each other like good neighbors. It's a great moment."

We broke into hearty applause.

At the Jordanian border station, I walked around in wonder as a policeman collected everyone's passports and entered his booth. Still clinging to my passport as he returned to his post, I walked up to his window and handed it to him last. He took it with a smile, put it on top of the pile, and repeated the refrain: "Welcome to Jordan." Then he took my blue passport off the pile and studied it carefully. He picked a rubber stamp from a group on his desk with slow deliberation, as if selecting just the right golf club. Then, with a flourish, he stamped the passport and handed it back to me.

As my fellow pioneers shuffled about on the blacktop waiting for their passports, a well-dressed man in his fifties approached, smiling broadly. He introduced himself as Mohammed Kalifa, a mechanical engineer from Amman, the Jordanian capital. He said he had traveled the 150 miles just to greet us.

"I came to see the first Israelis. I want to tell them that we are very excited about peace," he said.

How had a mechanical engineer gotten into the customs area? I wondered.

"*Mukhabarat*," whispered Nati Harnik, the photographer who was with me — "secret police" in Arabic. Nati, like many photographers, seems to squeeze such information out of the air itself, passing it on in credible-sounding, one-word mutterings: "CIA." "Prostitute." "Counterfeit."

Whether or not the man was indeed secret police or just a regular Jordanian who had come "to see," I'll never know. I was willing to believe almost anything in those first few hours, so bewitched was I by the feeling of being inside Jordan.

The bus rambled on to Aqaba. Passing through, I was struck by the marked difference from Eilat, which was built very much with the tourist in mind. Eilat opened up to the sea; its center was comprised of hotels, shopping centers, and restaurants built near the beach and around the lagoons. Aqaba seemed a regular workers' town, with its back to the sea. From its interior streets a few hundred yards inland you wouldn't even notice the water. Aqaba, it struck me, was a place for people to serve the king and to worship Allah; sun worshippers would do well to look elsewhere. The tall hotels of Eilat, seen from stoic Aqaba, seemed somehow surreal, a bizarre and frivolous nonsense.

It was clear to me then, looking back upon Israel, how the Great Rift was equally palpable from the Jordanian side, if not even more so. Seen from Aqaba,

Israel was an alien entity, an invasion of the Western world, insolent and out of place, filled with unpredictable lunatics.

In this context I had several startling interactions during my three days in Jordan.

In one instance I was confronted by three young Palestinians around a table in a cafe and told that "Israelis will die in this country." As they blew smoke in my face between drags on their water pipes, they insisted that "peace between Arabs and Jews cannot be!" I learned that one of the young men, named Hassan, had roots in Israel: his grandparents had come from the port of Jaffa near Tel Aviv and had often spoken glowingly of their lost home by the sea. He had grown up feeling the sting of their evacuation to the desert.

He helped make clear to me that while many Jordanians – especially the Bedouins in the south who stood to profit from tourism — welcomed the open border, many others still saw Israel as an alien nation and its people as regional interlopers. Some were quite unable to disguise their disgust at the presence of Israelis expecting to be served as guests. They, who had chafed at the successful persistence of the Jewish state — by means of galling military superiority — just couldn't brook the effrontery of this casual and curious incursion into their land.

This impression was crystallized in an exchange on our second night, when several members of our tour sampled the disco at our hotel in Amman. There was a wedding going on, and at first we were told that the disco was off limits. But as we were turning to leave, someone in authority observed that we were Israelis and reversed the decision.

As we were shown to a table, the singer on stage pointed us out to the other guests with delight. He then assured us, in English, that by our next visit he would have perfected a repertoire of songs in Hebrew.

After a pleasant half hour of drinking whiskey and chatting with some of the guests, our group grew tired of shouting across the enormous rectangular table where we were seated. Half the group got up and carried their chairs around to the other side where we could converse more intimately. Quickly a man in his thirties approached.

"What are you doing?" he demanded.

We tried to explain.

"You can't. You must sit properly at the table."

We tried to appeal to reason: "We're not disturbing anybody."

"Oh, it's just like Israelis!" the man exploded. "You think you own the world! This is OUR hotel. These are OUR tables. We have our OWN customs that you must respect!"

Red-faced, and apparently uncertain what he might do next, he stormed away.

The next day Jamal Halaby, head of the AP office in Amman, tried to explain.

"Here in Amman 90 percent or more are Palestinians," he pointed out in his jovial way. "Not all of them love Israel so much. They fear 'cultural imperialism,' you know."

Entering his office, Jamal introduced an elegant older man who sat on the couch sipping coffee as Yousef Kawash, a retired Jordanian general who had fought Israel in 1948 and again in '67. In pleasant conversation, General Kawash told me he was born in what is now northern Israel; his family was among the hundreds of thousands exiled by the 1948 war. He said that he was now a Jordanian and he had no problems with peace, if that is what the king wanted. But he added that Middle East stability depended on Israel completing the final peace agreement with the Palestinians.

"Otherwise everyone will suffer," he gravely predicted.

Israelis, meanwhile, were already enjoying the "dividends of peace," one of Peres's favorite phrasings.

Strangely enough, the Israeli economy had always done more or less all right. The isolation imposed by the Arab and Third World boycotts actually made Israel more self-sufficient, which fit in nicely with the Zionist ideology of economic independence pursued by the nation's founders. As a result, Israel, even when its population was small, did practically everything for itself. It produced cars, warplanes, submachine guns, home appliances, clothing, food, everything. There were four different types of Israeli beer at a time when hardly any Israelis drank beer.

But, economies of scale being what they are, not everything was the best quality, and not everything survived; the fiberglass Israeli automobiles, the Carmel and Susita, quickly became the butt of jokes and were quietly discontinued.

There were other problems, too. The country, constantly under siege, was spending a fortune on its military, a whopping one-third of its gross domestic product in 1975. This prevented the government from investing as much as was needed for education, infrastructure, and other areas that would help guarantee future prosperity.

In addition, the Arab boycott and Israel's pariah status throughout the developing world prevented it from exporting to most countries outside North America and Western Europe. This limited but highly developed trading arena helped set high standards for quality in Israel's industries (which today are a boon), but for decades total exports were suppressed by political isolation in a way no other nation except South Africa has ever faced so widely and for so long.

And when the world economy was starting to go global in the '70s and '80s, there was almost no foreign investment in Israel, another result of the boycotts and the instability. Israelis were amazed to travel to a place like Copenhagen and see the walls of downtown buildings radiating with neon signs advertising the products of multinational companies. Tel Aviv was far from poor, yet all you saw on the buildings was peeling paint.

Israel's economy also remained quite centralized. This had been natural enough during the nation-building phase: a nation under siege does not open up its currency markets. It does not sell its national airline to the highest bidder. It builds economic ramparts and digs in. But central control now held back growth.

In all these regards, the peace process was nothing short of an economic booster rocket. The Arab League annulled most aspects of the boycott, opening previously unknown export markets for Israel and freeing companies around the world to do business with Israel without fear of losing the poorer — but vast — Arab market. There was also a flood of foreign investment in the country because of the feeling that it was headed toward stability.

Exports grew 52 percent from 1992 to 1995, reaching a level that was higher, per capita, than that of the United States; foreign investments grew tenfold, from about $200 million before Rabin to more than $2 billion in 1995; tourist arrivals doubled to more than 2 million a year. As a result of all this, Israelis by the mid-'90s attained a per capita income of about $17,000, ranking them well within the range of countries in the European Union.

Defense expenditures, which in the 1970s accounted for about a quarter of GNP, fell to about 9 percent of it. Israeli trade missions toured the Arab world, from Morocco to Kuwait, sizing up possible investments and joint ventures. Deals on regional railways, importing natural gas from the gulf, and joint industrial parks were discussed.

This coincided with a mass immigration from the collapsing former Soviet Union, which began in late 1989 and during the decade brought more than 800,000 newcomers, many of whom were well trained and highly educated. The immigration helped catapult Israel to the number one place in the world, for example, in engineers per capita, with 135 to every 10,000 workers.

Helping take advantage of it all was a shift away from the centralized structure of the economy, which had actually begun in the late 1980s as a result of economic restructuring by the Peres-led unity government that ended hyperinflation. Here, despite differences in emphasis, Labor and Likud were uncharacteristically in agreement. A series of laws and policies was promulgated aimed at increasing competition, limiting cartels, and decreasing state involvement in the economy. And the government slowly began privatizing its assets, which in the mid–1980s included all the major banks and many of the key industries.

Between 1990 and 1996, as a result of the peacemaking, the immigration, and the reforms, Israel's economy grew by a combined 48 percent, with the greatest per capita growth by far coming in 1994-95 at the height of Rabin's peacemaking.

The numbers tell a staggering tale, but it was a much more visual and palpable phenomenon on the ground. Israel seemed to become a part of the Western world almost overnight, with every international outlet from McDonald's and Sbarro's Pizza to Office Depot, Tower Records, and Toys-R-Us setting up shop across the country. (This coincided with the general international expansion of American consumer companies in the '90s.) Cafes, bars, hotels and shopping centers were packed day and night. Office towers, heralded by a crop of yellow construction cranes, blossomed throughout the Tel Aviv area.

Subtle signs of the new prosperity were soon evident in the most unexpected places, like bread baskets in restaurants. In the old days, Israel was basically a one-bread economy, and all you'd find in that basket was the standard, white, soon-to-be-hard-as-a-rock variety of bread. Now the country exited the Stone Age of breads and entered a universe of fresh-baked baguettes and gebettas, special whole-wheat breads, and rolls filled with sunflower seeds and delightful new grains. Waiters seemed to lower their eyes in shame when they could not offer a special house bread, hot from the oven.

The companion to the economic boom, one feeding the other, was a positive outlook, or at least the surface manifestation of it. Polls showed that Israelis were among the most optimistic people on earth. And no wonder, for Israelis could see very clearly how well they were doing compared to their own recent past. Where families once made do with a single car, if that, now many had two or three. Funds freed up from the military budget were being poured into highway projects. Shopping malls sprouted on once-barren lots.

Only 15 years before, Israel had one state-run TV station, which not only broadcast in black and white but — in a policy that today seems surreal — suppressed the color even in its foreign-bought shows in order to discourage the purchase of "decadent" color TVs. Now there were 40 cable channels to choose from, about 10 of them Hebrew-speaking.

The introduction of cable and commercial TV in the early 1990s coincided with the start of the big peace breakthroughs, and this, too, played its part in the psychology of the times. Now it was not just Haim Yavin bringing the news from Israel, it was CNN and the BBC, it was dozens of channels from around the world, it was Seinfeld and Oprah and Jay Leno. Television fed the feeling of openness in Israel: happy, healthy, growing, good.

But this was TV — where the camera is either pointed at a made-up world, or where the real world changes itself for the camera. I knew, as all print reporters know well, that the real story is not always visible to the TV camera, at least not all of it. Frequently a print reporter, traveling alone, can pick up the more fundamental cadences of a place, a people, or a time. Away from the glare of the TV cameras, a different kind of truth is often visible.

One evening in Tel Aviv in October 1995, the leadership of the radical nationalist Zu Artzeinu ("This Is Our Land") movement convened in the basement of the Basel Hotel, an appropriately named venue for a meeting that they viewed as no less than an effort to save Zionism. Zu Artzeinu had carried out a series of mass protests against "land for peace" during the summer, but they seemed to be running out of steam.

I decided to attend the meeting, even though journalists were hardly welcome. This would be a party Yavin's news crews could not possibly crash, while a print journalist, looking pretty much like anyone off the street, just might.

I drove to the Basel Hotel, parked in the desolate parking lot, and marched up to the lobby, expecting resistance. There was no one except a drowsy man behind the counter — and no sign of any sedition. I shuffled over to the elevator, trying not to attract the attention of any cleverly concealed guards. Then the reception clerk noticed me. I froze as he shouted, "Hey, you!" I turned around and tried to look confused, hoping he would take me for a tourist. The man pointed distractedly toward the stairs leading to the basement. "Your buddies are downstairs," he said in Hebrew.

I thanked him and followed the stairs down to a little room where about eight rows of fifteen chairs each were lined up. They were two-thirds empty.

The movement's 33-year-old leader, Moshe Feiglin, was an earnest-looking, red-haired firebrand who had studied computer science in the United States. He was addressing his troops.

"It's every commander's nightmare," he was saying, describing a failed effort to mobilize protests against the peace process. "I said, 'Follow me,' and found myself alone."

I listened to Feiglin speak with quiet conviction for about 20 minutes. He may have been a radical, but he was a radical with a keen sense of reality. After two years of fruitlessly fighting the government, the right-wing rank and file, he said with resignation, "just don't want to fight the police and get arrested anymore."

The 40-odd activists — mostly unknown settlers and settler supporters who, like Feiglin himself, lived in the Tel Aviv area — were in a miserable mood. They spoke of their despair: despite the terrorism by Palestinians, despite the protests, there seemed to be no stopping the juggernaut of what most Israelis saw as peacemaking, but which they saw as surrender.

"We can talk openly because there's no press here," said one man. "We're among friends. But we don't have much hope."

I found myself sinking into my seat, then I caught myself. A real nationalist would not slouch. I sat up straight, then realized I was not wearing a *kippa*. Simultaneous with the thought, I found my hand searching around on the back of my head, unconsciously verifying its bareness and my larger feeling of being exposed.

Across the aisle I noticed an angry-looking youth staring at me. Then he walked up to the podium. I prepared for the worst: exposure and denouncement. But instead he went on to laconically describe his troubled effort to set up a Zu Artzeinu web site on the Internet.

Another man started to distribute pamphlets warning of the danger of a Palestinian state, as well as photocopied sheets containing the contact numbers for Feiglin and the rest of the group's leaders. I took one of each and stuffed them into my bag.

I scanned the room with what I hoped was the scowl of patriotism frustrated.

I saw people who were desperate. People who could see their ideological world collapsing before them and, I suddenly felt, people who would do anything to keep it from happening. I saw zealots.

In the back row sat a fiftyish woman whose handsome, determined face, ringed by black hair and a purple hat, was familiar to many Israelis from front-page headlines two years before. She was Miriam Lapid, the devout settler whose husband and son were shot to death by terrorists in Hebron in December 1993. Their murders set off a chain of back-and-forth violence whose ultimate expression, much closer now than anyone knew, would bring the peace train to a halt. I had no way of knowing that then, and neither did she, I'm sure. But I couldn't stop looking at her, and as I did my spirit sank deeper and deeper. For some reason I felt a sense of foreboding, as if something terrible was about to happen. But nothing did.

Mrs. Lapid spoke to no one, but she did not seem to share the gloom. She smiled the steady, radiant, incongruous smile of a visionary who sees something that others do not.

Darkness

A skull and crossbones, and a mantra: "The Land of Israel Is in Danger!" (photograph by Avi Ohayon).

Tens of thousands of people come to Herzliya just to enjoy one of its renowned eating spots. Evening after evening, the wealthy, the young, and the beautiful assemble in this swank beachside drag fifteen minutes north of Tel Aviv to see, be seen, and spend. While the hip metropolis to the south offers its own very fine restaurants, Herzliya is somehow just a little more chic. Maybe it's the drive up the coast.

Reclining in a cushioned wicker chair at a stylish bar along the beach or working at a desk in the cool confines of a mirrored building a block or two from the sea, where high-priced restaurants share quarters with high-tech businesses, your thoughts rarely turn to the rest of this sprawling suburban town. You certainly don't think of Theodor Herzl, whose name it carries. Secure in the conspicuous comforts of the dining district, you let the rest of Herzliya drop off behind the inland dunes, out of sight and out of mind in the great landed darkness behind the sea.

Indeed, in a country in which people are all too aware of which towns are Arab, which places are mostly Sephardic or Russian, and which are ultra-Orthodox — among many other distinctions — a place like Herzliya, with its veneer of ritzy repose, slips into a Zionist neutral, thought of simply as a place of privilege.

But Herzliya deceives you. For this town, you only learn later when something extraordinary happens, is one of the country's most diverse, mixed, and middle-class communities.

Not far from the sea, a few right turns from the coastal road on an approach from the south and Tel Aviv, sits a typical neighborhood of "inland" Herzliya. Its winding suburban streets are lined unevenly with cottages, bungalows, and other varieties of single-family dwellings, huddled under the orange and fig trees that grow in every yard. There is not much grass. Sitting upon a low dune, this neighborhood's lawns are rather more sand and dirt than green growth, but most do have gardens. There is the spreading shade of fruit trees, and here and there a flock of chickens running about. You can, in the middle of the afternoon, hear a rooster crow from time to time.

As with middle-class suburbs everywhere, what you remember most about a trip through Herzliya is how little actual human activity you discerned during your visit to its unrevealing streets. You go away with the feeling that it's just a series of quiet, pleasant neighborhoods, with quiet, pleasant people going about the normal business of raising families.

So for Israelis, it was a shocking revelation that a man who grew up to be an assassin came from this middle-class neighborhood. The hand with the gun did not emerge from some isolated religious stronghold, or from the occupied territories where Jewish settlers were fighting to keep their stakes, or from a lonely desert town of the disenfranchised, or even from the tumultuous big city where evil may lurk in basements and back alleys.

No. Although opposition to the peace plan was developing audibly from all those places, the gun emerged from Herzliya.

In the spring of 1995, Rabin and Peres began negotiating in earnest the future of biblical Israel, the West Bank. Far more meaningful to Jews than Gaza had ever been, the question of abandoning the West Bank had the power to set off tremendous protest. For many among the 150,000 Jewish settlers who lived in the West Bank, and their supporters in Israel proper, the idea of handing the land back to the Palestinians was almost like giving up on God.

Yet this is what in 1995 became the focus of peace talks between Rabin and Arafat and their negotiators: how and when and to what degree to give this land over to the Palestinians.

It was no surprise, then, that many of Israel's religious leaders began to speak out publicly not only against the peace plan itself but against those Jews who could give away their territorial birthright and rejoice in it to boot.

But it was not only spiritual and religious claims to the West Bank that fueled attacks on Rabin's peace plans. It was something far more tangible. Put in American terms, it was about life, liberty, and property. And the pursuit of happiness.

The people who had populated the territories, in particular the "holy" towns like Hebron, had done so at considerable peril to themselves. They were willing to take big risks for the things they believed in, risking even the safety and welfare of their children — not unlike Abraham risking Isaac. Moreover, they did so with the tacit approval, at times even encouragement, of the Israeli government. They moved their lives to these Jewish outposts, established homes and communities and a fabric of existence. Now the state was disavowing all that. No more new construction, no more tax breaks. "Maybe you can stay for now," Rabin seemed to be saying, "but doing so makes our peace efforts much more difficult."

Yet what was the alternative? Where were they to go? What awaited them elsewhere? No one in Rabin's government addressed these questions or tried to make the process any easier for the settlers. They were estranged from their government, and they felt scared and angry.

Rabin was not religious. He'd spent his life in service to a state and a people, not a religion. But he was also the head of the military when Israel overran and captured the "holy" lands. In Rabin's own assessment, no one was better authorized to rate the value of these lands to Israel's future than he was. It was on his watch that they were taken, it was he who stood at the graves of soldiers who had died fighting for them, it was he who had been elected as prime minister 25 years later at an opportune time in history to seal their fate. He was going to seize the opportunity, and he would not suffer guilt. When it came to moral authority, to measuring who had fought the most for Israel, few could trump Rabin, and certainly not the religious, so many of whom refused to even serve in the army.

Rabin yielded little to his detractors while never doubting his own integrity. Pure in his adherence to what his life had made him, he believed in rational compromise. He believed that compromise with Yasser Arafat helped create a foundation for a sustainable Jewish state in relative security.

Not only the settlers found themselves on the outside looking in. There were also the thousands of families who were not settlers but who were nonetheless devout, raising their children in the religious school system. Thanks to a compromise Ben-Gurion had put in place in the first years of the state, Israel was promulgating two vastly different images of itself and two or more vastly different sets of citizens — one in the "regular" schools, the other in the state-supported religious schools.

Although most were not settlers themselves, many of these so-called "national religious" Israelis believed in the settler movement and its principles, and through their fully sanctioned religious schools these beliefs were passed to the next generation of voters. Throughout the nation, therefore, opposition to Rabin's policies had an institutional home in every community — from Hebron to Haifa to suburban Herzliya.

Against a backdrop of continuing terrorist attacks, the Israel-PLO talks stumbled fitfully all summer, moving nervously between sites and missing several self-imposed deadlines for reaching an agreement. There was no question that Israel was to withdraw from the main Arab cities in the West Bank, but the Palestinians wanted to gain immediate control over more of the West Bank's rural areas than Israel was willing to cede. Also, the power-sharing arrangement in Hebron, where the situation was greatly complicated by the presence of Moshe Levinger and 500 settlers, proved a major sticking point.

Jews in the settlement of Kiryat Arba adjacent to Hebron announced that if agreement was reached they would form their own militia to resist Arafat's security forces. Down in the center of Hebron, Levinger accused the government of endangering the lives of Jews with its actions. "I say to Peres and Rabin: You are responsible for the murder of Jews because you are taking the army out of here," he thundered.

In June, Brooklyn-based Rabbi Abraham Hecht issued a religious ruling terming Rabin a *moser*— a deliverer of Jews into the hands of non–Jews — which is a crime punishable by death according to some interpretations of Jewish religious law. Hecht later apologized and retracted the ruling, but in Israel it became an increasingly popular refrain, usually issued in ways that kept the authors anonymous. In a rare case of courage in this regard, Rabbi Nachum Rabinovich of the Maaleh Adumim settlement repeated the claim that Rabin was a *moser* in a radio interview. Another ruling published in Israel in the summer of 1995 proclaimed that Rabin was deserving of the *din rodef*—the "punishment of the oppressor"—which implied a death sentence as well. On Yom Kippur, the holiest day of the year for Jews, some synagogues posted a ruling against Rabin entitled *Pulsa Denora*, an extremely rare curse in Jewish tradition, naming someone as deserving of death.

On July 12, 1995, the influential, 1500-member Rabbinical Association — which is connected with the right-wing National Religious Party and the settler movement — issued a religious ruling calling on soldiers to refuse the coming orders to withdraw from army bases in the West Bank. Rabbi Shalom Gold, speaking for the association, explained that an army camp should be seen as equivalent to a settlement and therefore its uprooting would be a violation of the biblical edict to "populate the land of Israel."

Rabin dismissed the action with a characteristic wave of his hand. "It is preposterous to imagine [the government] being threatened by a religious ruling," he said. "They will not turn [Israel] into total anarchy and a banana republic!"

But he underestimated the wrath growing against him among people for whom preserving the West Bank under Israeli rule had become the very essence of Judaism — and among those for whom Judaism was the very meaning of life.

Indeed, opposition to Rabin's policies was growing not only among the 140,000 settlers and the Orthodox. It was also growing among the ranks of the lonely religious, the citizens of the lost upland towns, the disenfranchised on the fringes of society — people for whom the rebellion provided a sense of belonging and purpose. All these people came together to form the heart of the resistance, and they were, by nature, an unpredictable assortment of personalities. Rationality could not be counted on; it could rather be counted out.

So the words that sprang from religion touched off a chain reaction among all sorts of would-be rebels. In synagogues throughout the country, on the campuses of religious seminaries and grade schools in Jerusalem and central Israel, in Jewish settlements in the hills and prairies of Judea and Samaria, the idea took root and began to spread: Rabin was a traitor. He must be resisted.

This incitement was being carried out by an extremist minority, but it was potent and it was loud. Occasionally a moderate religious voice was heard, like that of Rabbi Yehuda Amital, who condemned the application of ancient curses to modern-day politics as "nonsense."

The majority of Israelis were silent. In the hearts of many secular Jews there was an irritating dissonance: while free to condemn the religious from their cafe seats in Tel Aviv and Haifa, they were not quite up to the challenge of publicly defending their world view. It was too uncomfortable for their pacifist, liberal sensibilities to take on the religious and the settlers. Live and let live. Revile and let revile, even.

Furthermore, the controversy pitted the opportunity for peace — a rational desire — against the responsibilities of being Jewish, a much less rational matter that most secular Israelis were eager to leave alone. Yet the angry assertion that Judaism was synonymous with fighting to keep Hebron forced even secular Jews to consider what Judaism was. Some found answers in the idea of a universal Jewish morality, from Spinoza to Kafka, and others in the achievements of modern Israel. Others emerged confused and insecure in their identities.

Just getting the secular to the point of tackling these questions was a victory for the religious, and they used every tool at their disposal to elicit the individual Jew's sense of loyalty.

In 1982, when the government of Menachem Begin enforced a dismantling of Jewish settlements in the Sinai, he and his political supporters—those who had cast ballots for him—were at odds only with themselves; the opposition supported Begin's enterprise. In 1995, as Rabin moved toward his own return of land, the conflict was much more pitched, for it put half the nation at odds with the other half. Following in the wake of the divisive Lebanon War and the exhausting Intifada, the civil rift over Rabin's peace policies quickly became perhaps the broadest, most serious internal conflict Israelis had ever experienced, and it was getting more serious every day.

The mainstream Likud opposition, now led by Benjamin Netanyahu, was not motivated by the messianic zeal of the religious extremists. It opposed the Oslo Accords primarily on security grounds. But Netanyahu made a pact with the religious, and the settler and religious youth became the foot soldiers of his street campaign.

At a rally in Jerusalem, the captivating Netanyahu spoke from a balcony just above a draped canvas proclaiming "Death to Arafat." Many in the crowd of some 50,000 people—mostly settlers—were shouting "Death to Rabin" as well. Netanyahu ignored them.

I spotted a small blond boy of about six trying ferociously to shout about death with his tiny voice. He was leaning perilously over the railing of an elevated walkway.

"Where's your mother?" I asked.

"Right here," came a voice from behind me. She was a very young woman— I would have taken her for a high school student. She was attractive, with silky brown hair worn in the demure, shoulder-length style of the religious settler women. I inquired how she felt about her young son's homicidal rantings.

"I'm very proud," she said. "This is a government of murderers. Our country has been taken over by criminals who are selling it to the highest bidder!"

I turned to the boy and held him by the arm. "Why are you shouting 'Death to Rabin'?" I asked. "Don't you know it's not nice?"

He smiled sweetly, innocently, and replied, "Because he's a murderer and a criminal."

The right-wing and religious opponents of Rabin tried every possible argument in their assault on his policy, including some that were amusingly ironic. Some claimed that they were actually the ones who sought "coexistence" with the Palestinians—and indeed, Rabin's position that the land should be divided did suggest a despairing of the prospect of coexistence. The argument sounds good until you notice it does not include any offer for equal rights for the Palestinians; it's a colonial sort of coexistence.

And some even invoked "democracy," claiming that it was undemocratic to impose the Oslo Accords on the Israeli people when so many were opposed to them. This argument ignored the fact that the accords' very aim was correcting the spectacularly undemocratic situation in which Israel rules 2.5 million Palestinians by military occupation. And more important, it ignored the fact that whereas the Israelis were evenly split between the left and right camps, if the Palestinians in the lands Israel controlled had been allowed to join in a truly "democratic" vote — which no one on the right was proposing — Rabin's position would have certainly won an overwhelming majority.

In late July, in an effort to further galvanize public opinion against the coming West Bank agreement, Moshe Feiglin's Zu Artzeinu group organized several well-publicized efforts to establish "beachheads" for new settlements on West Bank hilltops. Since the makeshift settlements were not authorized — the government was opposed in principle to establishing new settlements, however fictitious — troops were ordered in each case to dismantle the caravans and tents and drag the settlers and protesters off the hill. The confrontations were effective in drawing attention to the settlers' ideological plight and creating a cause for supporters to rally around. In several cases the forced evacuations were accompanied by highly telegenic crying fits on the part of some women soldiers who saw too much of themselves in the protesters, or were simply overcome by the whole hysterical situation. Here were 20-year-old women forced to literally carry other 20-year-old women off these ancient hills of Israel. It was a preposterous publicity stunt, and the government seemed silly to be drawn into it, and yet something in these televised tears caused you to sit up and pay attention.

Was civil war possible?

The government pressed on. In September, in the Egyptian town of Taba on the Israeli border along the Gulf of Aqaba, the deputies of Peres and Arafat finally concluded the deal nicknamed Oslo II.

A few days later at the White House, with Jordan's King Hussein and Egypt's President Hosni Mubarak sharing the stage, Rabin and Arafat signed the accord, which detailed the extension of Palestinian authority to most of the cities and villages in the rest of the West Bank, accounting for nearly all its Arab population and about a quarter of its territory. In some areas Jewish settlements would be reduced to islands in a sea of autonomous Palestinian land. The phased withdrawals were to begin in mid-November and be completed in a few months.

Rabin, more comfortable now with his peace partners, spoke with delight about the surprising peace that had been achieved and the important items that remained on his agenda. "Ladies and gentlemen, look at us again," he said, glancing toward the only slightly younger Arafat in a fatherly manner. "Look at the scene on the stage, here in the White House. You are not excited anymore. You have grown ... accustomed to it. But in order for peace to be completed, in order for this picture to be completed and for the Middle East to become a jewel in the world crown, it still lacks two people: the president of Syria and the president of Lebanon. I call upon them to come and join us, to come to the platform of peace."

In the weeks before and after, as his words in Washington suggested, Rabin was of a mind to dramatically complete the peace process. Talks were scheduled to begin on the final status of the territories, in which the Palestinians would demand that autonomy be upgraded to independence and that they be granted partial control of Jerusalem, too. Those talks were to be completed by 1999, the end of the five-year "interim period." Although Israel had not yet formally agreed to the Palestinians' "final status" demands, the unusual device of talks under a deadline implied a degree of confidence in a successful outcome, suggesting that a final arrangement was, in one way or another, a foregone conclusion.

Rabin also appeared to be coming to terms with the idea of giving up the entire Golan Heights to Syria in exchange for peace, as President Hafez Assad demanded. A peace treaty with Syria, Rabin believed, meant Assad would call off the guerrillas fighting Israel in southern Lebanon and enable Israel to withdraw its troops from the border strip it controlled there, end the pointless bloodshed in Lebanon, and finally make formal peace with the Beirut government, too.

Egypt, Jordan, the Palestinians — and Syria and Lebanon next. Rabin was marching Israel steadily toward peace with all its neighbors.

The opposition was reaching a fever pitch.

At near-daily rallies against Rabin, protesters waved posters depicting the prime minister in a Nazi SS uniform and carried mock coffins labeled "Rabin." The cars of cabinet ministers were attacked by mobs several times; on one occasion, Housing Minister Benjamin Ben-Eliezer reported that he barely escaped without injury. Shin Bet Chief Carmi Gilon warned that Rabin and the cabinet were in danger; he urged Rabin to wear a security vest during all public appearances, to no avail.

Even in Israel, the warm, dry weather loosens its grip after September, and on a day here and a day there the wind takes on more of a chill, the sky a wintry hue. I felt a vague chill in my spirit, too. Something in the mood of the country, in the images of soldiers scuffling with settlers, in the drumbeat of crowds shouting "death, death," in the spectacle of religious leaders spewing biblical invective against the government — it all added up to no good. But such foreboding seems as connected to foreseeable reality as déjà vu is to the actual past.

Most Israelis read the newspapers and watched the news with detachment, as if surveying events in a foreign land. What was happening, what seemed to be coming, simply did not fit with the idea of Israel that most people held. The idea of Jewish violence against a Jewish government was, in light of the century's history, too unthinkable.

Rabin reacted to the attacks with the disdain he had reserved for opponents all his life. The settlers and the protesters "don't move me," he said. Using typically tortured Hebrew (even though he was Israel's first native-born prime minister), he termed his detractors "propellers," meaning that they could spin in place as they liked. At one point, when he felt he wasn't getting enough support from his coalition allies in the Knesset, he termed them "idiots." Rabin barely disguised his feeling of superiority toward most of his fellow politicians, be they his hapless cabinet ministers, most of whom were rarely included in his deliberations, or the opposition with its glib Netanyahu. Who were any of them compared to him — a pre-state underground leader, military hero, two-time prime minister, and Nobel Peace Prize winner?

At an appearance in October at a convention of immigrants from English-speaking countries, the 73-year-old prime minister was rushed by an unarmed man who seemed about to attack him before being caught by guards. Then, as Rabin tried to address the crowd, he was loudly heckled. When he heard the shouts of "traitor, traitor," Rabin, at last, completely lost his calm.

Angrily clutching the microphone, his face growing red and his voice hoarse, he shouted at the stunned crowd, his rage broadcast to millions of Israelis on national TV: "Shame! You should be ashamed of yourselves! Judaism was never about violence!"

On October 20, columnist Arye Caspi wrote in the *Ha'aretz* newspaper about the lax security surrounding Rabin: "I happened to be in a hotel lobby. Yitzhak Rabin walked in. Any one of the people in the lobby could have easily blown away the prime minister. Someone ... should start thinking differently, before the first bullet comes."

Had it rained, as meteorologists predicted, the demonstration might have been called off. But November 4, 1995, was a clear, beautiful day in Tel Aviv.

At Kings of Israel Square in the heart of the city, across from my apartment, I saw workers erecting stadium-like lighting fixtures and dragging TV and sound cables throughout the plaza, a huge open space that seemed designed by socialist bureaucrats for May Day parades. The first major peace rally in years was scheduled for that night, and popular musicians were to rally the crowd with songs prior to an appearance by Rabin. Security men set up barricades to separate the plaza from the elevated terrace from which Rabin would speak.

Israeli intelligence had warned that Islamic fundamentalist groups might try to stage a terrorist bombing at the rally, hoping to deal the peace process a coup de grâce by targeting its most ardent supporters. All afternoon, security agents scoured area buildings to make sure they were "clean." Snipers took up positions on the rooftops of the seven- and eight-story buildings surrounding the square. Parking in the vicinity was forbidden. Signs were posted informing residents that their cars must be moved or they would be towed.

Rabin had been reluctant to hold the rally, which was proposed by various supporters and promoted by Peres. He feared a small turnout that might end up only helping the opposition. Such fears were well-founded: Israel's peace camp was composed mostly of relatively docile characters whose temperament was ill-suited to fiery demonstrating or scuffling with thugs in the streets. They'd really rather be home watching TV.

But at 8 o'clock, as I went downstairs with Iris and my friend Eytan for the rally — we left our baby daughter, Maya, at home with a babysitter — it was evident Rabin's fears were unwarranted this time. A mass of people streamed toward the square, and it took considerable effort on our part to secure a decent view near the front.

Although I was not covering the rally as a journalist, I could not resist getting closer to where the action was: the terrace that loomed over the square. I asked Iris and Eytan not to move and set out to see if my government press card could get me into the VIP area.

Approaching the stage area, I was stopped by three private security guards in black and yellow uniforms. They informed me that to enter I must be checked out by a single Secret Service officer who was rotating among the various access points and would be back soon. I waited with the obedience of a man who knows that his special status — in my case, the little white press card issued by the government and bearing my picture and name — would be acknowledged.

As I stood there looking around, a woman whom I knew to be a TV producer appeared and breezed by the three men, mumbling that she had already been inside. She disappeared in the crowd even as the three debated among themselves whether indeed they remembered her from before. I was somewhat surprised, and a little upstaged, at the swiftness of her entry. But before I could decide whether to advise the three on enforcing their security strategy more evenly, another would-be entrant appeared.

"It's OK, it's OK," he said, waving a press pass like mine. "I've already been inside. I already passed security. I just went to get some cigarettes." Upon hearing this the trio were satisfied, and the anonymous figure went in.

Here was a conflict. On the one hand I wanted to get in without official reason, and toward that end the guards' incompetence might serve me well. On the other, security enforcement seemed to be in the hands of idiots, and that might not be so good. Was I there as a journalist or a citizen? I looked around, seeing nothing else out of the ordinary. I turned back to the three and spoke as a citizen.

"Look," I said, "are you putting me on? Are we on *Candid Camera*? What on earth is going on?"

The most officious of the three goons rose from his seat and demanded to know what I meant.

"If your system is to allow people to come in, go out, and then return without a new check, what's to prevent them from reentering with a grenade?"

The first guard was stunned into silence, but the second, who seemed to take my remark as evidence that I myself constituted a security risk, began shouting, "What do you mean, grenade? What grenade?"

Then the third — the brains of the outfit — said in a benign tone, "Why worry? Can't you tell that guy was a Jew?"

He smiled reassuringly, "Why would a Jew want to do any harm here?"

I recalled this exchange two days later, when the irony emerged through a forest of thoughts much dulled by a desperate lack of sleep.

About the time I was finally being let in to the secured area, Yigal Amir was arriving at the rally by bus. He walked through the crowd and settled in the area near Rabin's car, which waited near the terrace's rear stairway to whisk the prime minister away.

On stage, Rabin seemed amazed. Not only had more than 100,000 people showed up, but they were ecstatic, treating him and his ministers more like a rock band than a collection of old men in suits. He sat on the stage with Peres and other top officials. They were joined by businesspeople and artists, as well as the ambassadors of Egypt and Jordan. The atmosphere was euphoric, but when Rabin got up and approached the podium he was very serious. He leaned against it with his left hand.

"Allow me to say that I, too, am moved," he began, his voice booming through the square. For the gruff and taciturn Rabin to declare that he was "moved" was a dramatic thing, indeed.

A few meters away from him, surrounded by journalists, politicians, and hangers-on, I happily sipped a beer, joked with a CNN correspondent, and surveyed the huge crowd.

"I was a soldier for 27 years," Rabin continued, his words echoing off the buildings surrounding the square. "I fought as long as there was no chance for peace. I believe that now there is a chance for peace. A great chance — which must be seized."

Rabin said the violence of the opposition "must be rejected and condemned." He praised the PLO, which "was once an enemy and has now forsaken terrorism." He spoke of "the pain of the families of the soldiers" who did not return from Israel's many battles and promised, for their sake, to "exhaust every tiny possibility to move ahead and reach a comprehensive peace."

When he finished, a lustful applause arose from the crowd. It started with energetic approval, then kept building through a series of emotions: exuberance; pride; belief. With cheers and shouts it spread through the square, growing ever louder, creating a profound sense of purpose and unity.

Perhaps inspired by this, Rabin did something he had never done in public before: he hugged Peres, his long-time rival, his contemporary from the time the state was founded, the man with whom he planned to complete his mission of peace and ensure Israel's safety and prosperity.

In the parking lot beneath the elevated terrace, Yigal Amir took off his *kippa*—the signature of religious Jews—in order to better fit into the secular environment at the rally. His blue sweatshirt was untucked. He sat on a large potted plant beside Rabin's car and remained unaccosted by the security men nearby.

I left the stage and found Iris and Eytan in the crowd. They were both overflowing with good cheer. From the stage, a flurry of balloons was released and floated up toward the night sky.

Then Eytan pointed to where Rabin and Peres were waving to the crowd; amidst the celebration and hoopla he suddenly observed, "Look how exposed they are!"

We forgot about that moments later when Rabin was cajoled by singer Miri Aloni into singing the "Song to Peace" with her and Peres. The song, inspired by the musical *Hair*, had been denounced and briefly banned on the military radio station as defeatist when it first came out in the early 1970s, but it had since become the anthem of the peace movement in Israel. Rabin had a deep bass voice, but was no singer and he knew it. He hesitantly accepted a lyric sheet and, looking around with embarrassment, mouthed the idealistic words.

> Don't say "A day will come"
> Bring the day!
> And from every plaza,
> Hail peace
> And sing a song for peace
> Do not whisper a prayer
> Sing a song for peace,
> With a great shout!

Rabin folded the lyric sheet and placed it in his jacket's breast pocket. He then listened to rock star Aviv Geffen, an outspoken pacifist who never served in the army, sing about his longing for a friend who had been killed. The Rabin of a few years before might have avoided Geffen, but on this day he was elated at the young star's support. "You were great!" he told him. "Do you know Leah?" he asked, introducing Geffen to his wife.

Downstairs, Shin Bet agents created a "sterile zone" around Rabin's car, herding the crowd behind barricades erected some 50 feet away. But Amir, strangely, was allowed to remain with the police and security men. A videotape of those moments shows him talking to three policemen, who later said they mistook him for a plain-clothes security officer.

On the terrace, Peres and Rabin were preparing to leave. Peres made for the stairs. The happy Rabin stayed on, saying good-bye to a TV crew, and then, with a warm smile, to the sound man.

As Peres entered his car, Rabin began his descent down the stairs surrounded by six bodyguards. When he reached the bottom he was about 20 feet from his car — and from Amir who stood beside it with some others. As Rabin approached, one of his bodyguards paused and turned back to the stairs.

Amir waited until Rabin passed by him, reached into his right pants pocket, pulled out a Beretta 9-millimeter handgun, and — lunging through the hole created by the missing bodyguard — pumped a bullet into the prime minister's back. Rabin turned his head to his left for a split second, seeming almost to glimpse the young shooter through his glasses — and collapsed.

Before he was subdued by a swarm of police and security men, Amir managed to fire twice more, hitting Rabin again and wounding bodyguard Yoram Rubin in the arm. Rubin later said that Rabin was able to push himself into the car. Menachem Damti, the driver, jumped in and sped away.

The shots were heard throughout the area. Demonstrators, who had been dancing to South American music on the steps of city hall, rushed the parking lot. Police tried in vain to keep them at bay. The area flowed over with confused people.

From my mobile phone, I called our babysitter, who could have witnessed the shooting from our living room window across the street and two floors up. "I heard shots, or something," she replied with a professional babysitter's unflappable calm. "I went to the window and saw a car speed by."

In it, Rabin was stretched bleeding across the back seat, but Damti had no clear getaway instructions for such an emergency. He asked Rabin if he was injured, and the prime minister responded, "Yes."

His voice fading, Rabin whispered that his back was in pain but added it was "not too bad." Then he passed out.

"Drive! Drive!" screamed Rubin, the bodyguard.

Ichilov Hospital was only 800 yards away by the shortest route, but the way was blocked by people who had attended the rally, so Damti was forced to take a roundabout route almost three times longer. On the way, he was stopped at a police roadblock set up hours before to secure the rally area. Damti spent precious moments talking his way through but gained a police escort the rest of the way.

At the hospital, no one had been alerted. Damti had to stop at the gate and explain. Then, assisted by Rubin and the police officer, Damti carried Rabin into the trauma ward.

The duty doctor in the trauma unit was Nir Cohen, a 33-year-old former surfer with a prematurely graying beard who in recent years had lost his long blond locks to a receding hairline. Nir, a friend of mine, later told me how things unfolded in the emergency ward.

Just before 10 P.M., Nir was on a coffee break, chatting with his wife on the phone, when he heard a commotion outside in the hall. Nurses shouted that there was an emergency case on the way. "Gotta go," he said, cutting the conversation short and rushing to the trauma ward.

Nir admits that he was relieved to see that the man being dragged in by a panicked police officer and a civilian and being hurled face-down onto the operating table was not young—because he hated to see young people arriving in such bad shape.

"It was an old man, dressed in a suit," he recalled, as we sat in a steak restaurant just off what is now Rabin Square. He shook his head gently, lost in recollection. "A very old man, his face white as snow..."

In the heat of the moment no one looked closely at the victim's face or asked questions. The team of doctors started ripping off the suit. A few seconds later, Nir took a step back, recognized his patient's puffed-up, bloodless face, and gasped.

Rabin was unconscious and without a pulse. By 10:30 P.M., TV stations were already reporting that Rabin had been "seriously injured" in a shooting. I arrived at Ichilov Hospital as hundreds of shocked Israelis, many weeping and praying, gathered outside the locked main gates.

Ichilov is a huge compound, much of it built in the depressing socialist style that typifies public institutions in Tel Aviv. I once spent an aggravating two weeks within its bowels, suffering from mononucleosis; I recall it as a depressing, bureaucratic, and less than immaculate place. Since then Ichilov has been modernized and expanded, and during the Gulf War it had been somehow prepared to handle tens of thousands of people who might have been gassed by Saddam Hussein. Who knew then that, in a few years, a single patient would make it famous across the world?

In the confusion that night, I was able to sneak through the parking lot to the emergency room entrance, which was sealed off and seemed abandoned except for a panicked-looking Ethiopian immigrant soldier. "Are you with them?" he asked urgently. I imagine a simple "yes" might have gotten me inside and netted me the scoop of my career, but I hesitated, and the soldier regained his composure and demanded that I leave.

I walked down the driveway and out the main gate, where I saw people arriving from all directions. No one there knew yet what the fate of the prime minister would be, but I could see the seeds of his eventual deification in the groups of weeping young girls who sat and quietly sang folk songs around candles they had melted to the sidewalk. I couldn't help but think that for all of the peacemaking of Rabin's old age, the Woodstock-like atmosphere that was developing might have been too much for the famously unsentimental old warrior.

Then a photographer, a native of France not known for his affinity for Israel, emerged from the shadows, his face streaked with tears. "What have you done?" he shouted at me. "What have you people done? He was the best fucking thing you had!"

A group of right-wing supporters drove by in a white van, stuck their heads out the window, and bellowed, "The traitor is dead!"

The crowd stiffened. It couldn't be true. Rabin would yet emerge, perhaps in a wheelchair, to dismiss his shooter as a "propeller."

Inside, Peres, Leah Rabin, and most of the cabinet were waiting nervously near the emergency room. Yoram Lass, a Labor Party Knesset member and a doctor, came out of the hospital gates, his face drawn. "All I can say is the prime minister has suffered the kind of injury from which you do not quickly recover," was his tortured formulation as he spoke to me. "We will know more soon." Hospital director Gabi Barabash later said Rabin had only a slim chance of survival from the moment he was hit.

At 11:15 P.M., Rabin's top aide, Eytan Haber, emerged from the hospital gates. With dozens of reporters swarming around him, Haber struggled to read a short statement as an anguished "No!" arose from the crowd.

"The government of Israel announces with astonishment, great sorrow, and deep grief the death of Yitzhak Rabin, who was murdered by an assassin."

In a cramped police interrogation room about a mile away, investigator Motti Naphtali leaned toward the dark-haired young man.

"I accuse you of murder," he said quietly.

Yigal Amir perked up, seemingly incredulous. "He's dead?"

"Yes," replied the officer.

"I can't believe it!" Amir exclaimed. Then, in a hushed tone, he added, "I've done my job."

Amir was a 25-year-old law student who lived in the same Herzliya home where he had grown up and where his mother runs a day care center under the spreading branches of the fruit trees. His parents, devout Jews from Yemen, raised Yigal and his six siblings in a traditional Jewish way and gave them a religious education. Following his army service in the infantry, he became increasingly interested in politically oriented youth groups, eventually spending much time organizing weekend youth visits to the Jewish settlers in Hebron. He also became active in the demonstrations and protests against the Rabin government. Kicking up a fuss, he was dragged by soldiers off a West Bank hilltop at one of the Zu Artzeinu protests.

The charge sheet filed against Amir a month after the assassination said that he and his brother Hagai had considered many ways of killing Rabin, including creative solutions like blowing up his car or firing an anti-tank missile into his apartment from an adjacent balcony. In the end Yigal Amir decided he'd simply use a gun.

"Do you regret what you've done?" Naphtali asked.

"No," the young man replied, without defiance. Applying the radical religious dogma he had heard so often over the previous year, he explained that Rabin had been an "oppressor" of the Jews, for which there was only one suitable punishment: "He was executed."

Emergence

Benjamin Netanyahu rides to power on a wave of fury (photograph by Avi Ohayon).

Few things have the power to change our lives like the death of someone close. It destroys our illusions of certainty and replaces them with an arm's-length distrust of the world. It sobers us, drains our hearts, induces us to approach life more cautiously for a while. Above all, it is inscrutable; death chooses its forms and moments without pattern and without traceable purpose, leaving behind only unanswered questions about its workings and our own mortality.

A whole nation can be affected like this when a special leader, a once-in-a-generation personality, is prematurely stolen from life. Especially when he is gunned down by a fellow citizen.

Israelis were stunned by the killing of Yitzhak Rabin. For a brief moment in the wake of the assassination, the eternal deadlock in national politics was broken, and Rabin's policies enjoyed an overwhelming posthumous majority. But the moment faded, and the death of Rabin left Israelis facing a time of pain and tumult without his determined leadership. In his wake, an Israel much different from the one he believed in emerged.

A few hours after the killing, at two in the morning, Shimon Peres addressed a nation that was still wide awake. In one of his most graceful moments he eulogized Rabin and did not even mention that he would be the new prime minister. Perhaps he felt this would be an inappropriate topic — or perhaps, in the heat of the moment, he just forgot. It seemed obvious to everyone, however, that there was only one possible successor.

Around 4 A.M., still filing updates onto the wire from the office in my apartment, I decided to get confirmation of this detail and phoned government spokesman Uri Dromi. "You know, I really don't know myself," Dromi said. "I'm sure they chose Peres. Let me check."

I spoke to him again a half hour later, and he informed me that indeed the cabinet had held "some kind of vote" and chosen Peres.

Peres was a great anomaly in Israeli politics. He was part of the founding generation of '48 but, unlike many of his contemporaries, he was not perceived as a man of action. He was an intellectual, a thinker, somehow less accessible. Even though he tried harder than anyone else to woo those who shunned him, and polls showed the nation supported his policies, Peres never managed to win an election (his two years at the helm, from '84 to '86, resulted from a 60-60 tie). He was never loved or trusted the way Rabin was.

They were opposites, in many ways. Rabin had been the first prime minister to be born in the Holy Land. He spoke Hebrew in a guttural native accent, a combination of Germanic and Middle Eastern influences that made him sound like he was going to break his teeth when he spoke English. But it was unpolished Hebrew, littered with grammatical mistakes. And although he was widely credited for an "analytical mind," Rabin was ultimately a man of simple tastes who loved nothing more than watching soccer on TV. He held bureaucrats, intellectuals, and professional politicians in contempt.

The man born in Poland as Shimon Persky was basically all three rolled into one.

Although he arrived in Israel at age eleven, Peres never lost his Polish accent, which for Israelis always made him seem foreign and faintly comical. The "Peres accent" is a big crowd-pleaser for Israeli comedians.

Even as a young man he had seemed of a different time and place, drawing his slicked hair severely back on the top and sides of his head, looking more like an East European gentleman than a rough-hewn Israeli. He rose to the top not through the underground or the military but as a bureaucrat, riding on the mammoth coattails of Ben-Gurion.

Although his formal education was rudimentary, Peres is an autodidact who brags about his prodigious reading and his ties to authors and philosophers. He is always ready to fire off bombastic pronouncements, such as "We will take the salt out of the water, the sand out of the desert, and the hatred out of the people!" This unfortunate habit probably never won a single vote for Peres; the sophisticated cringed at his forced cleverness, and the less educated just thought he was strange.

Peres spent his teens in Tel Aviv, where his father hoped to raise his son as a merchant. But the studious youth was attracted to the socialist movement that flowered in Zionist Palestine and soon found himself at the Ben Shemen agricultural school instead. There, in the spirit of the times, he changed his name to something manly in Hebrew (Peres means "bearded vulture"), and there he met his wife, Sonia — courting her, in a reflection of his intellectual formality, by reading to her out loud from *Das Kapital*.

Peres likes to recall a story about his youth in Israel. As he tells it, he was already an ardent admirer of Ben-Gurion as a little boy and often daydreamed about working with the great man, then part of the pre-state underground. One day when Peres was sixteen, he was standing on a lonely patch of highway outside Tel Aviv looking to hitch a ride to Haifa. He was stunned when a car bearing Ben-Gurion himself pulled over. Speechless, he entered the back seat where he sat alone while Ben-Gurion sat up front talking with the driver. Peres tells wistfully and touchingly of sitting back there for the entire hour-long ride up the coast wondering how he was going to tell Ben-Gurion of his dreams. He never uttered a word.

The ride, however, and his brief good-bye to Ben-Gurion upon leaving the car, gave him all the additional inspiration he needed.

Peres went on to help found two kibbutzim, the communal farms that are Israel's unique contribution to the socialist experiment, called Geva and Alumot. Even then, with the kibbutz movement just starting out, Peres saw that the system would work better if it expanded beyond agriculture into industry as well, advice the kibbutzim would only begin adopting 40 years later to stave off bankruptcy. Peres earned scorn from his farmer colleagues for his nonconformist ideas and administrative bent. But he caught the attention of the bureaucrats who were laying the foundations for Jewish independence.

It was a hot, mosquito-swatting day in 1946 when Levi Eshkol, then a senior aide to Ben-Gurion who was always on the lookout for a promising recruit, arrived at the kibbutz. He asked Peres to leave the commune to take over the manpower branch of the Haganah, the underground militia. And this he did.

Still only in his early twenties, Peres quickly became a favorite of Ben-Gurion, and shortly after independence he was appointed Defense Ministry director-general. From this position, Peres was able to achieve far more than most combat generals in establishing Israel's defense capability, including helping build the air force and set up Israel Aircraft Industries. Over a 15-year period he also forged an alliance with France that helped arm the military and netted Israel its Dimona nuclear facility, considered by most Israelis today to be the key element of deterrence.

In the early 1970s, Peres was a junior cabinet minister under Golda Meir. After the debacle of the 1973 war, she resigned as prime minister, and the Labor party leadership picked Rabin, the hero of the Six Day War, to succeed her. The ambitious, 50-year-old Peres mounted a challenge in the party's central committee. Although he lost, the ploy established him as number two, and Rabin grudgingly appointed him defense minister.

Under Rabin, Peres was a relative hawk, lending the nascent West Bank settler movement tacit support, which Rabin interpreted as being aimed at undermining his position. When Rabin resigned abruptly in 1977 in response to a tempest over his wife's illegal U.S. bank account, Peres took over the party and lost the election — Labor's first defeat at the polls in nearly 30 years of statehood. He lost again, narrowly, in 1981. In 1984, even though Likud had run the country into Lebanon and the economy into the ground, the bloc led by Peres managed only a 60-60 tie in the breakdown of Knesset seats, leading to a prime ministerial rotation with Yitzhak Shamir. Peres received stellar marks from almost every quarter for his performance in his two years as prime minister, defeating rampant inflation and repairing the economy. Yet in 1988, with the Intifada raging in the West Bank and Gaza, he was edged out again by an electorate seeking a firm hand. After three (and a half) setbacks at the polls, the image of Peres looking forlorn became the great constant of Israeli election nights.

In 1992 the party made Rabin its leader and candidate and squeezed out a victory. Under pressure from the Peres wing of the party, and sentimentalists elsewhere, Rabin reluctantly appointed his old rival as foreign minister. Peres seemed to come to terms with his position as number two in the party, although he was always ready to lecture anyone who would listen about how all his defeats were either not his fault or not defeats at all (in 1981, for example, he improved Labor's seat total by a third compared to 1977, so even though his bloc lost by a whisker it was actually, in a sense, the party's greatest success ever).

But the key thing turned out to be that, as foreign minister, no longer the chief target of right-wing abuse, Peres was free to be a diplomat and not a politician. At this he was brilliant — and he pursued his dreams with a religious fervor.

By now Peres was a super-dove, convinced that peace with all the Arabs was within reach, convinced that borders were antiquated things and squabbles over them ridiculous. It seemed he could virtually feel history passing by, the same way that a true believer can feel the Holy Spirit brushing past a pew. With Peres generating grandiose plans behind the scenes, it was Rabin's job to be the skeptical details man and, in turn, to sell a skeptical public. It was a partnership that worked, leaving each to what he did best.

In the wake of the assassination, that equilibrium was lost.

None of the cabinet ministers and party members around Peres, all younger and less experienced, approached his stature. Indeed, he and Rabin were part of an exclusive and honored class of Israeli leaders. Members of the founding generation, they had been there at the beginning, 50 years earlier — one man helping lay the structure of the state, the other blazing its trails. Five decades later, they were the last members of that generation to head their nation, leading it together toward peace — one laying the structure, the other blazing the trail.

Now Rabin was gone. All the hopes and expectations fell upon Peres.

The stage was set for an electoral confrontation that for the first time would pit a representative of the founders against a product of the brash, modern Israel: opposition leader Benjamin Netanyahu.

Netanyahu was everything Peres was not. Although a powerfully intelligent man, he did not strive to appear intellectual, and he was certainly no dreamer. "We do not foresee a computer for every peasant," he once said, alluding sarcastically to the Peres notion of a "New Middle East" modeled on the European Union.

Netanyahu did not string together complicated metaphors. Instead he practiced effective sound bites and delivered them perfectly. He was a salesman, schooled in America and brimming with American slick. The silver-tongued former United Nations ambassador had spent his teenage years in the U.S. and had earned an M.B.A. from the Massachusetts Institute of Technology. Furthermore, he was the younger brother of national hero Yonni Netanyahu, the sole military casualty of the spectacular 1976 rescue of Israeli hostages at Entebbe, Uganda. It was a fine pedigree, but Netanyahu seemed to have a knack for needlessly undermining his own position.

In 1993, Netanyahu defeated a battery of Likud veterans in an internal election and succeeded Shamir as the head of the party. But only weeks before the national primary, Netanyahu went on Israel TV to confess to adultery and accuse a nameless Likud rival — apparently David Levy, his main opponent in the race — of trying to blackmail him with a videotape of his exploits. Years later Netanyahu retracted the charges, and nothing was ever proven in any direction, making the episode one of the more bizarre in the annals of Israeli politics.

As opposition leader, Netanyahu adopted a far right stand somewhat out of sync with his moderate-seeming appearance and speech. Many saw in his angry words the influence of his domineering father, Benzion Netanyahu, a renowned scholar of the Jews' history in Spain who was for decades deeply embittered by the feeling that Israel's leftist academic establishment was denying him his due because of his politics.

Netanyahu attacked the Oslo Accords from the outset as a disaster that placed Israel's security in the hands of an arch-terrorist. He blamed Arafat for the Hamas bombings of 1995 and brazenly exploited the carnage as evidence that the government was wrong. He was an articulate and effective enemy of the peace process — almost too effective for his own good. In the aftermath of the assassination, memories of Netanyahu criticizing Rabin as a leader who had "lost his mind," and his ideological association with the violent and extremist sector of society that had produced the triggerman, seemed to have crippled his political career.

The peace camp and the left-leaning intellectuals felt guilt at having taken Rabin so much for granted and having done so little to protect him. But with the passing of the weeks, as the shock waves dispersed, a new thought crept forward — one most on the left preferred not to discuss out loud: The assassination was good for peace. It gave Peres an unheard-of 30-point lead in the polls over Netanyahu and seemingly shattered three decades of deadlock in Israeli politics over the fate of the occupied territories. This was reflected in the posters that flooded the country: "Peace will be his legacy."

About two weeks after assuming power, Peres flew to Brussels to sign an accord of association between Israel and the European Union. In the brisk chill of the European capital, he was received with the respect reserved for those who are considered important historical figures even while still in office. Herzl's vision seemed to be coming true: Israel was being recognized as an extension of Europe. As Peres proceeded through the day of ceremony and adulation he gradually shed the cloak of bereavement that had enveloped him since that tragic Saturday night.

On the flight home, I was invited, together with a few other journalists, to sit with Peres at the front of the plane. It is one of the special prerogatives of the prime minister to rescue favored journalists from their overcrowded, noisy, and smoke-filled domain in the back compartment. We happily pushed past the curtain and the humorless security men wearing earphones — their eyes ever-trained on the jagged pens and dull-edged tape recorders carried by suspect reporters — and entered a world of spacious couches separated by neat tables. Five of us pushed into space enough for three, sitting across from Peres and his top advisor, the rotund and always calculating Uri Savir.

After a day of receptions and social drinks, Peres's tongue was loose and his fancy free. He spoke of his conviction that a peace treaty with Syria was within reach. Everyone knew that this would require the return of the entire Golan Heights to Syria, which was a very unpopular idea in Israel with weak support even on the left. But Peres believed Israelis would soon see that they were getting a huge return on their investment. By removing the Syrian veto, he reasoned, the deal would concurrently yield peace with some twenty Arab nations — all the countries of the region save the "rejectionist" Libya, Iraq, and Iran. The concept was very grand, very Peres.

In any case, Peres said, sinking into his seat, at this late stage in his career he was far more interested in tomorrow's history than today's politics. "If I have to choose between peace and popularity, I choose peace," he said earnestly.

In the following weeks Peres was as good as his word, moving ahead efficiently. In November and December, the government speedily withdrew Israeli troops from the West Bank cities of Jenin, Tulkarem, Nablus, Ramallah, Qalqiliya, and Bethlehem, as promised in the Oslo II Accord signed six weeks before the assassination. In January the Palestinians held their first-ever election, which Arafat handily won, gaining much credibility in the eyes of his people, the Israelis, and the world. Israel was to pull out of Hebron, the last West Bank city under occupation, in March. And Peres was still enjoying a 20-point lead in the polls over Netanyahu.

The peace process was at its high point.

In the days after the assassination, with Peres at his most somber and apolitical, cabinet colleagues began to pressure him to call a snap election in order to benefit from the sympathy vote, crush Netanyahu, and win another four years in power for Labor, enough to complete the peace process for sure. But Peres was fearful of gambling wrong and unsure of himself after so many humiliations at the polls. He refused the overtures, insisting that he preferred to take the negotiations as far as he could, hold the election as scheduled in October 1996, and win on his own merits. With the massive wave of sympathy generated by the assassination, it seemed the experienced Peres, the very symbol of the New Middle East, was the right man at the right time, a shoo-in at last, no matter when the elections were held.

And then, as so often before in his star-crossed political life, Peres suffered from a bedeviling combination of bad luck and needless mistakes.

On Friday, January 5, Hamas master bombmaker Yehiya Ayyash was handed a mobile phone by a friend who arrived at his hideout in Gaza City. The phone exploded, ripping off half of his skull.

Nicknamed "The Engineer," Ayyash had masterminded most of the Hamas bombings of the previous several years, often painstakingly building the bombs himself. Israeli intelligence held him responsible for the deaths of up to 80 Israelis and placed him at the very top of the country's Most Wanted list. Although Israel believed he was hiding in Gaza, Arafat's forces insisted he could not be found. Then someone found him.

Israel proceeded as it generally does in such cases, neither claiming nor denying responsibility but allowing an unmistakable smugness to prevail. Who else but our boys would have been so clever, so surgical, as to use an exploding mobile phone? The Hebrew press brimmed with self-congratulatory analyses and diagrams depicting exactly how the remote-control mechanism was set off. The information was attributed to Israeli defense experts.

Arafat was livid. There had not been a terrorist attack in Israel for months, and Arafat had worked hard to gain an agreement that Hamas would desist from further violence. He was convinced he had reached an understanding with the radicals and that it had been imperiled by his partners in Israel. Not only might

Hamas renew the attacks, but some Palestinians might even believe the not-so-farfetched idea that it was Arafat or his men who fingered Ayyash. While they would have been obligated to do so under the Israel-PLO accords, Arafat also knew he would be gaining no popularity with his people by turning over a man who had become a folk hero in some Palestinian circles. Arafat visited Ayyash's family and attended rallies in his honor, even referring to the slain militant as a martyr and hero.

Despite the official silence in Jerusalem, it was understood that the killing of Ayyash was a blow struck from Israel. It was fairly clear that such a high-profile attack would have required approval directly from the office of the prime minister.

Perhaps Peres thought the operation served justice or provided security. Maybe he was hoping it would lend him a touch of the military luster he still lacked. Or perhaps he feared the political implications if it had become known that Israeli intelligence had located the reviled Engineer and Peres had been too spineless to put him out of business.

A few weeks after Ayyash's death, almost three months after the Rabin assassination, the mood of the country was still in a state of flux. Peres still rode high in the polls, but from voters on the right the support was more out of guilt than conviction. The shock of Jew-against-Jew violence still weighed on their minds, and the atmosphere of moral outrage following the assassination lingered, cowing into contrition many Israelis who had previously objected to the peace process.

The assassination stayed on the front pages, helping maintain the outrage of the left and the guilt feelings of the right. Nearly a month after the shooting, an amazing videotape of the fatal moments finally emerged (the amateur videographer was said to have engaged multiple bidders in a complex financial negotiation). The state inquiry into how the security service could have allowed the killer to get so close did not wrap up until nearly five months after the shooting. And the trial of admitted assassin Yigal Amir stretched on longer.

All of these inquiries — with their daily twists and turns, colorful personalities, closed-door sessions, and media speculations — kept the assassination in the spotlight, which seemed to bode well for Peres.

But in a complex situation polls can mislead, especially if they ask a one-dimensional question like "Who would you vote for today?" Such polls don't gauge the sturdiness of the answer — whether, for example, it is based on ephemeral sentimentality for Rabin — and they gloss over the deep-rooted biases and neuroses that can cause many a traditional right-wing voter to return home at the last minute at the polls.

Indeed, Peres had led in many polls in 1981, 1984, and 1988, so he finally caved in to the urging of his advisors and decided to call early elections, moving the date forward to May. This was a compromise date that achieved nothing. It was too late to capitalize on the post-assassination sympathy that probably *would* have won him the election, and it was too early to enable him to achieve a diplomatic coup and build up independent momentum in the contest.

But what is most unbelievable is that the decision to move up the election was announced just as the traditional Islamic mourning period for Ayyash was coming to an end, marking the unofficial but well-understood beginning of revenge attack season.

I was in the headquarters of the army spokesman's office on the morning of February 25 when a soldier rushed into the room and blurted, "There's been an attack!"

A bomb had ripped through a bus on route 18 near Jerusalem's central bus station, killing 26 people, including the suicide bomber, and turning the vehicle into a smoldering wreck of twisted metal, shattered glass, and burnt rubber.

Peres visited the site, surrounded by bodyguards, and watched as ultra-Orthodox volunteers went through their grisly ritual of picking up pieces of flesh and limbs and placing them into small nylon bags for proper Jewish burial.

About an hour later, another man carrying explosives strapped around his waist drove up to a soldiers' hitchhiking station at a crossroads near the southern city of Ashkelon and blew himself up, killing a soldier.

The attacks occurred shortly after Peres had lifted the closure of the West Bank and Gaza that had been in place since the Ayyash killing, allowing Palestinians easy access to Israeli population centers. Peres quickly ordered the territories resealed and demanded that Arafat launch a crackdown on Hamas.

Weekend polls showed that the Peres lead over Netanyahu had been wiped out.

A week later, another militant blew himself up on another route 18 bus in Jerusalem. This time 18 people were killed, including a group of temporary Romanian workers. Again Peres visited the scene, absorbing curses and shouts of "Resign!" and "Go join Rabin!" from hotheads in the crowd.

Peres held a press conference. "We are at war with this horrible organization, the Hamas," he complained.

A day later, on the Jewish holiday of Purim, Hamas struck in the center of Tel Aviv.

Around 4 P.M. on an overcast but pleasant winter day, a Palestinian man got off a truck that had smuggled him from Gaza and approached the southern entrance to the Dizengoff Center shopping mall. Catching the glance of soldiers stationed at the entrance to the four-story enclosed mall, the bomber turned away. He proceeded to a series of cash machines on the corner of the street and then to the crosswalk, where he took several steps into the intersection and then pressed the button that sent a tiny spark to the twenty-five pounds of TNT he carried in his shoulder bag. He and fourteen people—half of them children—were immediately killed, and more than 100 were injured.

If you remember these times from television, this is the attack you probably recall. Shot from above by TV cameras that seemed to appear instantly on the rooftops of surrounding buildings, Israeli TV stations and CNN carried live and taped pictures from just moments after the blast. Below, the intersection outside Dizengoff Center was unsettlingly still for a while, pierced only by the muffled cries of the injured. Passersby rushed to the aid of the wounded, most of whom were not in the middle of the intersection but at its tree-lined curbs, cradled there by strangers tending to their wounds. Then the sirens came, and as the emergency vehicles started arriving a new chaos set in, with lights and stretchers and police and soldiers running this way and that, attempting to clear the area of civilians in case — and this is always the fear — of another explosion.

I was out of the city when the blast took place, but I was there in half an hour. A huge clock hanging on the outside of an over-street passage stood still at 4:10, holding the moment of calamity and making us aware of every subsequent minute that passed.

By the time the ashen Peres arrived, about an hour after the attack, the scene had transformed itself completely. The intersection was besieged on all sides by onlookers and hostile demonstrators, and the prime minister walked around for several minutes surrounded by hysterical-looking Shin Bet officers pointing their loaded submachine guns, with fingers on the triggers, in all directions at the crowd. Almost more than the bomb wreckage itself, this grim realization stunned me: the prime minister of Israel was clearly not safe among his own people.

There are only two key government departments headquartered in Tel Aviv rather than Jerusalem — the security services and the Defense Ministry. Just as the cabinet had gathered at the Defense Ministry following Rabin's death in Tel Aviv to hold "some sort of vote" for Peres exactly four months before, now Peres called them there again, this time to actually address national security. After four terrorist attacks in just nine days, the cabinet emerged to announce a series of extreme measures. In particular, they upgraded the closure of the West Bank and Gaza to include blockades of each of the scores of individual communities therein.

But could the attacks really be halted? The fact is that terrorists do not stand out from the crowd because many Palestinians can pass for Sephardi Jews or Israeli Arabs. Any bag can carry explosives. And the West Bank, bordering Israel along hundreds of miles of hills and valleys, is far from airtight, even during a so-called closure.

Given this, many Israelis were slipping into despair, frustrated by a sense of being sitting ducks. In a span of time that most people measure by the recurrence of their favorite TV program, the nation's collective heart had skipped a beat four different times as news of a bombing spread. Where did it happen? When? And the automatic inner calculation: Do I know anyone in that vicinity? Where are my wife, my brother, my parents? What bus do my children ride? Is my sister stationed near there?

It's hard under such circumstances not to give in to rage. And even supporters of peace who kept their cool began to question the prospects of conciliation with an enemy whose extreme elements were so cruel as to attack civilian shoppers on Purim, a holiday when children dress up and parade about town.

Now Peres was in trouble. Death was emerging again, this time differently, and peace was slipping precipitously away.

Down in Gaza City, in the heart of the Gaza Strip, Yasser Arafat was walking the precipice, too. He had stuck his neck out a good long way to see the peace process started and had gambled his leadership on seeing it through so his people could reap its benefits. Limited autonomy in Gaza and parts of the West Bank had been established just weeks before by the determined Peres, but future adherence to the agreements was being cast in greater doubt with each new bomb. Arafat had promised Israel security, and now his credibility was in serious question not only in Israel but around the world.

Arafat finally moved to shore up his standing and give Peres a boost. After two years of playing cat-and-mouse with the Islamic fundamentalists — tolerating them, essentially — he joined Israel in a serious crackdown, arresting hundreds of Hamas activists and shutting down universities and mosques that served the movement. In April he convened the PLO's widest body, the Palestine National Council, and rammed through a historic resolution annulling clauses in the PLO charter that called for Israel's destruction — a development Peres somewhat over-enthusiastically termed "the greatest event of the century."

U.S. president Bill Clinton also moved to support Peres. He joined almost 20 leaders from the West and the Arab world for a hastily organized "anti-terrorism" conference in Egypt just a few days after the Tel Aviv bomb. Clinton then traveled to Israel and showered its people with affection during a two-day visit that amounted to a barely disguised campaign tour on behalf of Peres.

It is hard to overstate the positive emotional impact that a visiting American president can have in foreign lands facing difficult times. John Kennedy won a place in German history with his rhetorical declaration, "I am a Berliner!" In that same city, Ronald Reagan cheered oppressed peoples throughout Eastern Europe with his hard-nosed demand: "Mr. Gorbachev, take down this wall!" Clinton had a similar impact on Israelis, magnified because they sensed he had a real soft spot for their country.

This was probably best seen when Clinton learned of Rabin's killing, eulogizing him with a simple, heartfelt phrase in Hebrew. It evoked the exact sentiment that most Israelis felt at the time, regardless of political disposition. With a crack in his voice, Clinton said in Hebrew, "Good-bye, friend."

The phrase caught on, and a friend of mine in advertising took advantage. Sensing the chord that Clinton's words had struck, he convinced his bosses to print several hundred thousand bumper stickers with the phrase "Good-bye, friend." For years they were visible on practically every other car in Tel Aviv.

At the new, postmodern opera center in Tel Aviv, Clinton stood beside Peres on the stage. He acknowledged the hard times but urged Israelis to stay focused on the goal of peace. "We know that overcoming adversity is the genius of the Jewish people," he said.

The support from other leaders — including Arab leaders who rushed to the anti-terrorism conference in Egypt — probably boosted Peres's credibility and warmed up the electorate for him, but there was no doubt that he had to stand and deliver on his own. Peres was facing a nervous people who had lost faith in the idea of a harmonious peace and who wanted to see some kind of reassessment from their starry-eyed prime minister as well.

The campaign began in earnest near the end of March, two months from the voting.

Peres's approach was badly misconceived. He did not understand that in the wake of so much mayhem he had to present himself in fresh terms, to convince people to stay the course using more sober, less euphoric arguments. Peres saw only peace and spoke of "four wonderful years" under Labor's stewardship. But many Israelis instead saw a grotesque period of unprecedented bestiality on both sides — from Baruch Goldstein's massacre of Muslim faithful in Hebron, to the human bus bombs exploding in the heart of Israel's cities, to the assassination. Peres utterly failed to understand how susceptible his people might have become to fear and doubt — and how this might make them turn away from him without thinking all that deeply about the alternative.

Equally important, Peres did not recognize how much the peace process itself had already affected the social-political landscape. The conflict between Israel and its neighbors had been, from the very beginning, an existential threat that united Israelis who otherwise had little in common. The paramount importance of defense on the national agenda was the consensus that had bound a diverse population up until the Lebanon war. The fissures in society uncovered by that war, and the Intifada that followed it, started Israelis down a path toward not just political but social division. Now the peace process — seemingly something around which Israelis would rally — paradoxically accelerated the splintering of public opinion on other political and social issues. It suggested that after nearly 50 years, the "external threat" could be removed from the top of every Israeli's list of concerns.

A nation born from the Holocaust, a nation that had fought five major wars — one every ten years or so — was now facing the possibility that survival didn't necessarily mean standing up alone against an entire hostile region, didn't mean riding a tank into Sinai or Lebanon, didn't mean casting a ballot first and foremost for the person most able to lead the next military charge. The peace process suggested that the leaders of the past had done their jobs; Israel had survived and flourished, had built its defenses to overwhelming effectiveness. Now was the time to move beyond survival.

But if for five decades survival had held first place atop every Jewish Israeli's list of national priorities, what had occupied second place?

The diversity of answers to that question is what Peres and his campaign did not take into account. He campaigned on peace and its dividends but did not push his vision beyond this to address the other issues that had been so long suppressed in the national psyche. It's possible that he simply could not push his vision beyond peace, even as other issues crept forward into the light. For example, Peres underestimated how angry and frightened for their way of life the religious population had become. He also didn't see how the nation's rush toward Westernization and talk of open borders with the Arabs made even secular people yearn for something more lastingly "Jewish."

He underestimated how detached a large portion of Israel's Sephardi population felt from his government, where only four ministers out of 21—none of them senior—were Sephardi, even though Sephardim made up almost half of the Jewish population. He didn't even notice how the Russian immigrants, whose massive support had been absolutely critical to Rabin's victory, turned against Labor after a member of his cabinet made unflattering references to them.

And he certainly did not anticipate how Israel's Arab citizens might react to his bombardment of southern Lebanon just six weeks before the election.

Israel had occupied a several-mile "buffer zone" inside southern Lebanon ever since it withdrew from a larger part of Lebanon in 1985. Its aim was to keep the populated areas of northern Israel safe from terrorist incursions; areas like Metula, a chalet-filled town in the shadow of Mount Hermon, or the kibbutz Misgav Am, proudly nicknamed by its residents "kibbutz at the end of the world." A terrorist attack there in 1980 killed two kibbutzniks, including a baby, and injured 12 others. A soldier was also killed.

Kibbutz elder Josef Abas, whose parents were the only members of his family to escape the Nazis in Holland, lived on Misgav Am during the attack. He and his family are still there. "There is no place else for us," he said plainly, as we sat in his small, Dutch-inspired living room.

"If we move away from the border we are relinquishing our land. No one has to tell me about the risks—I know. But this is Israel; how far would I have to move to be safe from terrorists here? There are no guarantees anywhere."

His words could have come from a West Bank settler.

In deference to thousands of people like Abas who live near the northern border, the powerful, high-tech Israeli army has done its share to provide protection. But all the technology in the world could not suppress the Soviet-designed Katyusha, a primitive rocket that had bedeviled Israel since the late 1970s, when it was used by the PLO. Twenty years later, it was serving the Hezbollah very well indeed. The militants launched the Katyusha from mobile units, and it had enough jump to sail over the Israeli-patrolled buffer zone and crash into the Galilee.

Six weeks before the election, following another round of Katyushas, Peres sought to punish the Hezbollah. In a military campaign that was unwisely named "Grapes of Wrath," Peres approved bombings of known Hezbollah locations in southern Lebanon. The raids began on April 10 and went off as planned for a week: Israel hit targets with precision artillery and air strikes and then showed off the results at news conferences. Then, on April 18, a raid went astray—far astray. Several shells landed in a United Nations refugee center near the town of Kfar Kana, killing more than 100 Lebanese. Within a few days, Peres meekly ended the bombing campaign with a U.S.-brokered cease-fire.

Despite all of these subtexts playing upon the mood of the electorate, few of the overconfident people around the prime minister chose to look beyond the surface of the polls, where Peres had regained a lead. Within a few weeks of the Tel Aviv bombing, with the help of Clinton and Arafat, Peres was again about 10 points ahead. But the lead was almost the same as the portion of the sample who declared themselves undecided. These were mostly traditional Likud voters still shamed into political self-denial by the assassination.

Peres's TV campaign — the centerpiece and albatross of the election effort — began with a baby gazing up from his crib at worried parents. "Can you imagine that in a few years he'll be a soldier?" the mother asks her husband.

The baby's imaginary voice implores the father, "Dad, now's the time to tell her that by then there will be no more wars. Why don't you tell her?"

But the frowning father says nothing as he picks up the boy and holds him tight. The mother strokes the infant's fair hair and a soft female voice coos, "On May 29, we will elect the man who makes peace. On May 29, we will elect Shimon Peres."

Another spot had Peres surrounded by adoring children, almost all of them European-looking Ashkenazim. Sitting around him in a circle, they hear Peres explain, with some exaggeration, that Israel's GNP "had doubled" because of his peace efforts.

"We've had four wonderful years!" Peres bubbles, as the kids nod happily. Presumably none of them were related to the hundreds killed or wounded in terrorist attacks in Israel's streets just two months before.

Netanyahu's campaign, masterminded by American negative campaigning guru Arthur Finkelstein, struck much harder and rang true. Pictures of devastation and carnage filled the screen as an announcer intoned, "Peres wants to entrust Israel's security to Yasser Arafat, and everything will be OK. Meanwhile, we live in terror."

A soft fade brings in pictures of a car burning after being hit by a rocket fired from Lebanon. "Peres wants to let [Syrian President] Assad take care of the Hezbollah, and everything will be OK. Meanwhile, we live in fear."

And then these words, one by one, filled the screen, read by an announcer with the deepest of voices: "There is no peace. There is no security. There is no reason to vote for Peres."

Later, Netanyahu strategist Eyal Arad admitted that the Likud campaign had waited in fear for Labor to unleash its doomsday weapon: videos of Netanyahu viciously attacking Rabin, speaking at rallies where some carried signs saying "Death to Rabin" and portraying the late premier in a Nazi SS uniform. Labor did prepare a campaign focusing on the assassination, in one ad featuring a smiling Yigal Amir as the announcer says, "Who do you think he's voting for?"

But the blow never came. Peres's campaign manager, Haim Ramon — who was revered for having managed Rabin's 1992 campaign — decided to avoid stressing the assassination. He felt it wasn't necessary to shake up the campaign with Labor's victory so clearly assured and his man ahead in the polls.

Peres toured the country under heavy guard and gave speeches to handpicked audiences. He hammered away at the message that peace equals prosperity — which, like economics itself, contains the dangerous assumptions that everyone understands the workings of the economy and that people are always rational beings. Peres should have sent some of his yes-men to visit the hundreds of thousands of recent Russian immigrants, whose lives had been spent under a communist planned economy, to find out what "growth" meant to them.

The message was, of course, easily understood by Israel's economic, academic, artistic and other elites, and these groups gave the prime minister solid, almost wall-to-wall support. But throughout the nation's smaller, more provincial towns, heavily populated by Sephardi Jews, the things Peres talked about did not resonate — and neither did the white and Western images in which his TV messages were clothed.

"We doubled the education budget," Peres boasted at an appearance in a poor suburb near the northern port city of Haifa. "For the first time, we have more teachers than army officers. We want a country of peace and science."

Netanyahu, he said, had no message for the future, adding that what his opponent proposed was "like making an egg out of omelets!"

Still trying to figure that one out, I decided to drive around the area, largely populated by working-class Sephardi Jews with roots in Morocco and other Middle Eastern countries. In a deteriorating neighborhood, I stopped in front of a group of youths and, touching a button, lowered a window on the passenger side of my beat-up Alfa Romeo. One of them came over.

"Listen, I just saw Peres campaigning around here. What do you think of him?" I asked, leaning over the gearshift. The youth, about 20 years old, laughed. "You a journalist?"

I admitted I was.

"Well, everyone around here is going to vote for him. We love our prime minister!" he laughed.

Now another kid came over and introduced himself as Oren. "My buddy just lied to you. No one here will vote for Peres," he said.

I asked why.

"Look around!" he replied, drawing my eye to the crumbling three-story stucco buildings around him with a sweep of his hands. "Peres loves the Palestinians; he gives them everything. And we continue to live in garbage. None of the Moroccans will vote for Peres."

Oren had made what sounded like an economic-ideological argument against Peres. But I knew — as anyone who lives in Israel for any time would — that there was more. A sad, sinister truth about human nature was driving our interaction and his politics.

Practically every study supports the observation that the more educated, the wealthier, the more professionally advanced an Israeli is, the more likely he or she is, statistically, to support the political left. There are exceptions, but the facts are irrefutable. And, although elites the world over tend to lean toward "social" parties in their countries, it is more extreme here than in any country I know. (America, of course, is a well-known exception to the whole premise, in that its business elite tends toward the right.) Here's how the electorate breaks down: most of the undereducated support Likud; the highschool-educated are fairly divided; the college-educated tend considerably toward Labor. In this campaign, almost all the leaders of Israel's institutions and establishments — the army, the judiciary, academia, business and industry, the artists, and the media — supported Peres, and many were on record with this. I knew it. So did Oren.

So Peres should have been worried, because the non-elites are always greater in number than the elites. When they see the elites so overwhelmingly behind one candidate, they can turn the other way out of spite alone, out of a desire to beat the elites in one of the few arenas where they can: the one-person, one-vote democratic process. Never mind about policy. This is politics.

I stepped out of the car, walked over to Oren, put my notebook in my pocket, and asked him what he does for a living. He told me he works in the nearby Strauss ice cream factory, where the Ashkenazi owners pay him about $3 an hour. It would probably take him a lifetime of ice cream creation to save enough to buy himself a one-room apartment in the run-down community where he already lives.

"Please," I said, "politics in this country is a very important thing. Maybe you really don't want peace. Maybe you want to reoccupy Gaza and go patrol it. Maybe you want to fight the Arabs all your life. Maybe you think Netanyahu will bring peace. But don't be an automaton. Think before you vote. OK?"

Oren looked at me in surprise, then promised he would. I believed him.

I had similar experiences in Bnei Brak, a suburb of Tel Aviv where more than 100,000 ultra–Orthodox Jews live. Followers — called *haredim*, or the "fearful" — wear black suits and grow their hair in sidelocks, which, for the secular, are the outward signs of who they are and what they represent. They devote most of their lives to the study and practice of Judaism. And they are a rapidly expanding sect that has mushroomed through a tremendous birthrate to about 8 percent of the Jewish population in Israel. Almost all of the ones I met seemed to hate Peres because of Labor's alliance with the aggressively secular Meretz party.

Here, too, I found myself being drawn into political arguments, especially when mild-mannered 40-year-olds declared that "none of the Arabs can ever be trusted!" Or that "secular Jews are not even Jews!" Or that "nothing matters" because "we are all in God's hands."

As far as I know, I failed to sway any of these people with my urging to "think." One after another they invited me to "come do the Sabbath with us. You will be enthralled, and you'll become a real Jew in no time."

Netanyahu deftly cultivated this population. In one appearance that he knew would be widely broadcast, he told rabbis that one of his most gratifying moments of life came when his son Yair proudly stood up and recited the religious song *Adon Olam*—"Master of the Universe."

Labor had hoped that at least some *haredim* wouldn't vote for a prime minister at all because of a change in Israel's electoral system. In 1996, for the first time, Israelis would cast two separate ballots, one for prime minister and one for a slate of party candidates for the Knesset. The prime minister had never been directly elected before—the position had always been awarded to the leader of the party that was able to form a majority coalition in the Knesset.

In the past the *haredim* had voted for small religious parties that had played Labor and Likud off against each other and joined whichever coalition offered a fuller pork barrel and a greater willingness to pass new religious laws. Even though they had tended toward the right since 1977, these religious parties were just flexible enough that on some occasions they appeared to control the balance of power. Now, however, the party vote was less relevant to the prime minister's seat. Labor hoped that rabbinical sages might tell their flocks that voting directly for a secular candidate like Netanyahu—a thrice-married admitted philanderer—would be a sacrilege. But this hope evaporated as one after another the rabbis bestowed his blessing on Netanyahu, falling in line with the hard-line political leanings of their constituencies.

Particularly disturbing to modern-minded Israelis was the campaign of Shas, a religious party specifically meant for Sephardi Jews. The party was founded by the eccentric but revered Rabbi Ovadia Yosef who had hoped to build respect and recognition for the small group of Sephardi *haredim* in the much larger and powerful world of Ashkenazi Orthodoxy. But Shas was not solely about religion; it was about exploiting a wider Sephardi alienation for political gain. In its aggressive ad campaigns, the party validated the social, political, and religious habits of many Sephardi Jews while peppering them with quasi-spiritualistic sub-messages aimed at stoking Sephardi pride. To the collective groan of the secular and the modern religious, the party also employed an array of medieval means ranging from lucky amulets to whispered curses against those who dared vote the wrong way.

Netanyahu was not exactly a natural with this constituency either, but when the ancient Sephardi mystic Yitzhak Kadoori blessed the Likud candidate a week before the election, many voters' hesitation vanished.

Also important was the support given to Netanyahu by the Habad movement, the followers of the late Brooklyn rabbi Menachem Schneerson, believed by some to be no less than the messiah. After receiving an explicit promise from Netanyahu that he would not cede more West Bank land nor allow a Palestinian state, in line with the late rabbi's most vehement preferences, Habad launched a huge poster and billboard campaign throughout the country under the slogan "Netanyahu is good for the Jews" and threw its considerable organizational apparatus behind him.

Time and again, Netanyahu succeeded in reaching out to voters who felt left out by the European, modern, intellectual, seemingly elitist Labor program.

Anyone who felt a little uncomfortable with any of those attributes in the Labor personality found an understanding friend in Netanyahu. His was a rainbow coalition of the disenfranchised and disgruntled.

Peres's limp campaign did nothing to counter Netanyahu's most brilliant move. Netanyahu realized that shouting "Reoccupy Gaza" would not win too many votes. Instead, despite years of pouring bile on the Oslo Accords to galvanize his supporters, Netanyahu suddenly announced that he "recognized" the new facts, and he tried to seize the more moderate center. Although he said he would not carry out the pending pullout from Hebron that the accords required, he promised to continue the peace process. But he would change it. There would be a new spin. It would be peace "in our way," he said. It would be, according to the slogan of the final weeks of the campaign, a "secure peace."

In closed forums Netanyahu reportedly promised settlers and religious leaders to kill the accords by making their implementation conditional on so much that the process would collapse. This Netanyahu persona seemed much more in line with his 1993 book, *A Place Among the Nations*, in which he made clear that he was deeply committed to the Likud ideology of holding on to the West Bank and Gaza above all else.

In his book, he referred to the West Bank's central highland and the Golan Heights to the north as Israel's "protective wall" that must not be abandoned. He also did not buy the PLO claim that it was willing to make do with only the West Bank, Gaza, and East Jerusalem. His book described the PLO as a "Trojan horse" that Rabin was foolish to bring into Israel. He went on to assert that the PLO had a "stages plan" to get these territories first, then Arab-populated parts of Israel like the Galilee, and finally Tel Aviv and Haifa. Ultimately, Netanyahu's book revealed him as having little faith in the possibility of peace with the Arabs — at least until the Arab Middle East became as democratic as the Jewish one, or for that matter as Western Europe.

In a meeting I had with Netanyahu a few days before the election, he expressed bewildering certainty that he nevertheless would be able to reach a final settlement with the Palestinians, striking a better deal for Israel than the "defeatist" Peres.

"What exactly would be the essence of that settlement?" I asked.

"Autonomy for the Palestinians," the candidate replied, looking steely and determined.

"But that's what they have now. They want an independent state. The government has let them assume they'll get it," I said. "How will you be able to make them sign on to autonomy forever?"

Netanyahu dismissed this with a wave of his hand.

"No responsible Israeli government can give them a state," he said dryly. Then, perking up, he added, "Autonomy exists in many places as a permanent solution." And, moving in for the rhetorical kill with a flourish of his eyebrow, he asked, "Did you know that the residents of Barcelona in Spain live under autonomy? And that they suffice with it?"

"But the Catalans are also full of Spanish citizens with the right to vote in Spain's elections," I replied. "Can you offer this to the Palestinians? If you did and they took it, Israel would cease to be a Jewish state."

Netanyahu didn't reply. He moved on to the next question.

The episode perfectly illustrated his campaign strategy. His arguments were seductive. They enabled Netanyahu to woo away from Peres members of the sizable Israeli majority who wanted the peace process to continue but were inclined to vote against him for various reasons — the terrorist attacks, the Labor party's 1950s mistreatment of Sephardim, his haircut, whatever. It's a safe bet that many of these swing voters, tens of thousands to be sure, couldn't tell Barcelona from Baltimore, much less bicker about its system of government. There was a wide-open market for Netanyahu's "secure peace."

I saw the tide in the street turning to Netanyahu. Peres, protected from the masses by his armored car and his army of politicos and pollsters, did not.

In the televised debate three days before the election, Peres's one chance to challenge Netanyahu directly, he did not. Instead Peres followed his campaign's strategy of trying to deny Netanyahu equal footing by ignoring his arguments and addressing him in a dismissive way as "Mr. Bibi" — using Netanyahu's nickname in the formal setting to make him seem ridiculous. But in the wake of the bombings and Netanyahu's highly effective campaign, it wasn't working. Peres just looked arrogant and tired, sulking as he absorbed Netanyahu's dead-on broadside: "Mr. Peres, it's not enough to be photographed with kids — you have to protect them." Netanyahu pounded away at a woozy opponent who for some reason did not use his ample power to strike back. And, like spectators at a boxing match, there were those watching who cheered ecstatically with each blow, and those who, waiting with increasing desperation for the counter blows that never came, pulled at their hair in red-faced anguish.

In the end, the election was not decided by the most energized fans of either man. It was decided by those tens of thousands of voters who did not know exactly where their vote belonged, people for whom the peace process had opened that cellar door to long-suppressed issues and new priorities, people who decided maybe now was the time to start making an independent statement.

People like my friend Zevi.

Zevi, in his early thirties, had always been a supporter of Likud. It was a product of his upbringing. His parents, who were immigrants from Romania, distrusted the Arabs and had little concern for whether Israel treated them in a way that would impress Amnesty International.

But as he grew older and became an anesthesiologist, Zevi's circle of friends became increasingly peopled with educated professionals with more liberal points of view. Soon Zevi found himself opposing his father, who felt, for example, that when a terrorist was captured alive he should be summarily executed by a lynch mob or the police, whichever came first.

"That's not exactly the way a civilized society works, you know," Zevi would say, shifting in his seat.

But his father would only laugh with derision. "And do you think they'd treat you with civility if given half a chance?"

Zevi always voted right-wing, telling himself that Labor's plan to give the Arabs the West Bank was not tenable because it would leave Israel indefensibly thin at the waist. When our peacenik friends would ask him what the better alternative was, he would reply with the resigned tone of a practiced doctor diagnosing a terminal disease: "There is none. There is no good solution."

Still, as the 1996 election approached, our friend Avi recognized Zevi's inner struggle. The two of them had been arguing about Israeli politics for years, and Avi understood that much of Zevi's political persona was defined by family tradition. He subjected Zevi to intense campaigning on behalf of peace and Peres, at one point even offering to pay for his vote. That was how strongly Avi felt about the peace process.

A week before the election, Zevi confided to me that he was still undecided. "Bibi's not so bad, but the people around him ... I don't know if I can vote for these people," he said.

It seemed to me that Zevi, like other Israelis this time around, was thinking about where he truly fit in the Israeli puzzle. In his case, it was not with the Kadoori amulet clutchers. For most Sephardi Jews, it was not with the party that featured so many blond children in its ads. For some Arab Israelis, even though they desperately supported the peace process, maybe it could not be with the leader who had bombed Arab children in Lebanon, accidentally or not.

Election days in Israel are fraught with tension, more so than in any other country I know. It's probably the only established democracy in the world where most people care mightily about who wins, because for more than 50 years the issues have been fundamental, dramatically affecting the everyday lives of its voters. At the polls, there is a reverent, businesslike silence, totally unlike American elections in which only the really dutiful turn out and where the polling place has all the formality of a backyard barbecue.

When the first (ultimately wrong) TV projections showed Peres just barely edging out Netanyahu, Avi knew that he had done the right thing in pushing and tugging so hard at his friend. Every vote, clearly, had been critical. He called Zevi. "Did you vote for Peres?"

His friend let him stew for a few seconds before replying, "Yes."

But in the momentarily precise yet ever murky and mutating DNA of the electorate, Zevi's vote and others like it had been offset. Peres lost by less than 1 percent.

Among die-hard Netanyahu supporters there was unbridled joy. But half of the country was truly in mourning, as if Rabin had been assassinated all over again. His widow, Leah, said she felt like "packing my bags and getting out of here." And even many of Netanyahu's centrist voters — the so-called "terrorism electorate" — were immediately apprehensive, as if they hadn't really expected their votes to actually turn everything upside-down. No one could say what the result would be for peace, for security, for society, for the economy — for Israel.

But one thing was clear. The '96 election showed that a new social and political reality was emerging in Israel. It was a reality in which Israelis began to distinguish and define themselves in new ways; in which they were aligning with parties that had vastly differing and largely conflicting visions of the future; and, strikingly, in which the elected parliament was a vivid reflection not of political positions but of identity.

Instead of having two big blocs dominated by Labor and Likud, the Knesset turned into an array of mid-sized parties strongly linked to sectarian groups within Israel's society, indicating clearly where the future fault lines lay. Labor's vote was overwhelmingly Ashkenazi. Likud's was mostly Sephardi. Almost all of the Russian immigrants voted for a new Russian party headed by Natan (formerly Anatoly) Sharansky. Israel's one million Arab citizens voted mostly for Arab parties. And, of course, there were the religious whose parties won a record 23 seats out of 120; of these, Shas won ten seats, getting a vote from one in five Sephardi Jews.

Almost everyone, it seemed, had voted according to an emerging sense of identity. Like Zevi.

Netanyahu ensconced himself in a suite in the Hilton hotel in Tel Aviv and dispatched advisors to the lobby to tell reporters in the vaguest of terms that the peace process would continue. He did not emerge in public until four days — four days! — after the election, as if he, too, didn't quite know what to do with his victory.

Somehow, in those four days, it struck me that for the first time Israel had a prime minister who was younger than the state itself, who had lived only a small part of its history.

Part II
Beyond

Citizens

Jews and Arabs meeting on Mt. Carmel, before the state was born (photograph by Zoltan Kluger).

On the morning of May 31, 1996, Shimon Peres woke up with an irreconcilable burden. Two days before he had been his country's prime minister, favored for reelection. Today, with the final results in, he was on his way out.

The last few days of the Rabin-Peres era were fleeting and jagged. There was no comfort for Peres or his supporters in the manner of his loss. He had not been beaten soundly; he had not been beaten by a foe he could graciously acknowledge. In the wake of the assassination of Rabin and the rancorous campaign that had followed, the defeat at the polls was almost unbearably bitter.

Pundits, newspapers, and the public at large immediately began to theorize about where Peres had gone wrong. With the election so close, almost any aspect of the campaign's march of folly might have cost him his office. And yet one electoral fact stood out from the rest, tantalizing in its irony and cruelty: just a few more Arab votes could have turned things around.

Peres knew that in the Jewish state it was not the Jewish sector of the electorate that was most devoted to his peace plan — it was the Arab sector. It was not the Jews who would vote for him in overwhelming percentages — it was the Arabs. And, in the end, it was not Jewish votes that Peres had lost with his ill-advised attack on Lebanon and the Kfar Kana debacle that followed. It was Arab votes.

Peres could have neutralized more of the negative response to the Kfar Kana incident had he made a serious and convincing effort to reach out to Israeli Arabs, especially had he done so quickly. But for reasons as steeped in history and culture as in political miscalculation, he did not. In his seven months as prime minister, Israel's prince of peace had not even bothered to appoint an Arab to his 21-member cabinet, although Arab legislators were critical to his slim parliamentary majority.

A small portion of the Israeli Arab electorate responded by not voting for prime minister, casting blank ballots instead. Although it is not known exactly how many blank ballots were cast across the country, the election commission had, by the end of the tally, discounted nearly 150,000 votes in the prime minister's race as "invalid." Many analysts believed these were primarily blanks, as did Israeli Arab leaders, most of whom had exhorted their people not to submit to the rabble rousers behind the blank-ballot campaign but to vote for Peres.

And most did. In Nazareth, for example, the largest Arab-populated town in Israel, a staggering 98.6 percent of those who cast ballots for prime minister voted for Shimon Peres. But 8.6 percent of the total ballots cast were invalid — most likely blanks. With Nazareth a fair representation of the Israeli Arab population as a whole, and with Arabs accounting for about 500,000 votes (out of a nationwide electorate of 3 million), it was easy to see that thousands of votes for Peres — perhaps as many as 40,000 — were lost this way.

Peres lost the election by just 29,000 votes.

It is a fundamental paradox of Israel's existence that although it has always been at war with the Arab world, the closest part of that world has always existed within Israel in peace. Today that Arab minority accounts for more than one in six of Israel's people. And although the Jewish majority has been reluctant to fully acknowledge that the fate of their nation is shared with an Arab minority, the Arabs have increasingly laid claim to the idea that they are, indeed, Israelis — citizens of the democratic, "Jewish" state with rights and a vote.

One of them is Mohammed Amin Tibi, a resident of Taibe, an Arab village about 30 miles northeast of Tel Aviv. One of the hundreds of thousands of Arab Israelis who had voted for Peres, Mohammed knew what Peres knew that morning: the hope for peace between Jews and Arabs had faltered at the polls, at least in part due to the reluctance of too many of his fellow Israeli Arabs to vote for Peres. And Mohammed knew more: he knew that his life as an Arab citizen in a Jewish state would not be making any more sense as a result.

When I first met Mohammed a few months before the election, he was a surprise guest in my home. It had been eight days since the assassination of Rabin in the square; now a memorial was being held for him there. My apartment on Ibn Gvirol Street, just across from City Hall and one flight up, was a natural pre-event gathering spot.

My friends were natural supporters of the Labor Party and its policies. They were almost all of European descent, well-educated, and successful in their fields. And all were Jewish.

Most lived in Tel Aviv, a short drive — but a spiritual universe — away from Mohammed's Taibe. They saw Arabs every day — working at construction sites, staffing kitchens in their restaurants. They saw and heard Arab politicians on TV and radio programs, airing concerns particular to their constitutuents. They knew very well that one out of every six Israelis are Arabs, and that the country had virtually incorporated territories with millions more. Many may even have had at least some sympahy for the struggles of an Arab minority living in the Jewish state.

And yet, it's safe to say that few if any of my friends — despite their pro-peace sentiments — had ever had an Israeli Arab in their homes, except maybe as a laborer. I'm certain none of them could say they had a real Arab friend. So Mohammed, upon crossing my threshold, was something of a curiosity to a whole room of Jews who considered themselves "enlightened."

Mohammed, a math teacher, is an Israeli citizen with full equality under the law, and, as we learned, he wholeheartedly supported Rabin's peacemaking with the Palestinians. Indeed, in a very real and confusing way, Mohammed himself *is* Palestinian. He is different from the Arabs of the West Bank and Gaza only by an accident of history and by the demarcation of cease-fire lines in 1949 that left his family on the Israeli side of the border.

Yet despite his support for the late prime minister, it was no small leap of good faith for Mohammed to come to my home in Tel Aviv. Israel's Arabs, though ostensibly equal citizens, are nonetheless effectively second-class in many respects, living their lives in mainly Arab towns and villages clustered inland, behind Israel's cosmopolitan — and Western-oriented — coastal cities. Places like the church-filled town of Nazareth, Mohammed's Taibe, the Bedouin community of Rahat, and the village of Abu Gosh, known for its Middle Eastern restaurants, just off the highway outside Jerusalem.

After the assassination, Mohammed felt the urge to step out of Taibe. He called my friend Eytan, a Jewish Israeli he had met several months before at a convention for high school teachers. They had remained in touch by phone, drawn together less by natural affinity than by the shared ideal of an Israel in which ethnic origin didn't matter.

Mohammed's arrival at my door with Eytan took my other guests by surprise. Obviously unfamiliar with such a situation, they stepped carefully, going out of their way to be nice to him. Mohammed began by amiably answering their questions about his Arab community.

"In Taibe, there is real bereavement over Rabin," he said with sincerity. "Because of Rabin's peace process, we [Arab citizens] felt for the first time that there was a chance for the country and the region to become normal, and for us to be able to say we are Israelis without feeling and sounding ridiculous. For the first time, I felt the Israeli prime minister was my leader, too.

"It is a tragedy," he said. "We Israelis must now join together to remember him and complete his work."

Some of those present smiled at Mohammed's use of the phrase "we Israelis." I couldn't tell whether their looks held condescension, trepidation, agreement, or just surprise.

We went down to the square, which was packed with more than 200,000 people, and pushed our way forward until our progress was impeded by sheer mass. Leah Rabin, the prime minister's widow, made a short speech in which she addressed her slain husband directly, a practice that many in the crowd found cloying. Then came a parade of Israeli popular singers performing the melancholy tunes that always dominate Israeli radio stations after terrorist attacks or other sorrowful events.

The "Israeli sound" is most easily identified in these tuneful ballads. Israeli performers—whose music typically ranges from American-style folk to soft rock, employing smooth, full rhythms with some Middle Eastern hints in the background—have made a distinctive contribution, even winning the annual European song competition on three occasions. The country's top stars tend to be poetic balladeers, people like Arik Einstein, David Broza, and Hava Alberstein. Their Hebrew songs, even if they occasionally tip their hats to Middle Eastern influences, are not the stuff that appeals to the Arab population, which favors the wailing, high-pitched tremolo of true Arab music.

Nonetheless, Mohammed was familiar with the words being sung in the newly renamed Rabin Square, in the same way that I am familiar with the words to John Denver songs—more or less through osmosis.

"Where are there more men such as this man, who was as the weeping plains?" sang pop icon Shlomo Artzi, who a week earlier had been noticeably absent from the rally where Rabin was slain.

Standing unobtrusively, almost pensively, in the crowd, Mohammed intermittently sang along, looking quietly down at the ground.

Israel's national anthem, "Hatikva," was the last song played at the memorial. It is a bending, mournful melody, rising quietly and slowly from instruments and throats as if rising from the ages themselves, expressing the burdens of the Jewish soul across the centuries. As its first notes floated skyward, a tremendous chorus arose:

> As long as in the heart a Jewish soul beats,
> Forward, toward the east, an eye watches Zion,
> We have not yet lost our hope, the hope of 2,000 years,
> To be a free people in our land, the land of Zion and Jerusalem.

Mohammed held his head up during these phrases, trying good-naturedly to mouth some of the words. And while no sound emerged from his hardened throat, he had a dignity about him that I could not resist acknowledging. Swept up in the moment, I approached him and whispered: "I don't want to sound like I'm patronizing you, but I want you to know that I am impressed and grateful that you are here tonight, and singing 'Hatikva' too."

Mohammed looked me in the eye for a moment, cocked his head with a smile, and responded: "Please don't be offended. But you know, I have to tell you that even though I sing this song, it is not really my anthem."

The early Zionists didn't do much planning for the potential presence of Arabs in Israel. Some of them believed — wrongly — that the land they had designs on was basically empty. In Russia, early Zionist Moses Leib Lilienblum wrote, "We were Semites among Aryans, a Palestinian tribe from Asia among the lands of Europe.... Why be foreigners in foreign lands when the land of our fathers ... is still empty and can, together with its environs, contain us?"

Few counted the Arabs already there, or foresaw that more Arabs would be attracted to move to Palestine when it was under British rule, or that declining death and infant mortality rates in the twentieth century would yield a population explosion in the region, especially in Palestine. The rise of Palestinian and Arab nationalism in this century was also not widely foreseen.

In his utopian novel, *Old-New Land*, Herzl foresaw the Jewish society as one that would borrow only the most progressive habits from all others and as a result would cultivate a prosperous harmony with its neighbors. An Arab character named Rashid Bey explained it this way, responding to a traveler who asked him why his people accepted the Jewish influx so readily: "The Jews made us richer — why should we be angry with them? They live among us like brothers — why should we not love them?"

One notable exception was right-wing leader Vladimir Jabotinsky, who insisted that out of respect for the Arabs one should expect to have to fight them. In his book *A Hebrew State* he wrote, "The greatest folly would be to depend on the notion that our settlement will bring the natives much economic advantage. It is true — but no people ever sold out its national aspirations for a slice of bread and butter."

In any case, few then questioned the notion that Jews would be the eternal masters of the land by virtue of the great majority they would doubtless enjoy. Indeed, after 50 years of statehood, the Jews of Israel are still the unquestioned masters of the land — but they do not enjoy the luxury of a great majority.

If anything, this quiet, powerful math is what unsettles Israel's Jews more than anything else. Since the 1960s, Israel's Arab citizenry has quadrupled, entirely by birth. The Jewish population increased only 2.5 times, and this was aided tremendously by immigration.

This fact of life is what every Jewish Israeli knows as the "demographic threat." Ironically, this is the real reason why many so-called peaceniks support dumping the West Bank and Gaza. Those territories hold 2.5 million Palestinians, too many — on top of the 1 million Israeli Arabs — to preserve Israel as Jewish and democratic.

The patterns of Jewish settlement in the first half of the century were such that when international mediators tried to come up with a solution to dividing the land between the Zionists and the Arabs, a natural map emerged that would yield two states.

The partition plan proposed by the United Nations allotted the Jews a state in most of the Mediterranean coastal plan and the Negev Desert in the south, and part of the Galilee around Lake Kinneret (also known as the Sea of Galilee) in the north. At its inception it would have 538,000 Jews and 397,000 Arabs — but its Jewish majority was expected to grow dramatically with the unlimited immigration of Jewish refugees whose arrival had been blocked by the British authorities.

The Arab state in Palestine was given part of the Galilee, the southern tip of the Mediterranean coast bordering Egypt (now known as the Gaza Strip), and most of the center of the country, the hilly region that today constitutes the West Bank. It would have 804,000 Arabs and 10,000 Jews. Jerusalem, which had a substantial Jewish population, was to be an "international city" surrounded by Arab land and with no territorial link to the Jewish state.

To Jabotinsky's disciples in the so-called Revisionist movement, the plan, in denying the Jews not only Jerusalem but the heartland of Israel, was an abomination. But the mainstream Zionist leadership, led by David Ben-Gurion, was inclined to take what it could get, as was most of the population. The truncated Jewish state may have looked ridiculous on the map, rather like a bunch of sausage links, but it was better than no Jewish state at all. In any case it constituted an amazing achievement only 50 years after Herzl's *Judenstaat* raised condescending chuckles in the foyers of Eastern Europe.

Arab leaders and activists rejected the partition outright. To the Arabs, in those days of global capitulation by European colonists, the possibility of a European-Jewish state in their midst seemed not only unnatural but also an unnecessary compromise. They saw it as one last colonial thrust toward capturing the

Holy Land, which so many past crusades had tried and failed to conquer and hold. The Arab nations, themselves newly independent and fighting their first fights, would repel this last crusade as well.

The plan was put to a vote in the UN General Assembly in November 1947. Jews around the world listened intently as each nation's name and vote were declared on the radio. In the opening pages of their fabulous book, *O Jerusalem!*, Larry Collins and Dominique LaPierre capture this moment beautifully through their description of Golda Meir sitting in her small Jerusalem kitchen alone, wringing her hands as she tracked the voting on a small napkin.

In those days, as the world was coming to terms with the horror that had befallen the Jews in Europe, the Arabs didn't stand a chance. The partition was approved by a vote of 33-13. The Arab population responded to the vote with strikes and violence in Palestine and elsewhere in the region. In the city of Aden in southern Yemen, 76 Jews were killed. It took but a few more months for the British to pull out of Palestine altogether, and war began in earnest.

On May 14, Ben-Gurion gathered the leaders of the pre-state Zionist movement together in what is now an innocuous old building in a bar and business district in southern Tel Aviv. In a small, echoing auditorium, he declared the State of Israel.

Ben-Gurion said the new nation would be open to Jewish immigration and would guarantee all its citizens equality and freedom. He called on the Arabs "to cooperate with the independent Jewish nation for the common good." This did not happen. Arab armies attacked Israel from the north, south, and east, and war raged for about a year. At the end of it, Israel controlled all the territory allotted to it by the UN plan and somewhat more, including half of Jerusalem and a corridor leading to it, captured by a unit led by the young Yitzhak Rabin.

The Palestinian Arabs ended up with nothing to call their own. The Gaza Strip was seized by Egypt, a small profit for the proud nation of the pharaohs that rendered its war effort an embarrassment. Transjordan, so named because it lay across the Jordan River, captured the west bank of that not-so-mighty river, creating two new names for history: the renamed Hashemite Kingdom of Jordan, proudly straddling both banks of the river, and its newest acquisition, the henceforth-to-be-capitalized West Bank. Jordan thus took over the land the UN had envisioned as the key zone of the Palestinian Arab state.

The Palestinian Arabs also lost the part of the Galilee that was to be theirs — in this case to the Jews. Furthermore, in the course of the war more than a half million Arabs fled the areas that came under Israel's control and, although it took Israel decades to come to terms with this, many of them were expelled by Israeli troops. These became the famous Palestinian refugees, living for subsequent decades in miserable camps in Lebanon, Syria, Jordan, the West Bank, and Gaza, and now numbering millions.

For the 156,000 Arabs who remained in Israel when the guns fell silent, there was citizenship and a vote, but little of the utopia promised in the Proclamation of Independence. In many cases the Arabs suffered land expropriations.

Many who remained in the country but had fled their homes were listed as "absentees." About 1500 were expelled from "security zones" in various parts of the country. And a "military administration" was applied in Arab communities, allowing the army to detain the locals without trial, enforce random curfews, and impose house arrests. The most tragic single result of this approach to managing the Arab population came in 1956, when 49 villagers, returning late from work and unaware that a curfew had been imposed, were gunned down by Israeli forces. Ben-Gurion expressed shock at the massacre, yet all its perpetrators were freed from jail by 1960.

The military administration was finally lifted in 1966, but that didn't change the basic dynamic. Indeed, the original Arab community of 156,000 has since grown more than 600 percent. The Arab population's growth rate is falling, but it still far outpaces that of the Jews. Many Jews still feel their majority is not secure (even without the West Bank and Gaza), and for many of them the Israeli Arabs remain, first and foremost, a classic potential fifth column.

Mamoun is an English teacher who lives in the town of Deir El-Asad in northern Israel. It is a fairly typical Arab setting, snug along a hillside. Although just a few hundred yards from the Jewish town of Karmiel across the highway, in spirit it is miles away.

"We have almost no contact at all," Mamoun said. "Whenever I walk into Karmiel people look at me in a strange way. I am a foreigner there, and I can feel their suspicions."

Mamoun was born in the same Arab village where he still lives, where his family has resided for 500 years. He is in his fifties. He has resigned himself to the idea that he will most likely live his whole life as a second-class citizen, and although he understands Israel's particular situation, he can't help feeling a sting. "They just don't know me," he said. "And I don't think they want to."

The cultural differences are daunting. Language, religion, history, myth, morality, modernity — all are realms in which Arabs and Jews come from different points of view.

Sometimes interaction can lead to amusing misunderstandings. Two teenage boys, one Jewish and the other Arab, both Israeli, were trying to set up an "exchange program" in which Arab and Jewish families would trade homes for a weekend to see what life in the other community was like. After a week of seeking interested families, the two boys got together to compare notes.

The Jew reported he had lined up 30 families for the exchange. "How many do you have?" he asked his Arab partner.

The answer came: "Two."

"Two? That's not enough! My families add up to 80 people."

"Mine add up to 100."

I heard this story from the young Jewish Israeli who was involved, who learned that in the Arabic community, families are not defined by the isolated nuclear groupings of the Western world, but by the much larger clan. "It was incredible," he said. "Their lives, their family situation, it's all so different—yet we know almost nothing about it. How can we have a healthy nation with people we know nothing about?"

It's not true that Jewish Israelis know nothing about their Arab counterparts. But what information does get promulgated tends toward the spectacular, the outrageous—things that cement stereotypes rather than supplant them with facts. One particularly well-known example is the periodic occurrence of Arab "honor killings."

At the rally, I had to ask Mohammed about this repugnant practice, which happens from time to time and is always widely reported. I started the delicate inquiry by getting his name wrong.

"Ahmed," I began.

"Mohammed, my friend, Mohammed."

"Of course. Sorry. Why is it, Mohammed, that the Israeli Arabs can't seem to part ways with this culture of killing women over issues of family honor? Don't they understand that in a modern country this just can't be?"

The question was on my mind because a few weeks before, in a well-publicized incident, an Israeli Arab youth had axed his sister to death on the main street of the village of Daliat-el-Carmel to the rousing cheers of neighbors. The young man reportedly believed she had soiled the family honor by leading a modern life in a Jewish town nearby.

Mohammed pondered the question for some time and finally replied, "This issue is more complicated than it would seem."

I couldn't grasp these complications. "Yes, but doesn't it bother you personally? Let's say your sister is a prostitute. You're not going to drag her to the main street in Taibe and ax her to death, are you?"

Mohammed looked at me for a long time. He must have decided that this was not the time, or I was not the audience, for a discourse on the demands and constraints his culture placed on him. "In my culture it is said, 'Let us cross that bridge when we reach it.' OK?"

Whatever he thought in his deepest heart about the girl who was slain in the town square, about his sisters, about traditional versus modern and Western mores, he did not reveal it.

Mohammed also managed to unnerve my friend Nir, then a doctoral student in physics. Nir attempted to establish commonality with Mohammed through their mutual training in math. But their discussion quickly turned to politics. Mohammed tried to join the two subjects in explaining the positive impact Rabin's peace policy had on the attitude of Israeli Arabs toward their country of citizenship.

"It has changed it completely," he declared. "360 degrees."

Nir smiled, as if to suggest that anyone was capable of such an error in heated conversation. "I don't think you mean 360," he said, patting Mohammed on the back.

"Believe me, my friend. It's true," Mohammed replied.

"You mean 180 degrees, I think," I interjected.

Mohammed was insistent. "No! The full 360!"

Although Nir is certainly in favor of peace and coexistence with the Arabs, like many Israelis he has doubts about them in his heart. Seizing on to this error after Mohammed had left for Taibe, he could barely contain his eagerness to repeat the story as proof of Arab backwardness and the burden it implies for Jewish Israel.

"A math teacher!" he exclaimed.

Despite obvious cultural divergences, communication breakdowns, and a seemingly immutable mutual suspicion between the Jews and the Arabs, Israel's Arabs have been quiet enough that most Jews are content to convince themselves that "everything is fine." But then, most of Israel had similar illusions about the occupied Palestinians of the West Bank and Gaza before the Intifada blew them to bits. The Jews had no idea such resentment and discontent had been building up. After all, they figured, the Palestinians were much better off under Israeli military rule than they had been under Jordan. Jobs. Access to Israel's markets. What was the problem?

A similar Jewish attitude now applies to Israel's Arabs. From the Jewish point of view, their Arab co-citizens have a lot going for them — citizenship in a democracy, some economic opportunity, stability. Compared with the Palestinians of the territories, or most of the Arabs of neighboring countries, for that matter, the Israeli Arabs live on easy street.

If Israel were just another dictatorship, the local Arabs might truly have reason to count their blessings. But Israel is supposed to be the region's showcase democracy. It has invited scrutiny, claiming membership in the upper echelon of enlightened places. Its Proclamation of Independence declared that the "State of Israel will maintain complete social and political equality for all its citizens, without distinction on the grounds of religion, race, or sex."

Israel was founded on the slippery slope of self-righteousness. The experiences of the Jews in Europe, culminating in the Holocaust, gave the state's early leaders a keen sense of justice. The new nation was intent on setting itself apart, on establishing standards that would stand as a mighty rejoinder to every injustice that had been wrought on the Jews. And, given the Jewish belief that somehow they were, indeed, a special people, the country had to reflect the specialness that was used to justify its very creation.

Yet many of Israel's lofty aspirations remained unfulfilled in the subsequent decades of Arab-Jewish conflict. Surrounded on all sides by enemies for so many years, Israel gradually lost some of its quest for purity, focusing instead on survival. Given the circumstances, Israel could not honestly embrace its Arab citizens — not while their brethren strove for Israel's annihilation.

And so, for half a century, the Israeli Arabs have been set aside, watched over to varying degrees, but mostly left undisturbed to go about their business. "Complete social and political equality," though, went by the wayside.

In its 1997 report, the Association of Civil Rights in Israel, the nation's premier advocacy organization, asserted that Israel's "worst infringement"—

outside the West Bank and Gaza, of course—was "discrimination against the Arab citizens of the state."

"Many government ministries continue to ignore the needs of Arab citizens," the report said, "and the discrimination against these citizens is found in almost every facet of life, though it is particularly acute in the fields of housing and education."

Since the association is not only a watchdog and advocacy group but a direct service provider representing individuals and groups in their cases against the government, it has a deep reservoir of examples to support its official findings. It claimed some organizations that require "army service" as a prerequisite to employment do so only as a means for turning away Arab applicants, as in the case of the company seeking ice cream vendors, hardly a position that demands great military skills. In another example, the electric company, one of Israel's largest employers, informed ACRI that it had recently increased employment of Arabs by 20 percent—from five to six. One finding was shocking: based on a national survey done in 1994 but not published in Israel until 1996, two-thirds of Jewish high school students opposed equal rights for Israeli Arabs.

Despite the considerable presence of Arabs—in greater concentration than that of African Americans in the United States—few places in Israel are truly integrated. The Arabs live mostly in their ancestral towns and villages. Some live in Arab neighborhoods in the big cities. In very few places are Jews and Arabs next-door neighbors.

One exception is the rambling neighborhood that abuts the millennia-old harbor of Jaffa, snug against the Mediterranean Sea. Jaffa's Old City sits quite unmistakably on a bluff overlooking the waves, aglow after sundown as the carefully planted spotlights set the ancient sandstone walls ablaze. Spreading out like a lava flow from this lighted dome are the alleys and streets of modern Jaffa, a district of Tel Aviv that today is shared by Jews and Arabs in remarkable harmony.

On any day of the week in Jaffa you can meander through one of Israel's largest flea markets. On rainy days, which occur with some regularity during the mild coastal winters, you can hopscotch from warehouse door to warehouse door for hours, wandering through receding tin-roofed interiors piled high with the collected treasures of the centuries. Carved woods from Hungary, intricate lamps from Persia, decorative ivories and pewters from India, elaborate hardwood wardrobes crafted in Spain and Morocco. All this, and the welcoming, relaxed hospitality of the market purveyors, both Jews and Arabs, who sit in rockers by the overflowing front opening.

"Come, sit, get out of the rain," you will be entreated. "Have some coffee or tea with us."

On one memorable visit to this *shuk*, a pair of elderly men, proprietors of neighboring stalls, invited me to sit, even though I wasn't buying. I sat down for a few minutes.

"This is what we do in Jaffa," the Arab man explained. "We sit, we drink, we play cards.... Life is good!"

His Jewish friend nodded with an open smile and not a trace of contradictory subtext.

Jaffa's population of 60,000 is roughly two-thirds Jewish and one-third Arab. The Arab population has been here for generations; the Jewish residents, other than a tiny fraction, are more recently arrived. Most came in the years just after the 1948 War of Independence, moving into Jaffa due to its immediate proximity to the Jewish city of Tel Aviv, taking over the houses and shopfronts abandoned by the Arab residents who had left. In this way, Jaffa developed as one of the few places in Israel where, street after street, Jews and Arabs came to know each other as neighbors.

But Jaffa's easy-going race relations also spring from the city's history as a trading port, a history that is traceable as far back as 2000 B.C., when Jaffa was the main port. In the trading environment of the wharf, a Jew's money was as good as an Arab's — or a Greek's, a Spaniard's, or an Indian's — and that's a philosophy that still holds sway. People who share a common appreciation for making a trade, earning a profit, and managing business affairs wisely tend to develop a mutual respect. In Jaffa, this is a principle as old as the sea. Jewish-owned shops are interspersed among Arab shops. Some are co-owned by families that have been doing business together for decades. And there is an understanding among those who have been here for generations that diversity and harmony are good business — they attract tourists.

For tourists and locals alike, one Jaffa name stands out above the rest. It is engraved and painted in gold lettering on an oak sign that hangs out over the main thoroughfare from the Tel Aviv beach area. It reads, "Abulafiya and Sons. Bakery" — in Arabic, Hebrew, and English.

Hamis Abulafiya is in his late thirties. He is one of five brothers who run the family enterprise that, in addition to the bakery, includes a large real estate concern, an investment house, and a restaurant. All together, it is a portfolio worth millions of dollars, making the Abulafiyas one of the wealthiest Arab families in Israel.

Their fame, however, comes from the bakery, which is open all night and all day throughout the year, serving up from a huge brick oven an assortment of pastries, finger pies, and breads to hundreds of customers an hour. Peak time is usually about two in the morning.

Hamis Abulafiya is accessible and embracing. On just about any night of the week after 10 o'clock, Hamis can be found at the Abulafiya restaurant in Old Jaffa, which occupies a 3-story stone building with a spectacular view of the sea. It is here, sitting in a corner booth and eating food off the plates of his guests, that Hamis has time to visit with friends. Here, one learns a little of his family history: how his great-grandfather started the bakery in the late nineteenth century; how his grandfather continued and expanded it, making the decision to keep the family in Israel after the War of Independence; how his own father died when he was still a boy; and how he and his brothers grew up and took charge.

Like Mohammed, Hamis is a passionate and sincere spokesman for coexistence between Arabs and Jews, and is almost physically pained by events that undermine that ideal. I remember his eloquent and sad statement about the Arab-Jewish conflict. "My beautiful people are at war with my beautiful country," he said.

Although his family is Muslim and some of his brothers are observant, Hamis was educated at the Christian convent in Jaffa. Now, nearing 40, he is considering enrolling in a program of Jewish studies at Tel Aviv University. "God decided for Jews and Arabs to share this land in the Middle East," he explained. "To do this I must know about you, I must know what is behind your thoughts, because I want to respect you."

While Hamis has his idealistic side, he is, like many Arab Israelis, ultimately a pragmatist. He has no illusions about his status as an Arab in a Jewish land. While he embraces both his "country" and his "people," he has a sharp and unyielding awareness of how difficult a line fate has forced him to walk.

Following a February 1997 helicopter crash in the north of Israel that killed 74 soldiers in a freak accident, Israel was in a state of shock and depression. Hamis decided not to play music in his restaurant for three days. On the evening of the second day, a Jewish patron sitting in the upstairs dining room asked for music. After several attempts by the staff to explain the policy, Hamis himself went to the man's table and gently but firmly clarified why no music would be played. It was a policy decision he made for a number of reasons, not least because of the memory of his father's death as a young man.

"I remember the way my grandmother cried and wailed that night," he recalled. "It is just like the way the mothers of these young soldiers cry today, the way they cry every time a life is lost. It is very sad."

But the pragmatist in him acknowledged another good reason why he should not play the music for a few days: "I know that if I play music too soon after this helicopter crash, some Jews will point and say, 'See, he is happy about the deaths!'

"To be an Arab citizen in Israel," he added, "you have to show that you are more loyal than anybody else."

But Hamis concluded that the pressure put on him to demonstrate loyalty ends up backfiring. Because his genuine acts of loyalty are not assumed to be trustworthy, he feels "pushed to act artificially."

This comes from an Arab who is wealthy, who has flourished in Israel, whose family is recognized by Jews and Arabs alike as having made considerable contributions to the country. If a man like Hamis can so easily feel his loyalty in question, the more typical Arab citizen must feel it twice as vividly.

The Israeli Arabs' loyalty to Israel has been most severely tested by the peace process. On the one hand, Arab citizens like Hamis have historically supported the left because they have wanted their fellow Palestinians to have a state—

which might make them feel less guilty about being Israelis. It would also make the region more of a normal place, helping dissolve the barrier of hate and mistrust between Jews and Arabs in general.

On the other hand, for Israeli Arabs it is nothing short of sand down the throat to see their Jewish political allies on the Israeli left so powerfully motivated to dump the territories because of the "demographic threat" posed by a large Arab population. That would include both Israeli Arabs and Palestinians. After all, the left's argument only works if getting rid of the West Bank and Gaza reduces the Arabs to a "manageable" minority. Well, are the Israeli Arabs, at some 20 percent of the population, "manageable"? For Jews on the right, the high birthrate of Arab citizens themselves is cause for alarm.

Right-wing leaders point out that Israeli Arabs constitute about a quarter of all the babies born, suggesting a possibly "unmanageable" demographic future. Ariel Sharon frequently argues that Israeli Jews ought to get used to living among the Arabs and drop the illusion that by ripping off pieces of the country they can create an Arab-free state in the Middle East.

The creation of a Palestinian state in the West Bank and Gaza also raises a different fear for Jews: that once such a state existed it wouldn't be long before Arab communities within Israel began a solidarity movement of some kind that would undermine the Jewish state from within. Perhaps some communities would try to secede from Israel and join Palestine.

For years Jewish Israelis have scrutinized their Arab co-citizens for signs of such secret "Palestinian sentiment."

And some may have found what they were looking for after Baruch Goldstein's massacre of Palestinians at the Tomb of the Patriarchs in Hebron in 1994: Arabs ran riot in the northern Israeli town of Nazareth, in the Negev town of Rahat, and even in Jaffa.

I went to Jaffa to have a look.

"We had to display our anger at what happened to our brothers," explained Bilal Abu Shaab, a 16-year-old who had thrown stones at police and got clubbed for his efforts. "But the police didn't seem to understand and acted like these were the occupied territories. They would never have applied such violence against Jews!"

When I pressed him, Bilal said that he felt "half Israeli Arab and half Palestinian."

But Yousef Asfour, an older demonstrator, hushed him, fearing that this admission of split identity would be widely reported and construed as proof of a threat.

"We understand that this is Israel and that's all there is to it," Asfour declared, speaking a little like a politician. "When peace comes, the West Bank and Gaza will be Palestine, and I will be an Israeli of Arab origin exactly like you have Americans of Irish origin."

Exactly how many Arab Israelis secretly wish they were part of a Palestinian state, or to what degree they would be loyal to it, or in what way they would ever act upon this — these are questions that cannot be answered for certain. What is very certain is that in the minds of most Jews, consciously or subconsciously, being Israeli means being Jewish. You see it all the time — starting with the issue of the country's population, which almost everyone will tell you is 5 million. "Six million," I always say, earning blank stares. "You're forgetting the Arabs."

It was quite a big deal when the Israeli national soccer team started its first Arab player. His name was Rifat Turk. Not long ago I listened as a friend of mine described the now-retired Rifat to a soccer fan from the United States.

"He's a pretty good-looking guy, in that soccer player way," my friend said. "A big smile, dark eyes. He almost seems Israeli."

Rifat is an Israeli citizen. He was born here, grew up playing soccer in a small town, and became a national star. His life story became a favorite with a media that seemed surprised to find a friendly, photogenic, articulate Arab in the land. Today he coaches the Taibe soccer team and shouts instructions to his Arab players in his perfect Hebrew.

Yet he rates no better than "almost" Israeli.

The sidelined role of Israeli Arabs in politics also illustrates their estrangement. Arab voters have traditionally backed Arab parties, which, it was well understood, would always join any Labor-led coalition in the Knesset. During Israel's first 50 years, the left held power for 35. Yet never has an Arab been invited to serve in the cabinet.

This was particularly striking in the case of the government that Rabin set up in 1992. Although the five "Arab" seats in the Knesset were critical to his absolute majority of 61 out of 120, Rabin was determined to have a "Jewish majority" for his policies. Thus he tempted the Shas religious party, powerfully detested by much of his constituency, to join him, which it briefly did. When Shas quit a year later and resumed its natural alliance with the right-wing opposition, Rabin still would not bring the Arab parties into his ruling circle, preferring to govern with a minority coalition supported by the five Arab legislators from the outside. The Arab parties seemed to have no alternative. They could hardly join the Likud in opposing the peace process.

Then came the 1996 election, the first in which the prime minister would be directly elected by the voters. Shimon Peres desperately needed Arab votes and plenty of them.

On the afternoon of election day, when it became clear that the vote was close and Arab participation not particularly high, Peres himself got on the phone at Labor election headquarters and started imploring party activists in the Arab areas to get their people to the polls. An Arab cabinet minister might have come in handy then.

A few months before, in the middle of the wave of terrorism that gripped Israel, I was sitting in a cafe on Allenby Street in Tel Aviv. Suddenly my mobile phone rang. It was Eytan. He had just received a call from Mohammed inviting him to Taibe. Mohammed was concerned that the peace he valued so much was falling apart and felt he had to do his part for knitting Arab-Jewish relations back together.

"I want you to come to Taibe, and let me show you around. I want you to see that not all Arabs are maniacs who blow themselves up on buses and kill children and old people," Mohammed told Eytan.

Eytan reluctantly agreed. Although he was very much in favor of Arab-Jewish equality and coexistence in Israel, and although he wanted to foster his nascent friendship with Mohammed, he was a little scared of visiting Taibe, which was famous mainly for gang violence. So he convinced me to join him.

At the appointed hour the next day, Mohammed met us at the gas station near the Taibe turnoff from the main road. It would not do, he explained, for a regular Israeli like Eytan to be banging around the unmarked and unpaved inner streets of the town in his own fancy car. We climbed into Mohammed's jalopy and proceeded to the first stop on the tour, the high school where Mohammed teaches math.

We were received like VIPs. The principal met with us for about a half hour to discuss society and politics. He personally apologized for the folly of his fellow Arabs in staging the terrorist attacks. He promised that the people of Taibe would do everything possible to balance things out by voting for Shimon Peres in the coming election. "Don't worry," he assured Eytan, who nodded.

Next Eytan was trotted before a chemistry class. After listening to a few prepared recitations from the children, who told him that Hebrew was their favorite class, he was asked to say a few words. My friend deepened his voice an octave and spoke like an ambassador from the Ministry of Education. "I wish you great success in your studies," he said, gesturing broadly with his arms.

The children were attentive, and Eytan continued. "I hope your end-of-year exams go well, and that you all advance to the next grade, and that eventually, many of you will attend even our university in Tel Aviv."

The kids listened wide-eyed, as if such a prospect was the height of all imaginable achievement.

I had at first been focused on the apparently elaborate efforts that Mohammed and his colleagues were making to assure we felt welcome, demonstrating the virtues of their school and its students. But now I realized that Eytan, not Mohammed, was the really interesting player in this scenario. He was so unaware of himself, so unaware of the elevation he placed between himself and the children. He did not realize that in his uncharacteristic use of hand gestures he was unconsciously adopting a stereotype he associated with Arabs.

The tour continued. Mohammed took us to the kindergarten and introduced his son, the first of only four planned ("I am modernizing," he says). He drove us up a hill to show off the fort-like villa he is building on a site that, typically, has no arrangements yet for electricity, sewage, or water — probably the result of the deep-seated government disposition to hinder the growth of many Arab villages, primarily through cold bureaucratic manipulation. Permits for all kinds of basic infrastructure are routinely turned down or delayed, often for years. Whereas Jewish towns get regular government investment to renew infrastructure, improve roads, and beautify landscape, Arab communities are poorly maintained.

Indeed, a handful of Arab villages that pre-date the state are simply not acknowledged by the government at all, part of an intransigent effort to relocate Arab citizens to locales the state prefers. Such "anonymous" villages, which do not appear on maps, struggle in the shadow of thriving Jewish communities, forced to access water and electricity through makeshift — illegal — hookups. So Israeli Arabs like Mohammed, if they want to build new homes for themselves, sometimes just get going on the project without utilities.

Still, Mohammed readily recognizes the advantages he enjoys as an Israeli citizen. As we climbed all over the half-finished concrete edifice and marveled elaborately at every emerging room, he bragged about driving to the West Bank to round up cheap Palestinian workers to build the house.

"When I am in the West Bank, I feel more Israeli than Arab," he said. "I am like a king over there!"

At Mohammed's brother's house we were treated to a Middle Eastern feast as the brother proudly told of the anti–Hamas rally he had organized that morning. And at the home of a colleague of Mohammed's, we discussed the changing role of women in Israeli Arab society and smoked sweet-scented nargila water pipes produced by his fashionably dressed wife.

Then, with the mood at its most fraternal, I received a pager message: another bomb had exploded in Tel Aviv, this one just outside Dizengoff Center, the main downtown shopping area. There were many feared killed, dozens of injured, and extensive damage to the area.

It was Purim, a festive Jewish holiday. Iris had off from work and had been planning to go shopping with our one-year-old daughter, Maya. I struggled with the mobile phone in hopes of reaching them at home, but it was impossible to get through. Eytan tried to call his mother on his own mobile phone — it seems practically all Israelis have one — but couldn't get through either.

"What are we going to do?" Eytan shouted, looking at me wildly. "These bastards aren't going to stop!"

His liberal, forthcoming persona melted away, replaced by fury and immense frustration. "We have no choice but to hit at them with all our might!" he ranted. "Crush them!"

Wordlessly, Mohammed drove us back down the hill to Eytan's car at the gas station. He hugged the distracted Eytan as they parted. "Oh, Eytan," Mohammed said, conjuring up his first and only words. "Eytan, my friend ... at this time, I am ashamed." His eyes held sadness, a plea, and resignation at the sight of all his good works so rudely undone.

A few days later, police arrested an Israeli Arab who had smuggled the Palestinian suicide bomber out of the Gaza Strip, hidden under the passenger seat of his truck, and dropped him off down the street from Dizengoff Center.

Siblings

Ethiopian Jews deplane, adding to the ethnic cocktail (photograph by Nathan Halpert).

One afternoon in an office in Tel Aviv, I found myself looking across a desk at one of Israel's most recognizable politicians. He is tall and slender, with an easy smile and a direct manner. What makes him so particularly recognizable, however — in Israel, at least — is that he is black. Born and raised in Ethiopia, in fact. His name is Adisso Masalla.

For many people, the news that there are "black" Jews comes as quite a surprise. After all, the operative notion of Judaism is that the Jews are the descendants of biblical Abraham. According to the Old Testament, Abraham's grandson, Jacob, was anointed by God as "Israel," his descendants thereafter were known as the "children of Israel," and the land in which they dwelt was "the land of Israel." All this suggests that, at some point at least, the Jews were "one people."

Yet a casual glance around modern Israel makes clear that the "one people" notion doesn't fully account for the interventions of history. Israel's Jewish population today is comprised of European, Middle Eastern, and North African immigrants who reflect the physical traits common to each region, from the dark Persian to the blonde Scandinavian. Yet no group stands out more strikingly or underscores Israel's surprising racial diversity more powerfully than the black Jews of Ethiopia.

When I mentioned this to Masalla, he looked at me with a big grin and, in delightfully accented Hebrew, remarked, "When the first representatives of Israel came to Ethiopia some decades ago, we were surprised to find that all Jews *weren't* black."

We both laughed. In one breath, Masalla had deftly and subtly laid out before me a number of unspoken messages: that maybe the biblical Jews were not exactly "white"; that no single group of modern Jews writes the book on Jewish history by itself; and that being Jewish in Israel is not by itself always a universal equalizer. But then I'd known this last fact for a long time.

When I was about seven years old I had an experience with my friend Moshe Aharoni that first made clear to me that all Jews were not on equal footing in the Jewish state. Like everywhere else, little boys in our neighborhood were classified as "good" or "bad." I was shy and studious, hence "good." There's not much glory in this label out in the street, so I was always looking for ways to prove it false. I secretly envied Moshe who, as a recognized troublemaker, enjoyed some status.

One day when he was playing in my apartment, our different personalities briefly drew together. Standing on the third-floor balcony off the living room, Moshe eagerly challenged me to throw my treasured little Matchbox cars toward the fancy villa adjacent to our apartment building. I was reluctant to do something so reckless. But Moshe persisted, and after he threw the first car himself, landing it in the neighbor's flower garden, I could resist no more. I hurled a car into the bushes and then gestured for Moshe to take his turn.

"No. This time you go first!" he said.

That seemed fair enough, so I did. It landed harmlessly on the patio. And since I was now reveling in the adventure and sense of freedom that we were sharing, I took charge of the proceedings and tossed a third car as well. This one smashed through the villa's bathroom window.

Soon an elaborate investigation was underway, with neighbors knocking on doors and piecing together evidence. Eventually the pack, led by the rich owners of the villa, concluded that the projectile had come from my family's apartment. The adults confronted Moshe first, and to my surprise and dismay he broke down and confessed everything. Then they turned to me: had I taken part in this dangerous conduct?

I could have stood tall with Moshe, and maybe helped ditch my label at last. But here our paths diverged as suddenly as they had joined. Looking at the group of adults clamoring for my answer, I grasped a fundamental truth: Moshe and I were operating under different conditions. He had answered based on his. I would do the same.

It was not until many years later that I more fully understood the racial dynamic that was at play. At the time, I simply identified the crucial difference in who Moshe and I were perceived to be. It was not just "good" versus "bad." The essence was that I was Ashkenazi, the son of Romanian immigrants, whereas Moshe was Sephardi, the son of Iraqi immigrants. In those two words, Ashkenazi and Sephardi, everything was understood — and across Israel today, in many quarters, it still is.

The stereotype basically says: Ashkenazim are educated, law-abiding, and reasonably refined. Sephardim are backward, shifty, and crude.

As a child, I was barely conscious of this. But confronted by the stern adults and their difficult questions — and the sight of a hopeless, convicted Moshe — I suddenly sensed, for the first time, Israel's ethnic dynamic having an impact on me, and I was overcome by a blissful awareness of the advantage it provided.

"I have no idea what's going on," I declared. "Moshe was on the terrace by himself. I was reading in my room."

Moshe stared at me with wide-open eyes, saying nothing. To my amazement, the lie worked: everyone believed me. Not only my parents, not only the other adults, not only the victims, and not only my friends — even Moshe's close friends believed me. David, the leader of our group and himself (I now realize) a Sephardi, later advised me to take Moshe's effort to frame me in stride. "You know his kind, always telling grandmother's stories," David said, using the Israeli term for tall tales.

Moshe stopped coming over, and we never discussed the episode. But whenever I saw him I felt shame, and I could never look him in the eye again.

Israel was not supposed to have an internal racial dynamic that distinguished Jew from Jew, that put one above the other. It was not intended to be a place where there was serious disagreement about cultural tastes, or where "intermarriage" among Jews would become almost as dreaded a proposition to some parents as it had been when it involved gentiles. It was not supposed to be a place where Jews could feel nearly the same sense of disenfranchisement as they had in the countries from which they had come.

And yet, a significant chasm exists between the Ashkenazim and Sephardim. For example, Ashkenazim are four times more likely to get a university degree, the same as in 1975. They earn 30 percent more, on average, than Sephardim. Top professionals and business leaders are usually Ashkenazi. All ten prime ministers have been Ashkenazim. No Sephardi has ever headed the Mossad, Secret Service, or military intelligence. Only two Sephardim have ever been foreign or defense minister.

Lawyer and activist Ofer Bronstein (who, despite the name, is Sephardi) has lobbied for years for greater Sephardi rights. He predicts that as soon as Israel resolves its disputes with the Arabs, the Ashkenazi-Sephardi problem will explode. "This will become our number one concern," he says.

As a project in nation-building, Israel was primarily conceived by and for the Ashkenazi Jews of Europe. In the late 1800s, Europe's Zionist visionaries looked out upon the world with the satisfying sense that their home was the center of Judaism and that their people, these Jews, were the once and future "nation of Israel."

Indeed, prior to World War II, Europe's Jews were the great majority of the global Jewish population. At the turn of the century, they numbered about 15 million, far more than the 2 million or so who lived in North Africa and the Middle East. Many of them had a common language in Yiddish, and they shared the European continent and the intertwined fate of its nations. And while in the wake of their eighteenth and nineteenth century emancipation in Western Europe some Ashkenazim toyed with the notion that they were French, German, or English first — and Jews second — most lived in less tolerant Eastern Europe where there was little effort or desire to assimilate them. Whether the city of Chernowitz was ruled by Austria-Hungary, Russia, or Romania, its Jews tended to consider themselves (and be considered) Jews first — and in many cases, Jews only.

So the Zionist notion of a single Jewish "people," with its insular European perspective, seemed viable. Where there were objections to Herzl's plan of creating a modern Jewish state in Palestine, they were based on cosmopolitan ideas ("We should strive to assimilate instead") or pragmatism ("It doesn't make sense to leave Salzburg, with its tasty strudels, and move to the desert").

After Herzl's death, the mantle of Zionism was adopted with vigor by Chaim Weizmann, a Russian-born professor of chemistry, who moved in 1904 to England, which would in a few years take over the administration of Palestine from the collapsing Ottoman Empire. He was able to persuade the British to produce the next milestone toward fulfilling Herzl's vision: the 1917 Balfour Declaration. In it, British Foreign Secretary Alfred J. Balfour assured Jewish financier Lord Rothschild that "His Majesty's government views with favor the establishment in Palestine of a national home for the Jewish people, and will use their best endeavors to facilitate the achievement of this object."

The Balfour Declaration was opposed by anti-Zionist Jews, pro-Arab British, and many Arabs, but it set the stage for organized Jewish settlement of Palestine. Three decades later, however, the British claim to the Herzl hall of fame was forfeited when, succumbing to Arab pressures, they tried (with only partial success) to close the gates of Palestine precisely at the time when the Jews needed it most: as the Nazis were slaughtering 6 million of them during the Holocaust.

The Holocaust created new momentum in the world—especially in the United States and among its victorious but guilt-ridden European allies—for the realization of Zionism's goal. For the first time the creation of a Jewish state seemed not just possible but likely.

By the end of the war, almost a half million Jews already lived in Palestine, most of them immigrants from Poland, Russia, and elsewhere in Europe. Several tens of thousands had lived there since long before the birth of Zionism, mostly as a result of a steady trickle that had begun on a grassroots level centuries before (in 1892 Jews constituted almost two-thirds of the 42,000 residents of Jerusalem).

This was something, but it was far from enough for a serious state. The Zionist leaders had always counted on the immigration of millions of Jews from Eastern Europe, the great repository of world Jewry, once the state was established. But in one of history's brutal ironies, the Holocaust very nearly wiped out the East European Jews, compelling the United Nations to approve a Jewish state but robbing it of the population for which it had been intended.

So who would people the new State of Israel? Ben-Gurion and his fellow founders pondered this question with some urgency even as they fought a year-long war, in 1948 and 1949, to secure and expand Israel's UN-sanctioned borders. Although the young state prevailed in the war, its leader concluded that to survive in the long term it must increase the population dramatically and quickly. In his first major act of nation-building after the war, the Ashkenazi leader of the overwhelmingly Ashkenazi State of Israel decided to act with haste to open the doors to the Sephardim, whose communities had existed for centuries in the Middle East and North Africa. Emissaries were dispatched throughout the Arab world.

Zionist needs were not the only reason for this. In many Arab countries, official hostility to the creation of Israel had jeopardized the lives of local Jewish populations. Whether they had been happy where they were or not, many Sephardi Jews now found they had little choice but to flee to Israel to escape the danger. On top of this, many of the Sephardim were highly traditional and welcomed the birth of Israel as a divine and wondrous thing.

And so they came.

From the southern reaches of the Saudi peninsula came 50,000 Yemeni Jews, most in an Israeli airlift known as Operation Magic Carpet. Some 120,000 Iraqi Jews arrived between 1950 and 1952. More than 300,000 Sephardi Jews streamed in from Morocco, Tunisia, and Algeria, and some came from as far as India. By

1964, Sephardim had become the majority among Israel's population of 2 million Jews, a majority that lasted until the collapse of the Soviet Union brought a great Ashkenazi immigration wave in the 1990s.

The Sephardi influx was not homogeneous. As with the Ashkenazim, there were distinctions based on country and region. The Jews who came from Iraq, for example, were generally better educated than those who came from Yemen. Likewise, the Jews who came from Morocco were mainly people from mountain and provincial regions. They had survived through their skills as craftspeople, while most urban Moroccan Jews, who were more Europeanized, moved to France.

But Ashkenazim watching the newcomers stream in typically saw an indistinguishable and forbidding mass. The Sephardim, getting off the trains and buses at reception camps, were something unfamiliar to their European siblings. Some wore a headdress, a fez, long robes. Their language was Arabic. There was an abundance of dark skin and dark eyes, not the more European traits of many Ashkenazim. The first meeting of the two groups was a shock for both.

My father, an immigrant himself in those early years, remembers boarding a bus and being conscious of a group of Arab fellow passengers — until he realized they were Sephardim.

In April 1949, the respected *Ha'aretz* newspaper published an article on the North African immigrants, saying openly what was on many people's minds. "This is the immigration of a race such as we have never known in this country," wrote commentator Aryeh Gelblum. "We are dealing with a people whose primitiveness is a record. Their degree of education borders on total ignorance, and even worse is their total inability to absorb anything spiritual. In general their level is only somewhat superior to that of the Arabs, Negroes, and Berbers of their countries."

Gelblum, who had spent an indeterminate amount of time in an immigrant transit camp, recounted one incident in which a Bulgarian Jew, by insisting that everyone wait patiently in line for food, inadvertently provoked "an African [who] immediately produced a knife and cut his nose."

Gelblum railed on: "In the Africans' living quarters you will find filth, card games for money, drunkenness and prostitution.... Above all these is a fundamental problem — the absence of any ability to assimilate into the life of the country, and first and foremost a chronic laziness and hatred of labor.... Unlike in the case of poor elements from Europe, here even the children have no hope. Raising their level from the depths of their ethnic origins is a matter for generations!

"What can we do with them? How to 'absorb' them? Have we given thought to what will happen to the state if this will be its population? What will be the face of the country?"

Closing with a bit of prophetic political analysis, the author added, "Perhaps it is no wonder that [Menachem] Begin and his Herut Party [the forerunner of Likud] are demanding the immediate immigration of all these hundreds of thousands. They know that ignorant, primitive and impoverished masses are good for them and only such an immigration can bring them to power."

In the Israel of the 1950s there were powerful racial forces at work between the Ashkenazi power-holders and the Sephardi newcomers, including the kind of racism evident in Gelblum's screed. Almost all the people in positions of power were Ashkenazim, including the government leadership. Given the times and their own family backgrounds, it was natural for them to grant preference to the thousands of Holocaust survivors still arriving from Europe every month. The extraordinary suffering of the Jews in Europe was, after all, the cause that moved the world to accept Israel's creation. With so few resources and so many newcomers, the authorities were constantly forced to weigh competing interests. This, ultimately, was an equation in which the Sephardim could never quite come out ahead.

In 1949, Ben-Gurion's cabinet debated whether it should favor a wave of immigrants from Poland in the distribution of subsidized government housing — implicitly prolonging the period others would spend in the squalid transit camps that had so revolted Gelblum. Cabinet Minister Yitzhak Rafael argued in favor, saying, "If we release the Polish Jews from the camps and give them housing they will get along easier than the Oriental [sic] residents of the camps would, because they have among them professionals needed for the economy. This will be a blessing to the economy."

Rafael went on to say that "Polish Jews come from good living conditions. For them camp life will be more difficult than it would be for Yemeni Jews, for whom the camp is itself a salvation."

This view of the Yemenis reflected the prevailing wisdom on Sephardim in general. The Ben-Gurion government made other decisions along these lines, including the housing of most Sephardi immigrants in small desert and mountain "development" towns. These places, such as Dimona, Netivot, and Kiryat Shmona, were hastily built not only to absorb the immigrants but to serve national purposes like dispersing the population, settling the Negev Desert (a pet project of Ben-Gurion's), and buttressing the borders.

Although some Ashkenazim also lived in these outlying communities (like my parents, briefly), their cultural affinity with the people in power and the education and skills they had brought with them from Europe enabled most to make a hasty retreat to the country's intellectual and economic centers in Haifa, Tel Aviv, and Jerusalem. Most Sephardim, lacking these tools, went nowhere. The development towns became their virtually exclusive domains — again until the 1990s, when the Russians began to pour in and to be offered subsidized housing in these same places.

Almost all the Sephardim I talked to on this subject agree that Ben-Gurion was not a bad man. "He just didn't understand," they say.

But while Sephardim today may not think badly of Ben-Gurion, whose decision to send them to the boondocks helped cement their lower-class status, they are still punishing his political successors with a vengeance.

It seems to be a trait of human nature that when two groups, coming together for the first time, interact on an unequal basis, it is extremely difficult to ever root out the inequality and establish a new arrangement considered fair by both. Neither group can ever quite see things as the other does; barriers have stood between them, they have come to understand the world from opposite sides of those barriers, and even when the barriers are gone there remains a "wall of the mind."

This is evident in many countries in which a dominant group has attempted to absorb a second group without offering it significant control over its own assimilation or destiny. America, for example, still struggles with its racial divide, despite the Civil War, despite civil rights.

Beginning in the late 1980s, Germany undertook the reunification of two non-equal groups. Though this started with the speedy demolition of the world's most famous wall of bricks, it could take generations to tear down the far more resilient wall of the mind.

As in these other cases, Israel sealed its fate when it failed to give its newcomers, so clearly at a disadvantage, a sufficient role in the building of the nation. The Sephardim were welcomed not as full siblings at the family table, but as distant cousins who could eat in the kitchen — and work there if they wanted — while decisions about the family estate, which really belonged to the Ashkenazi side, were being made elsewhere in the house.

Haya is an intelligent, gregarious Sephardi woman in her forties. She grew up in a development community for North African immigrants in the rural south of Israel. Her parents arrived in the early 1950s from Tunisia, where they had been respected members of a mixed Jewish-Muslim community. Haya remembers her father telling stories of a happy childhood in Tunis, recounting how he sometimes played with the children of the king. But her memories of her father in Israel, and her own youth, are not so idyllic. "It's the ego," she said emphatically. "First you kill the ego, and then everything else goes after that."

Haya describes how a whole generation of Sephardi men were "broken" by the Israeli system that set them up for failure in the early years of the state. It's a common story: no job, no money, declining respect from the children, declining self-respect, alcoholism, and, finally, family breakdown and frequent criminality. The cycle often recurs in the next generation. It's hard to break.

Haya took a hard look at her reality, at the way life was for many Sephardi women, and broke the cycle. "I didn't want my life to turn out like my parents' had," she said. "I looked around me and saw the way women were treated, and decided that it wasn't for me. But it was hard, real hard. It's not easy at all to break away from your family and parts of your heritage. You feel like maybe you are abandoning parts of yourself ... and really, it took me until I had become a full adult to be able to do it completely, to be the person I wanted to be."

Haya is proud to say she is Sephardi and proud of those parts of Sephardi culture and tradition that she has chosen to retain. She still prefers her music with a Middle Eastern ring to it, for example. As a teenager she had sought it out at the only place she knew it could be found, the sprawling, tumbledown, now-defunct Tel Aviv bus station, which back then housed rows of crumbling shops in which homemade cassettes of Middle Eastern music were on sale.

Haya still cooks her family's meals with the flavors her mother brought from Tunisia. On Passover, she sings with her children the Sephardi songs that are passed from generation to generation outside of the official *Haggadah* (the story and prayer book) of the holiday.

But there are also many things that Haya chose to leave behind. One of her early decisions, for example, was to refuse dates with the Sephardi men she grew up with, rejecting their often rigid attitudes toward male and female roles. She has also limited the role of religion in her life and in that of her family, reducing it primarily to the telling of Jewish history to her children and the celebration of holidays. And, as an adult, married to an American, Haya went back to school to study Sephardi-Ashkenazi relations and business.

Although she broke the cycle for herself, she looks at fellow Sephardim with a mixture of sadness, disgust, and determination. "Look at the prison population," she says. "That's my barometer of progress. As long as I see so many young Sephardim in there I know that the situation in Israel has not changed nearly enough." Almost nine in ten convicts are Sephardim.

In July 1959, in the ramshackle Haifa neighborhood of Wadi Salib, a drunken Moroccan immigrant was shot while resisting arrest during a barroom brawl. False rumors — that he had been killed — quickly spread through the Sephardi community. The next day, a crowd gathered outside the local police station, shouting for justice and protesting police brutality. Police eventually stormed and dispersed the crowd, leaving 13 police officers and 2 civilians injured, 32 protesters in jail, and extensive damage to shops, cafes, and other property.

The riot was a rude awakening for many Israelis who had no idea how much anger the Sephardim were harboring. And although it's been four decades, the name Wadi Salib still awakens the fear of a Sephardi vendetta.

In the early 1970s, a more organized series of protests erupted in low-income Sephardi neighborhoods in Jerusalem. This time, the spark was probably Sephardi bitterness over the tax breaks and mortgage advantages awarded newer immigrants from the Soviet Union (a first, smaller, Brezhnev-era wave), the kind of financial aid no less needed by veteran Sephardi immigrants who had become the bulk of Israel's poor.

Prime Minister Golda Meir met with several leaders of the protests, who called themselves the "Black Panthers" after the American civil rights group. The famously plainspoken Meir later declared the Panthers "not nice."

For the first 25 years of the state, Meir's Labor Party had been the undisputed king of the Israeli political hill. Even the immigrant Sephardim voted largely the Labor way, believing that what was good for the country was good for them, naively taking for granted that the patronage promises of Labor candidates would be fulfilled, or simply believing that it was the "Israeli" way to vote. But the 1973 Yom Kippur War changed this, particularly for the younger generation of Sephardim.

The debacle of the war hobbled the Labor Party. Although Meir resigned in disgrace after it became known how her mismanagement of intelligence information had left Israel exposed to attack, the party had a difficult time reviving its standing. When Yitzhak Rabin resigned as prime minister a couple of years later, the party took another hit.

The Likud opposition, hapless for almost three decades, took full advantage. Likud leaders attacked Labor as out of touch and blamed it not only for the war, but for destructive economic and social policies as well. Likud trumpeted "free economy" ideas as the antidote to the bureaucratic, initiative-stifling, semi-socialist regime Labor had instated. This was a tune that resonated in Sephardi ears.

Encouraged by the idea that under a freer economic system they might be able to stake a bigger claim, Sephardim, especially the younger generation anxious to improve on the stagnant lives of their parents, voted en masse for Likud. Their dreams were not elaborate: many hoped to open an auto garage or a small shop, and the plan was simply to do a little better by their children than their parents had been able to do by them.

Begin's Likud party—along with its religious coalition partners—won in 1977 with major support from the Sephardi portion of the electorate, firmly establishing a Sephardi-Likud alliance that has persisted ever since. Labor, unable to break it, is at a perpetual disadvantage. Gelblum's 1949 prophesy was totally fulfilled.

According to an analysis by Professor Asher Arian and Michal Shamir of Haifa University, 53 percent of Sephardim voted for Likud in 1977, while only 29 percent voted for the Labor party (the rest voted for religious and small, mostly right-wing parties). In 1992, according to the study, Likud's share among Sephardim was 41 percent—still high, considering the party received just over a quarter of the overall vote. (In 1996, in many Sephardi areas Netanyahu won 80 percent of the vote.)

Labor and its brood—now mainly Ashkenazim and Israeli Arabs—find the Likud-Sephardi alliance a great vexation. After all, the conservative, militaristic policies of Likud—which absorb so many resources—would appear to be the opposite of advantageous to an economically underprivileged group. Young Sephardim are probably the majority of the foot soldiers on the front lines of conflict, whether in Lebanon, the West Bank, or the Golan. Israel's poor, who desperately need the greater prosperity that comes with peace, are mostly Sephardim, too. Thus, in an era that offers a realistic prospect for peace between Israel and its neighbors, the left cannot grasp why Sephardi keep pulling the right wing lever. The chance for Israel to reach its full economic and social potential, it seems to them, is hindered by each such vote.

Sometimes Sephardi voters try to describe their support of the right in socio-ideological terms, explaining, for example, that having "lived with the

Arabs" in their countries of origin, they "know their mentality." This is a code for saying that their native Middle East perspective teaches them the Arabs cannot be trusted and understand only strength.

But the real motivation in many Sephardi votes is psychological, a manifestation of their struggle to distinguish themselves from the Labor-voting Ashkenazim as Israelis of equal standing. I suspect that subconsciously some Sephardim may even think that by acting like fiercely nationalist Israelis, they could never be viewed as quasi–Arabs themselves.

The Sephardi-Likud alliance is also, undoubtedly, an electoral protest vote against the Labor party for its perceived wrongs during their difficult absorption in the early years. It was Ashkenazim sent by the Labor party (or Mapai, as it was known then) who deloused Sephardim with DDT powder in the immigration camps and who created an economy based on patronage and connections the Sephardim didn't have. It matters far less that Labor's policies today might offer Sephardim a better future.

"It's hate of the past," says Haya.

The 1981 election — in which Begin was narrowly reelected — demonstrated how badly Labor had become estranged from the Sephardim. At a Labor election rally in Tel Aviv several days before the vote, comedian Dudu Topaz (born Goldberg) told Labor supporters that he was happy to see his audience was the crème de la crème. "The *chakh-chakhs*," he said, using a term meaning "lowlifes" that usually refers to Sephardim, were with Likud. The remark caused outrage that Begin capitalized on, sarcastically affirming that he indeed welcomed all *chakh-chakhs* to his camp.

That same campaign saw the advent of graffiti in heavily Ashkenazi North Tel Aviv directed against the "Ashke-NAZIS." In Sephardi development towns, meanwhile, the decidedly Ashkenazi Peres was verbally abused and pelted with tomatoes.

In September 1997, Peres's successor at the head of the Labor Party, Ehud Barak, decided to formally apologize to the Sephardim for their treatment in the 1950s. Barak conceded that the immigrants were routinely sent to border towns to fend for themselves without adequate means and declared that their pioneering contribution had never been properly acknowledged.

"I'm sorry," he told crowds great and small across the country, in a tone as earnestly doleful as a former military chief of lifelong privilege could muster.

If the Ashkenazi-Sephardi divide was purely a matter of politics and policies, the differences might have dissolved by now. But at the heart of the conflict lies a struggle for cultural dominance that began with Herzl himself. For all his Jewish nationalism, he was assimilated into Europe and greatly admired its culture. In *Der Judenstaat*, he wrote that the Jews, once in Palestine, "should there form a portion of a rampart of Europe against Asia, an outpost of civilization as opposed to barbarism."

Today, the opposing forces among Israel's Jews could be variously described as West versus East, Europe versus the Middle East, liberalism versus conservatism, modern values versus traditional values. Just about every aspect of the clash between Jews fits neatly under one of these headings, pitting most (but not all) Ashkenazim against most (but not all) Sephardim.

Whether the clash is over tastes in food, music, and dress; the role of religion in society; attitudes toward gender roles; attitudes toward education; family structure and practices; or even the visual image of the ideal Israeli — all are part of the Ashkenazi-Sephardi divide, and all are part of some larger social conflict affecting not only Israel but most countries.

In this battle the Ashkenazim have had most of the weapons on their side — namely, control over mass media and most consumer industries — enabling them to shape Israel in an Ashkenazi image, in the image of Europe, in the image of whatever it is they want the country and its people to be.

The Ashkenazim also have another advantage: in cases of "intermarriage" — currently one out of every four weddings — the children tend to adopt Ashkenazi identification and ways. It's just natural to identify with the dominant culture.

Although they are only about half of the Jewish population, and less than half of the total population, the Ashkenazim are everywhere on TV and in advertising. Israeli diaper ads look like they were made in Scandinavia. Most Israeli models could be German or Italian, which goes double for TV personalities. Television dramas tend to glorify the glamorous lives of Ashkenazim. When Sephardim appear, it is typically to portray lowly or laughable characters. In comedies, if a character is an imbecile, then he will almost certainly be using the Sephardi guttural *h* and *a*.

Israeli school curricula are focused on the Western world; little of the surrounding nations' history is taught. Relatively few Jewish students — even Sephardim — learn Arabic.

Israeli music, as well, is heavily flavored by the European style. Only in the last decade did Arab-influenced pop, the kind Haya and her generation once went to the Tel Aviv bus station to hear, become more accepted. This is the result not simply of market forces, but of market forces finally unleashed: Israel had maintained a state monopoly on radio and delayed the introduction of independent stations until 1993 (incredibly, three years later than Romania). I suspect private radio was deliberately delayed in Israel at least partly in an effort to control and influence public tastes. Even today, many Ashkenazim openly detest the Oriental sound, considering it to be "painful to the ears" and "backward-sounding."

Increasingly, though, a synthesis can be found. Singers like Boaz Sharabi and Ehud Banai (Sephardim) and Yehuda Poliker (whose parents are from Greece) combine the Eastern and Western sounds into a mix that might be uniquely Israeli. Predictably, they are very successful.

One result of the media emphasis on Ashkenazi appearances and tastes was seen in a 1996 study by sociologist Malka Aharonson on kindergarten children's attitudes toward ethnicity. Her findings, published in *Yediot Aharonot*, found that the kids — including the Sephardim — strongly associated Sephardi appearance with evil, while admiring European, or Ashkenazi, appearance. They also desired Ashkenazi friends and wanted to grow up to be Ashkenazim.

The group — a representative sample of 100 Jerusalem children — were shown pictures of people who seemed either Ashkenazi or Sephardi. Almost all the Ashkenazi kids and half the Sephardi youngsters said they wanted to look like the person in the "Ashkenazi" picture. The reasons they gave were: "He's blond and I like that color" or "He looks nice." When asked who was more likely to be wanted by the police, the vast majority chose the "Sephardi" picture.

The survey raised a short-lived fuss, with politicians demanding that advertisers switch to more Sephardi-looking swimsuit models to persuade the nation's youth that these were positive role models, too.

Vicky Shiran, a criminologist whose parents immigrated from Egypt, said she felt the pervasive pro-Ashkenazi messages so powerfully that, as a child, "I would tell other children I was from France, not Egypt. I was ashamed of my identity. Everything about society here told me it was bad. I only shed this recently when as an adult I began to realize how twisted it was."

Nonetheless, through television, radio, the music industry, the fashion industry, and the news business, the controlling Ashkenazi Jews either by nature or by design promulgate images of Israel that are nearly exclusively European.

And, in official Israel's continuing, subliminal efforts to court Western culture, practically every arrival of a visiting Western celebrity is treated like a major event, often including an audience with the prime minister. Arnold Schwartzenegger, in Tel Aviv to launch a franchise of Planet Hollywood, reveled in his own meeting with Rabin in the summer of 1995. "I met with your prime minister," he briefed reporters. "We talked about the important issues like the peace talks with Syria, and all the problems you are having here with the Golan Heights."

Sometimes I hear one Jew admonishing another on the street for being too Western-leaning: "Where do you think you are? This is the Middle East we're living in, not Switzerland or America!"

This criticism is also used by right-wingers to deflate peaceniks perceived to harbor unrealistic expectations about future harmony with the Arabs.

But there is a subtler side to what at first seems like a simple statement of geographical fact. When uttered by a Sephardi to an Ashkenazi, the underlying message can be: "And perhaps you, my friend, do not really belong."

It speaks to the simple truth that the Sephardim, for all their occasional ranting against "the Arabs," are on the whole not uncomfortable with their identification as "Middle Eastern." They have something money and connections can't buy: a native harmony with the surroundings.

For most Ashkenazim the words "Middle Eastern" raise immediate negative associations and denial, but at the same time their attitudes can be strangely dualistic. Alongside the need to feel European, they often go to considerable lengths to try to fit into the Middle East. They yearn to be tanned — for where is there a more obvious misfit than a pale blond person in the sun-scorched Middle East? (This tapered off somewhat after Israel became notorious for its high rate of skin cancer.) And the Ashkenazim share and probably lead a nationwide disdain for daintiness and refined behavior perceived to be somehow alien to the region, and most consider Arabic slang and invective to be the coolest.

Indeed, the one "European" quality that most foreigners quickly notice that Ashkenazim have successfully shed is politeness. This is a little ironic, for the Arabs themselves are not this way at all: few things offend Arabs more than Israelis' sometimes loud and painfully direct speech and behavior.

So becoming "Israeli" has been a challenge for the Ashkenazim, too. They are, they know, somehow affiliated with Europe and its history and culture. Yet they were rejected there and now find themselves in the Middle East, trying to carve out a persona that is distinctly theirs—something that is at once both clearly Israeli and yet more bound to Europe than the Middle East.

All this raises a question Israelis take pains to sidestep.

If the Ashkenazim are, in the final analysis, a type of European, then are the Sephardim not a type of Arab? After all, the Arab nation includes people of many faiths besides Muslims; there are Maronite and Coptic Christians, Druze, Bedouins, and people of other faiths. The Sephardi Jews have their ancestry in the Arab world. So wouldn't Sephardi Jews *have* to consider themselves Arab in some way?

Most of them say no. And it's obvious why. The conflict with the Arabs does not permit the Sephardim to identify themselves as part of the Arab nation. Doing so would undermine Israel's resolve and raise impossible questions about their loyalty. It would also have the explosive effect of defining the Arab-Israeli conflict in religious terms, a tangle more difficult to undo than a national dispute. And the identification of so many Jews as Arabs would be fatal to the hopes of Israel's dominant classes that theirs somehow be considered a European state. So society—from official Israel down to the person on the street—does everything to sweep this question under the rug.

For example, when police or reporters describe a Sephardi suspect or character, they use the ambiguous term *hazut mizrahit*—"Eastern appearance"— never "Arab appearance." When Ashkenazi Israelis try to temper their revulsion at the Arab elements the Sephardim have introduced into their culture, they often refer to the resultant cultural mix as being "Mediterranean" as opposed to "Arab." Sephardim singers describe their music as "Mediterranean," too, even though you are not likely to hear it in Cannes or Naples. The Mediterranean option is an increasingly popular way to describe Israel's cultural niche, because it is something almost everyone can accept. Most of those who want Tel Aviv to be like Vienna will make do with Barcelona as a model, and if others are thinking of Tangiers when they say "Mediterranean"—well, that's their business.

Meanwhile, when Israelis argue in the street, someone is still apt to step in and assert, "Calm down! It's OK! After all, we're all Jews, right?"

Such insistence on the seemingly obvious is so ingrained, so demonstrative, that I'm sure it reflects the deep-rooted need to affirm that it is indeed so—that Israeli Jews are one people, appearances to the contrary notwithstanding.

In the early years of the Zionist movement, and throughout much of the existence of Israel, there was a deliberate effort to create a new Jewish culture that all Israelis could adopt. The early Zionists, for all their appreciation of Europe, were profoundly repelled by the meek, bookish stereotype of the European Jew and were determined to transform it in Israel. The ideal Israeli was portrayed as a rugged farmer-soldier, tanned as opposed to pale, gruff as opposed to thoughtfully intellectual. Jabotinsky wrote mockingly of the European Jew as typically "frightened and humiliated." The "other," he wrote, the New Jew, "must be proud and independent."

Thus many Ashkenazim argue today that not only the Sephardim suffered cultural repression. They argue that most of the Ashkenazi immigrants to Israel also did not stack up against the ideal of the New Jew—the native-born *sabra*—that the Zionists were trying to fashion. They, too, were made to feel inferior, to be ashamed of their Yiddish. The German immigrants of the 1930s, with their famously pedantic ways, were held to particular ridicule and awarded the group label *yekkim*, which as far as I know means nothing but sounds as ridiculous in Hebrew as it does in English. Even Holocaust survivors were held up unforgivingly against the standards of the New Jew, and were judged harshly for inadequacies in this regard. In the dangerous reality of the Middle East, it was felt, Israelis could not afford to be meek or mild-mannered.

I myself remember trying hard to be more like Moshe and the other Sephardi boys in my neighborhood, whose rougher ways seemed in some way closer to the unattainable *sabra* ideal than the central European manners I learned at home.

But the New Jew was an Ashkenazi invention. It was European Jewish thinkers who came up with the idea that there was a need to "remake" the Jews in some way. All the philosophy behind the nation-building of Israel—the creation of the institutions of state, the resurrection of Hebrew, the strategy behind the immigration, the drive to win world support, the special role of the army, and even the post-independence effort to bring in the Sephardim—were authored by Ashkenazim.

The Sephardim who came to Israel after the state was created were perfectly happy to be what they were—Moroccan, Iraqi, Yemenite Jews. Once in Israel, they were swept into someone else's agenda.

Still, all the cultural engineering had a practical reason. Israel might not have mustered the cohesion to meet the tremendous external threat posed by the Arabs if it had not attempted to mold the various Jewish immigrants into a unified society. Social engineering—in Israel as elsewhere—was seen as an essential part of nation-building and, to some extent, it actually *did* create a new Israeli culture. Today, after 50 years, there is a distinctly Israeli way of doing many things, a distinct manner of social interaction, certain widely held attitudes.

Not all of them are positive, of course. Israel exhibits a machismo, on one hand, and a passivity on the other, that can be troubling. There are high rates of domestic abuse, highway death, and service-sector inefficiency. Criminal negligence in the public and private sector often raises a furor yet rarely gets seriously punished. Government inquiries and investigations into scandal are often cynical and politicized, resulting in plenty of drama but little real change.

On the up side, Israeli culture is distinctly informal and interactive. There is little artifice of formality in business, government, or social life. Pretensions have little place. People interact as equals based on their ability to converse and argue effectively. There is a stunning degree of social interaction in public among strangers — constant kibitzing, debating, and finger-wagging. It is behavior that in America would never fly, not even in small rural towns.

At some level, Israel has produced a distinct set of cultural traits, some from its Jewish nature, others from its diverse ethnic and geographic roots. Yet there is no question that while Israeli Jews may genuinely desire to be "one people," there is nonetheless a struggle over just what kind of oneness they are going to have.

And today, more than ever, there are forces that openly and successfully work against the idea of a "Jewish people," instead splintering Israeli identity along ethnic lines. Perhaps the most prominent such force has been the ultra-Orthodox Sephardi party Shas, which has grown spectacularly since its 1984 birth, despite being hit by a series of corruption trials that would have wiped most other parties off the political map.

Shas's original constituency of Sephardi ultra-Orthodox Jews might, at most, have been able to muster enough votes for two seats out of the 120 in the Knesset. But Shas wins the votes of great numbers of Sephardim, most of whom, perhaps, are traditional, but not religious. And this occurs despite a sorry record: one former Shas Knesset member, Yair Levy, served almost three years for embezzlement, another was implicated in a corruption scandal but never tried because of his Knesset immunity, and the party's political leader, Aryeh Deri, was forced to resign as interior minister in 1993 to face trial on charges he accepted $170,000 in bribes, and was eventually convicted.

Shas's political growth was based on its shrewdness in broadening its appeal beyond its religious beginnings, offering solutions to the pragmatic concerns of Sephardim (like a long school day for their kids), supporting a "traditional" approach to Judaism, and, not least, appealing to their "Sephardi pride."

Shas managed to secure funding for its network of religious schools in Sephardi communities, using the money to provide an extended school day and hot meals in poor neighborhoods where both were critically needed. That in these schools the children would be inculcated against modern science, non-religious art forms, and democratic values — perhaps ultimately condemning them to future poverty — turned out to be a less pressing matter for many working parents than having some place to put their kids.

The party played on the idea that it was the only force looking out for the everyday needs of the Sephardi downtrodden, a claim that, while supportable, also promoted the divisive idea that their constituents' condition was mainly caused by the Ashkenazim.

Its political rallies and campaign ads made sure to tout the traditional Jewish practices and values familiar to many Sephardim. In a particularly memorable and telling Shas campaign ad in 1988, Rabbi Yitzhak Peretz, who was then the Shas political leader, declared that "one trembling Jewish mother lighting the Sabbath candles is worth a thousand professors who teach our children that man comes from the apes." The visual showed a traditional Sephardi woman reverently lighting candles against a background of billowy curtains. Eight years later Ashkenazim scoffed at Shas's "secret weapon" in the 1996 campaign — holy amulets distributed by the aged mystic Kadoori — but the rabbi and his lucky charms were an amazingly effective attraction wherever the campaign road show went in Sephardi Israel.

Just how closely Shas had tied itself to the self-image and pride of Sephardi Israelis became apparent in January 1997, when a major scandal erupted involving Netanyahu and, once again, Shas leader Deri. In a story that broke on Israel's state-run Channel One, it was alleged that Deri, still facing the earlier bribery charge, had traded Shas support of Netanyahu for a personal favor. All Netanyahu had to do was appoint a crony of Deri's to be attorney general, ensuring proper handling of the charges against him.

When it was leaked that the police were considering an interrogation of the revered Rabbi Ovadia Yosef, Shas activists and die-hard supporters threatened that they would not allow the officers to even reach the sage's home. Benny Elbaz, a former pop singer who had traded his guitar for a prayer shawl, warned that the party's constituency would stage their own *intifada* if Yosef were made to answer to the police. The implication that the rabbi was above the law was an unprecedented challenge to the rule of law in Israel. From Netanyahu's government, hanging by a thread, came only the meekest protest.

In April the police stunned the nation by recommending that Netanyahu, Deri, and two others be prosecuted. But six days later, the state prosecutor awkwardly announced that there was not sufficient evidence to indict anyone but Deri. Within hours, hundreds of Shas supporters gathered around Ovadia Yosef's house as he consulted inside with his sons and advisors. They threw rocks and attacked TV crews and reporters that tried to approach. Around midnight, Yosef published an announcement charging that Deri had been scapegoated and that the group "has no faith" in the state legal system whose leaders — mostly Ashkenazim "are driven insane with hatred for Sephardi Jews."

A few days later, about 20,000 screaming Shas supporters rallied in a Jerusalem stadium demanding the charges against Deri be dropped. David Yosef, the rabbi's son, addressed unspecified representatives of Israel's despised establishment: "We will have no part of you, because you hold our sacred Torah in contempt.... When will you relent, along with the media, from your hatred of religion and Sephardic Jewry? The public is sick of you and accepts your authority no longer."

Deri attended, sucking hard on his pipe as he listened to this speech. Then he was carried up to the podium on the shoulders of his fans. There, he delivered what amounted to a writ of divorce to Israel's Ashkenazi-dominated secular democracy, his words clearly underscoring what the coming cultural battle in Israel is about.

"My oppression is not political but religious and ethnic," he bellowed. "The grand Zionist vision has failed, and now the secular people fear that we, Shas, will change the secular nature of the country. They consider [us] primitive ... this establishment that in the early years of the state sent us to live in development towns in intolerable conditions. But the more they humiliate us the greater our power becomes!"

Not all Sephardim bought into this message, of course. Many in subsequent days called for an end to the incitement. But these were mostly Sephardim that had made it, people like Defense Minister Yitzhak Mordechai, who wrote in the *Maariv* newspaper, "Let's stop the separatism and the useless pettiness.... We are all one people." But even some Ashkenazim disagree with Mordechai. In 1989, Amnon Dankner, a highly respected newspaper columnist, made it clear that, for him, being "one people" demanded that Israelis be one *Western* people. "I am sick of diminishing my own cultural heritage, of tiptoeing around them and lavishing praise on them," he wrote of the Sephardim in *Ha'aretz*. "All this talk — 'Please, don't be angry, we recognize the tremendous heritage you brought. It's true that we had Heine and Freud and Einstein, and the magnificent synthesis between Judaism and Western culture, but you also had nice things: hospitality, respect for elders, a great patriarchal tradition' — if I hear this nonsense one more time, I'll scream!"

In a complement to what Gelblum had written four decades earlier in the same newspaper (Israel's most liberal), Dankner continued, "Israel, which began as an Ashkenazi country, has slipped in the Oriental-Levantine direction. The Israeli public domain has become increasingly Levantine in the negative sense of the word."

The anticipated wave of Russian immigrants would change all that, Dankner predicted: "A half million Jews or more who love to learn and read, see theater and go to concerts, people with education. And their children — obedient, polite children, serious and studious. The heart rejoices at the injection of optimism all this will bring to the deteriorating fabric of our society."

Since then almost a million Soviet immigrants arrived in Israel. In many ways, they lived up to Dankner's hopes. Largely because of the arrival of the "Russians," Israel now has the highest concentration of engineers and medical doctors in the world. They have played a tremendously disproportionate role in Israel's high-tech emergence as well as in the economic boom that coincided with the years of their arrival. To the relief of many Ashkenazim, they have made Israel much more "European."

But are they becoming Israelis? Partly.

On the one hand, so many came at once that there was enough of a Russian center of gravity to spawn a half dozen Russian newspapers, several Russian rock bands, a Russian theater, and Russian "ghettos." But the younger generation of immigrants is, as always, the spearhead of absorption: you can hear them picking up Israeli accents, and as you count the Slavic names in army combat rosters it becomes apparent that a surprisingly high number of volunteers to such units — perhaps as many as a quarter — are new immigrants, eager to accelerate their assimilation.

Among their elders, not all have found jobs in their chosen professions. Doctors working as laboratory assistants, writers sweeping the streets, and physicists driving taxis are not uncommon. A few immigrants — some of whom apparently faked their Jewish credentials — have helped bring to Israel a vibrant Russian mafia, complete with gangland murders, prostitution rings, extortion, bribery, and all the rest.

There have been problems with the religious establishment, too. Israel's Law of Return enables anyone with a Jewish grandparent to immigrate as a Jew and receive automatic citizenship. But the Orthodox rabbis only recognize a strict maternal line of descent, a criterion that would leave many of the immigrants (estimates say up to a third) as non-Jews. In Israel, where there is no civil marriage, this means that unless such people, who consider themselves Jews, can arrange (and will accept) a Christian or Muslim wedding, their only choice is to marry abroad (such marriages are, absurdly enough, accepted and registered by the Interior Ministry). And ironically, Russian Jewish victims of terrorist attacks, as well as fallen soldiers, have been refused burial in Jewish cemeteries by the religious authorities on account of insufficient Jewishness.

All this has been closely watched by Israel's first big group of immigrants, the Sephardim. It has been hard for many of them, still struggling, to witness the rapid ascent of the Russians. Their bitterness has been heightened by the redistribution of state resources toward the newcomers, who have also taken over many local governments – especially in what were once exclusively Sephardi "development towns" — due to their huge numbers.

Some of this had been foreseen. Even as Yitzhak Shamir's Likud government welcomed the first arrivals in 1990, a member of the disbanded Black Panthers, Yamin Suissa, argued publicly that Israel should stop welcoming foreign part-Jews and concentrate on taking care of those already here. Cabinet Minister Yitzhak Peretz of Shas warned that too many of the former Soviets were not Jews at all. But the country's elite, still dominated by Ashkenazim and supported by the Zionist ideal of "gathering in" the exiles, was eager to have the Russians come.

In this light, it is a little amusing to consider the official dismay in 1994 when it was widely reported in the media that up to 300 million Indians could claim links to the ancient tribe of Menashe, one of ten exiled from ancient Israel. Hundreds of thousands were believed to be preparing to apply for immigrant status. Shortly thereafter, there were reports that one overly zealous rabbi had discovered a tribe of native Peruvians also claiming Jewish roots. Soon, it seemed, half the population of the Third World might be drawn to Israel, declaring themselves Jewish. The Israeli establishment stood on its hind legs.

Politicians pointed out the obvious: such immigrants could be motivated not by ideological but by economic reasons, now that Israel had grown prosperous. Yossi Beilin, an outspoken liberal in Rabin's cabinet, recommended changing the Law of Return to toughen the criteria for would-be Jews immigrating. "Many people are ready to move to Israel to become instant citizens just by claiming they are Jews. There are tribes in India, in Eritrea, in Burma, who claim they are Jewish, lost tribes of Israel, or whatever," he said.

Yair Tsaban, then the immigration minister, termed the Indians "a curiosity" and advised them to wait for the messiah before applying to immigrate.

One group that did make it from the Third World are the Ethiopian Jews, who now number some 60,000 in Israel.

Theories about their origins abound. Some scholars believe that the community began with the mass conversion of a small African tribe in some prior century. Others assert that they are actual and direct descendants of King Solomon, who ruled the Kingdom of Israel in the middle of the first millennium B.C.

Discovered in 1867 by French Jewish scholar Joseph Halevy, they remained mostly isolated until Begin decided in the 1970s to press for their emigration to Israel. Most arrived in two airlifts, Operation Moses in 1985 and Operation Solomon in 1991.

Back in the office of Masalla, the first Ethiopian to win a seat in the Knesset, we began talking about race relations among Jews and the treatment of the Ethiopians by their Jewish siblings. "They like us," he said of his fellow Israelis, Ashkenazim and Sephardim alike. "But they like us at a distance. As long as we don't live next to them, with the smell of our foods and our African clothes. They like us to be in a different building, you know. I don't blame them, really. No one likes to suddenly be surrounded by people who are very different."

Still, Masalla was outraged in January 1996, when it was revealed that Israeli health authorities were taking blood donations from Ethiopian Jews and then automatically discarding them for fear that they were tainted with the AIDS virus. The riots that resulted led to fears that the Ethiopians' frustration ran more deeply than had been thought.

Shula Mula, an Ethiopian student and community activist, told me that many of her friends were increasingly angry and "unless something dramatic changes fast, the Ethiopian Jews will become a disaffected minority no different from the blacks in America."

It can't be said that Israel isn't trying: as of 1996, more than half the Ethiopian families had bought homes with unprecedented government grants of up to $120,000, far more aid than is or has ever been available to other immigrants. But the community lags badly in education and income. And the visible racial distinction between the Ethiopians and their fellow Jews is always a factor. There are occasional reports of racism in the army. In one case a group of soldiers reportedly tried to turn an Ethiopian recruit into a "slave," and in another an Ethiopian soldier was advised by an officer that the medical clinic was off limits to blacks.

In Beerotayim, a mobile home site used for transitional housing for both Russian-speaking and Ethiopian immigrants, which I visited in 1995, a de facto segregation had installed itself, with the Russians moving to the northern half of the compound and the Ethiopians to the south side. The Ethiopians there said they disliked the Russians and couldn't believe that they were Jews. The Russians said the same thing about the Ethiopians. Occasionally, tensions developed into stone-throwing incidents across the unpaved road between the two halves of the camp. Sometimes, a stray stone would make a dent in a wooden sign that hung from the fence above the entrance to the processing center.

"Welcome to Israel," it said.

God

Messianic moment: Shlomo Goren, the army's chief rabbi, at the Western Wall (photograph by David Rubinger).

Every spring in Israel, the State Comptroller's Office — a body akin to the congressional Office of Management and Budget in America — publishes a comprehensive report on the general state of government. The 1998 report, issued in May by veteran State Comptroller Miriam Ben-Porat, a former Supreme Court justice, found the usual instances of malfeasance, impropriety, and inefficiency in various dimly lit corners of government activity. But her report went beyond the usual. It singled out what Ben-Porat had found to be the single most consistently and improperly "favored" sector of society — the ultra–Orthodox.

The report focused on how ultra–Orthodox representatives in government, both in the Knesset and in the administration, used the power of office to improperly give "preferential treatment" to ultra–Orthodox institutions and causes in the allotment of government funds.

Asserting that in 1997 the ultra–Orthodox — about 7 percent of the total population — had received a "disproportionate share" of welfare funds, subsidized housing, and other government handouts, Ben-Porat criticized key ultra–Orthodox political figures, including acting Housing Minister Meir Porush, who represented the particularly conservative religious party known as United Torah Jewry.

Most damaging was the state comptroller's finding of systematic fraud in the allotment of state subsidies to ultra–Orthodox yeshivas, religious institutes of higher learning. Ben-Porat found that the yeshivas inflated the number of students they claimed in order to get more funding. Yeshivas used multiple scams to inflate the figures — dead students, former students, made-up students, students at other institutions — and she found evidence that the practice was common throughout the ultra–Orthodox yeshiva system.

Did the Ben-Porat report in Israel's fiftieth year contain extraordinary findings? Not really. The yeshiva scams had been reported before, though in less detail. So had the allegations of preferential treatment and abuse of government power by the ultra–Orthodox. What was new was that an official organ of the state itself was leveling charges that for years had surfaced only in political and social arenas.

Still, despite a public uproar following publication of the report, the ultra–Orthodox remained resolutely unapologetic. As they had so many times in the past, they simply circled the wagons, denied the charges, and mounted a counteroffensive. Such distrust and disregard for outsiders had protected them in the past.

The ultra–Orthodox are an integral part of the government bureaucracy. They have become, through the years, increasingly powerful and increasingly entrenched. Indeed, ultra–Orthodox conflict with the rest of society is directly related to the growth of their political power and their willingness and opportunity to use it. At a fundamental level, the conflicts themselves — over everything from "disproportionate" budget allocations to Sabbath blue laws to education policy, army service, marriage, and peace with the Arabs — are not the real issue. The real issue is the government structure that allows so much religious influence in matters of state and the growing rage about this within the secular majority.

No one knows if Israel will ever solve this ungodly tangle.

Herzl recognized the role that Judaism had played in preserving his people during 2,000 years of Diaspora. For Jews the world over, the Torah had been the common root of identity, the shared wellspring of custom, and a primary source of guidance, ritual, belief, and law.

But Herzl's writings show he wanted to deny Judaism a major role in the reborn Jewish state. He justified the return to Zion in historical and practical, rather than religious, terms. It was the place where the Jewish people "came from," he reasoned, making it the most compelling and logical place for them to establish the state they required. Moreover, Herzl and his contemporaries conceived Zionism as a secular movement at a time when secular nationalism was emerging throughout Europe. (In this he was supported by leading Zionist thinkers such as Max Nordau.) The era of priests and princes, baronies and kingdoms was ending, they reasoned. The new world order would be built upon national identities. The Jews would be a part of this.

Herzl may have underestimated the transcendent role of religion in keeping the Jews focused on their "national homeland" for millennia. When Jews completed their annual Passover celebration with the famous toast, "Next year, in Jerusalem," it was not simply because they knew their forebears had come from there. It was because many of them truly believed that God had given that land to the Jews. Herzl was exceedingly optimistic to imagine that such basic religious conviction and the more elaborate Judaic practice that had flowered around it could be laid aside in the creation and management of a state.

Not surprisingly, Herzl outraged and was dismissed by the most devout of Jews. Some believed the Diaspora was God's way of punishing the faithlessness of the children of Israel. Reprieve could only be won, they believed, through community-wide humility and strict adherence to the faith. Only then might God return the Jews to their biblical homeland or appoint a messiah to lead them toward some greater place or plane of existence. No one saw the very earthly Herzl as the messiah.

Among the most conservative strain of the Orthodox, Zionism was rejected as blasphemy, just another swaggering conceit of modern man, another illusion that he could control his destiny without deference to God.

They did what they could to discredit the ideals of Zionism. When, for example, lexicographer Eliezer Ben-Yehuda moved to Jerusalem at the turn of the century and began to almost single-handedly promote the teaching of Hebrew as an everyday language (forcing his wife and children to speak it at home), he was excommunicated by the local community of ultra-Orthodox, who considered Hebrew a holy tongue to be reserved for prayer. Ben-Yehuda was even jailed briefly after the religious persuaded the Ottoman rulers of Palestine that he was practicing sedition by advocating Jewish self-sufficiency.

Yet, with the passage of the decades and the increasing likelihood that the

Zionists might actually succeed in creating a state in the ancient land of the Jews, the ultra–Orthodox could no longer afford to remain outsiders. By the time Israel was founded in the wake of World War II, many of the ultra–Orthodox were reasoning that if a Jewish homeland was being created it must be by God's hand. Their compromise, in many cases, was to move to Palestine yet not recognize the trappings of statehood or the authority of the civil administration. They answered to a higher power.

Oddly, despite the religious disdain for the machinery of state and Herzl's reciprocal notion that religion should not play a role in matters of civil law, fundamental powers were granted to the religious segment of society right from the beginning. The departure from Herzl's vision began in 1948, when Ben-Gurion, in one of his first acts as prime minister, decided that on top of all the other challenges facing his fledgling nation he did not need internal religious opposition as well. Also concerned that the young Jewish state might lose its moral advantage if it was seen by the outside world as being in conflict with some of the Jews themselves, Ben-Gurion decided to try to gain the support (or at least minimize the aggression) of the religious with a series of special regulations that today form the basis of the so-called "status quo" on religious-secular relations.

First, all issues concerning "personal status"—primarily marriage and divorce—were handed over to an Orthodox Chief Rabbinate. This basically ensured that no Jew would be able to marry within Israel except according to Orthodox religious prescription, with spouse approved and ceremony officiated by an apparatchik of the religious bureaucracy.

The rabbinate was also empowered to set religious dietary standards based on Jewish law, ensuring that meat, dairy, and other foods are kosher, or religiously pure. All food producers or importers who want the "kosher" label on their products (which most do, so as not to lose the religious consumers in what is already a fairly small market) must undergo inspection by the rabbinate's food patrol. Restaurants that want certification must meet religious standards of environmental purity. And the rabbinate can force its will on any government-sponsored entity that serves food, including the public schools and the military.

Ben-Gurion's second special regulation allowed the religious to run their own school systems — paid for mostly by the state. In consequence, today there are three separate school systems for Jewish Israelis to choose from (Arab Israelis have yet a fourth system).

The first is an open public school system where kids study according to a curriculum similar to that of most Western countries. One notable difference, however, is that in Israel's public schools Bible study is a requirement for all students. It is not introduced, however, in a cloak of religion. Here, the Bible is treated as history, taught with a reverence similar to that accorded colonial history in America. These schools educate about two-thirds of Israel's children.

The second is a state-run religious school system — also open — which also teaches the basics but places far more emphasis on religion and ensures that the students pray each day and eat according to strict religious code. This system is the choice of a class of religious people in Israel who are called "national religious," an allusion to the fact that they are both religious and nationalist (when the label was created, many of the ultra-Orthodox opposed the very existence of the state). This system is both monitored and funded by the government, and it operates with an extended school day so that there is enough time to cover both mainstream subjects and a thorough religious curriculum. This system educates about a quarter of Israel's youth.

The third system Ben-Gurion allowed for is referred to as "special education," a euphemism for ultra-Orthodox schooling. It is, indeed, special. Alone among Israeli schools, including the Arab schools, this system operates with virtually no state oversight. (In Ben-Gurion's day, this is what passed for separation of religion and state.) The religious are free to design the educational program as they see fit — at great expense to basic science, math, and non-biblical history. About a tenth of Israel's Jewish youngsters currently attend these schools.

To these two major compromises was added Ben-Gurion's agreement that students of yeshivas be exempt from army service. At the time, this applied to several hundred young scholars. Today, it has become one of the major means for the ultra-Orthodox to turn secular malcontents into converts, and almost anyone willing to succumb to Torah study at 18 can evade the army. Tens of thousands do so every year.

The legions of yeshiva students not only are lost to the army but often to the economy. The ultra-religious lifestyle often yields large families at a very young age, and these become wholly dependent on state welfare arranged by the religious parties in the Knesset and doled out according to the calculations of the ultra-Orthodox institutions that control their lives.

Although Ben-Gurion gave the ultra-Orthodox a considerable base of state-sanctioned power within society, they did not take full advantage of it until after the 1967 war. Two things happened then that changed things.

First was the sudden emergence of a new kind of messianism that felt that the conquest of biblical Israel could only have been brought about by God, a sign that it was time to reclaim the land. As religious scholar Avi Ravitsky, a founder of the moderate religious movement Meimad, put it: "For three generations [up until the 1960s], there was a well-designed Zionist framework for Israel. Zionism ran the engine and pulled the train; the influence of Judaism was confined to the dining car. But 30 years ago, a new generation of youthful religious moved from the dining car to the engine. And they changed the agenda for Israel."

Ravitsky points out that the period from the time of Herzl to the Six Day War was the only time in Jewish history when Judaism was not the force leading the Jewish people — Zionism was. There was a keen desire among many religious to restore the old order, but they had no design, no plan. Again, 1967 changed that.

Second, up until the time of the war, the forerunner of today's Labor Party was in total control of the government and the Knesset, with broad-based voter support. But the disaster of the Yom Kippur War a few years later ended the reign of Labor and strengthened Likud.

Starting in the mid-1970s, with the general electorate evenly divided between Labor and Likud, the religious parties had the opportunity to play a central role in deciding which party rose to and stayed in power — they held what is called "the balance of power." In exchange for funding and religious-based legislation, the ultra-Orthodox parties played the left and right off each other, promising their critical Knesset seats to whichever major party promised them more.

Although at all key junctures since 1977 they went with the right, this strategy worked very well.

The ultra-Orthodox were critical coalition allies for the right-wing governments set up in 1977 and 1981. The 1984 Labor-Likud "unity government" temporarily stripped them of their powers. In 1988, they flirted with both sides, making demands sufficiently difficult as to compel Likud leader Shamir, the seeming victor, to turn to the Labor Party and establish another unity government.

The ultra-Orthodox played a major role again in the 1996 election, when more than 90 percent of their vote went to Likud candidate Netanyahu. Indeed, the ultra-Orthodox Habad movement mounted a highly energetic street campaign featuring the slogan "Netanyahu Is Good for the Jews," which probably turned the tide of the campaign. The message was that other candidates — and their secular supporters — were not only *not* good for "the Jews," but might not really qualify as Jews themselves.

This course of events — taking the ultra-Orthodox from outsiders in prestate times to the ultimate insiders decades later — has led many in Israel to rue the day Ben-Gurion made his compromises.

Yosef Dan, an internationally renowned history professor at Hebrew University in Jerusalem, takes it even further. He blames the secular segment of society for keeping its eyes closed for too long, for letting the religious claim moral superiority and get away with it, for creating a culture of passivity when it comes to religious assaults on secular values. Above all, he faults Ben-Gurion and his spiritual successors — meaning the average, secular Zionist Israeli — for ceding control of the spiritual domain to the ultra-Orthodox.

"The notion that the ultra-Orthodox in Israel are the sole representatives of traditional Judaism, and that they faithfully and accurately follow old traditions, is ludicrous," he said one day in his office in Jerusalem. "I can say with some confidence, as a historian, that this is completely untrue."

Dan continued, "The ultra-Orthodox [as they exist today] are a direct result of the policies and culture of secular Israel itself. If anything, the ultra-Orthodox are not our grandfathers — they are our descendants!"

That the average secular Israeli accepts Orthodoxy, even ultra-Orthodoxy, as the definitive manifestation of the Jewish religion is well-documented. Survey after survey, vote after vote, shows a secular deference to the predominance of this stream of Judaism, which manages the portfolio handed over by Ben-Gurion in '48. Israelis will joke that "the synagogue the secular person doesn't attend is Orthodox."

Yosef Dan has modified this maxim slightly, taking into account the growing sense of anger among the secular even as they still accede to religious controls and influences in their lives. "All of Israel is ultra–Orthodox," Dan says with some relish. "Only part hate it."

The eighteenth and nineteenth centuries in Europe changed Judaism. The Enlightenment — the great intellectual movement that rejected biblical religion in favor of rationality and reason — took hold and inexorably altered communities and nations. Extraordinary forces, including industrialism and urban migration, swept across the whole of the continent, disturbing not only patterns of settlement and ways of life but patterns of behavior and ways of thinking. Indeed, more and more Jews felt the need to rebel against the ways of the *shtetl*, the small Jewish towns throughout Central and Eastern Europe.

In a fictitious *shtetl* called Anatevka, the setting for Shalom Aleichem's nineteenth-century story "Tevye the Milkman," the struggle between the irresistible forces of change and the traditions of family and community became epic. Little Anatevka, underfed and overworked, became the town that told the story of the reckoning between Enlightened Europe and the Old Jewish World.

A century later, Tevye became widely known as the sad and lovely hero of *Fiddler on the Roof*, which opened on Broadway in 1964. Tevye's pride, humility, and grace in the grip of forces far beyond his control represent the larger heroism of Jewish adaptation and survival through a period of stunning change in Europe. Anatevka, swept up in the winds of change, represented every Jewish village in Eastern Europe, where people reluctantly gave up what they had in order to survive.

Stories like this one were originally written in Yiddish, a sort of pidgin German that the Jews had adapted for their own use and later filled out with Hebrew, Slavic, and other components. Spoken throughout Central Europe starting in roughly the ninth century, it existed for centuries primarily as a spoken tongue. It was not considered a refined language and relatively little serious literature was written in it.

But with the emergence of the Enlightenment in Europe, and the associated outburst of scientific inquiry, philosophy, and writing, Yiddish entered a brief heyday of literary prominence. Just as Jewish thinkers, scientists, and inventors were playing their well-known roles in the re-creation of European civilization, Jewish writers were also flourishing. Some were students of the new wave of thinking; others were inspired by a desire to defend traditional Jewish ways. Among them, they captured thousands of stories of Old World Jewish life, just as that very way of life was being irrevocably transformed. The dramatic sweep of the Enlightenment had unleashed the creative spirit and progressive thought that would lead to the careful chronicling of the Old Jewish World while simultaneously ushering it almost entirely out of existence.

Almost.

Europe was changing, and European Jews were changing with it, giving birth to great Jewish writers, scientists, and thinkers — one of whom was Theodor Herzl. But there were also deeply devout groups of Jews, many centered around the scholarly institutions of various respected rabbis, who took to the trenches and dug in. These are the ancestors of today's ultra–Orthodox. Of all Jews — maybe even of all religious people — the ultra–Orthodox were the least willing to submit to the Enlightenment.

The early Enlightenment thinkers did not completely deny the existence of God, but they did reject much of the myth of God. They may have believed in a God who designed nature and gave it original life, but not one who periodically reappeared to perform miracles or issue directives to humanity. Later thinkers denied God altogether, giving rise to atheism. Either way, it was a direct challenge to both Christianity and Judaism.

But ultra–Orthodox Jews were confident in their beliefs. They believed they were the keepers of the very word of God: Jewish priests and rabbis had literally transcribed the holy texts of the Old Testament letter by letter for generations. For them, the Enlightenment was of no relevance. The word of God was not subject to empirical testing. They would practice their religion as they always had, regardless of how far astray other Jews wandered.

The determination of the ultra–Orthodox to stave off the encroachment of modern thinking and values 250 years ago is still what defines them today. Stepping quickly down the stone alleys of Jerusalem's Old City, the bearded, black-hatted faithful are still locked in a world view, lifestyle, and even wardrobe that have been transported largely intact from Poland of the 1750s, all the intervening splendors and spasms of human change notwithstanding. Even by Herzl's time, in the late 1800s, the distinctness of the ultra–Orthodox segment of the Jewish world was clearly established.

That long-established distinctness, now coupled with political power, has become a force agitating to turn back the clock for all of Israel.

Indeed, the political power that the religious have amassed through the years has made them strikingly uninhibited in their attempts to mold the social environment of the state. The Orthodox have variously tried to legislate morality, to enforce unwieldy religious standards in public institutions, to control the schedules of roadways and elevators, and to deny legal standing to other forms of Judaism. Occasionally they protest that their religious values place them above civil law.

Examples of the conflict abound. When I attended a press event at one of Israel's small army outposts along the Lebanese border, I was confronted by what strikes me as one of the more ridiculous, yet insidious, examples of religious assertiveness.

The base sat on a windswept bluff that rose to a crest where the Israel-Lebanon border runs, marked by a pair of barbed-wire fences. From the crest, soldiers looked down upon a dry Lebanese valley with nothing to distinguish it but a dusty town. Lurking somewhere within that vista was the fearsome Hezbollah militia.

Housing a ragged little outfit of maybe 100 men, the base included two dozen small shacks that served as command, barracks, mess, and supply, all huddled in the shadow of the bluff to remain invisible from the other side. It monitors a stretch of border to prevent incursions by Hezbollah guerrillas and to protect Israeli towns and kibbutzim located nearby. The soldiers I met were young — 18 to 20, generally — and were serving one of the more hazardous and uncomfortable duties that the army offers.

Although there are over 100,000 Israelis serving in the military at any given time, combat and near-combat positions are only a part of the overall program. So when combat soldiers around the country started demanding to have cornflakes added to their breakfast menu, it seemed like an easy way for the army to raise morale. In March 1997, the story broke into the Israeli media because the Chief Rabbinate had vetoed the army's attempt to deploy the cereal. Unfortunately for the soldiers, many of the smaller bases, like the one I visited, did not have sufficient refrigerator space to store the milk for the cereal separately from the meat served at dinner. (Jewish dietary law requires that dairy and meat be kept separate.) Thus did Israel fail to close the cornflake gap.

The prohibition of cold cereal for the troops had nothing to do with running an army. It was all about the power of the Orthodox and their daily battle to preserve Judaism. There were undoubtedly some troops who slept more soundly in their bunks knowing that their world was safer for kosherness — for up to a third of Israelis do keep kosher to varying degrees. Should they have been forced to violate their religious beliefs just because others wanted cornflakes? Wouldn't abandonment of kosher rules in the Jewish state's military be a repudiation of Judaism? Is such a thing reasonable?

Even cornflakes can raise this kind of debate here.

And elevators, too.

Israeli journalist Lily Galili, writing in the newspaper *Ha'aretz*, reported on the battle destroying neighborly relations in her Jerusalem high-rise. The 22 families in the building, mostly secular but with a substantial religious minority, had lived in harmony for 20 years, until just after the 1996 elections, when a planned modernization of the building's two elevators sparked bitter discord. The new elevators, it turned out, were equipped with the option of a "Sabbath mode," which, when activated, made the elevator go up and down all day long, with or without riders, opening automatically at every floor. This unusual mode was developed to help religious Jews more completely observe the Sabbath. According to rabbinical interpretation of the Scriptures, God's commandment that the faithful rest on the seventh ("Sabbath") day means not only "do not work" but also "do not create." The activation of a dormant elevator by the pushing of a button, and the further command for it to stop at a given floor, are thus interpreted as a type of creation, what with all the electrons flying around. Hence, according to some, they are a violation of the spirit of the Sabbath.

Of course, to the non-observant, a Sabbath elevator can become, week after week, a nuisance and a waste of time. To them, installing the Sabbath mode into the elevators effectively put them out of commission. And to call such a change an "upgrade" seemed preposterous. Nonetheless, the religious residents of the building argued that their lifestyle must be respected and a way must be found to prevent some of the more elderly religious from having to walk the stairs in the absence of a Sabbath elevator.

The house committee convened. Some secular residents said that not only did they oppose the Sabbath mode of the elevator, but they also feared that it would make the building more attractive for religious Jews and draw more of them to live there. Words like "fascism," "the rights of the minority," and "the future of the country" filled the room.

When the vote was held, the religious minority mustered an 11-11 tie. Apparently, some of the secular residents cast votes in favor of the Sabbath elevator and a little inconvenience in the interest of better relations with their neighbors.

The tie, however, was not good enough to activate the Sabbath elevator. Galili quoted neighbor Moshe Rigel, a member of the religious camp, as saying he felt like he was "exactly in the middle of a cultural war. I feel like an oppressed minority. I feel hatred, just like abroad."

Just like abroad. It was a telling expression. As Rigel intended it, the remark meant that in his view an anti–Jewish discrimination — meaning anti-religious — was emerging in Israel itself.

There is some truth to the notion.

When Rigel felt his Jewish faith was being attacked in the house committee, it was not simply a matter of religious discrimination. In his mind, being ostracized for his practice of Judaism was the same thing as being ostracized for being Jewish. That's how it had been when he lived abroad.

But his would-be persecutors — all fellow Jews — were not voting against the idea or fact of being Jewish. They were voting against the imposition of religious doctrine on those who did not choose to observe it. Furthermore, in their minds there is a difference between opposing religion and opposing Jewishness. But it may be that for people like Rigel, who live by a strict interpretation of what it means to be a Jew, the distinction is lost.

In his book, *In the Land of Israel*, Amos Oz describes the changes in his Jerusalem neighborhood between the time he was a child growing up there and the time he came back as an adult. Where there was once a thriving, diverse mixture of secular and religious, intellectuals and craftspeople, hacks and hagglers, there remained only the ultra–Orthodox, who "the fathers of Hebrew literature, Mendele and Berdyczewsky, Bialik and Brenner and the others, would have banished ... from the world around them and from within their souls," if they could have, Oz wrote.

"In an eruption of rebellion and loathing, they portrayed this world as a swamp, a heap of dead words and extinguished souls. They reviled it and at the same time immortalized it in their books.

"However, you cannot afford to loathe this reality, because between then and now it was choked and burned, exterminated by Hitler. Nor can you even afford yourself a measure of secret admiration for the incredible vitality of this Judaism, for as it grows and swells, it threatens your own spiritual existence and eats away at the roots of your own world, prepared to inherit it all when you and your kind have gone."

Fifteen years after he wrote this, Oz expressed strong, but ultimately inconclusive, opinions about the role of religion in the state of Israel.

He suggested in our meeting that the clash between religion and modernity that began with the Enlightenment in Europe was still being waged in Israel today and was an "undecided battle." Nor did he believe either side had the advantage. On the contrary. He sat back in his rickety chair and predicted that religion in Israel would remain "an uncomfortable reality as far as the eye can see."

Just as Oz depicted religious Judaism in a battle with "modernity," Professor Alon Kadish, chair of the History Department at Hebrew University, saw it in a battle with "Westernization." "I believe a process of materialism is weakening religion," he said.

Unlike the intellectual assault on religion that began in the 1700s, however, today the foe is more powerful. While the devout may have been immune to the winds of intellectual freedom in the eighteenth and nineteenth centuries, today's religious are far less immune to the allure of materialism.

As evidence, Kadish described an Orthodox community near Jerusalem where a loophole had been found to the religious prohibition against owning a television set, that purveyor of secular values. A shop in an alley rents them by the hour, and it is apparently raking in the shekels. He also spoke of an ultra-Orthodox family whose gift shop in Jerusalem makes good money from tourists seven days a week. The family goes through a weekly pretense of "selling" the shop to an Arab each Friday afternoon and "buying" it back each Saturday night — avoiding violating the Sabbath while maximizing profits at the same time.

But patchwork solutions alone cannot protect religion from change. So the religious political parties are pro-active, seeking to "Judaize" Israel more and more. This is a constant, difficult struggle, albeit one that was made much easier by the results of recent elections.

Beyond the issues that could be tackled in parliament, the electoral success emboldened religious activists on all levels. Soon after the 1996 election, ultra-Orthodox ruffians began attacking and throwing stones at women in "immodest" dress — lacking sleeves, knees exposed — in parts of Jerusalem outside the Mea Shearim neighborhood that for decades had been considered "their domain." (Assaults on immodest women inside Mea Shearim have been tolerated for years.)

Next came an assault on Israel's Supreme Court, a bastion of secular humanism that had offended the ultra-Orthodox (and other right-wingers) for years with its cosmopolitan and liberal legislating from the bench. Among other things, the court in the 1990s struck down laws banning the import of non-kosher meats, upheld the right of women to serve on local religious councils, and forced the government to recognize conversions to Judaism performed by rabbis of the less strict Reform and Conservative streams.

A few months after the 1996 election, the Court blocked a government effort to shut down Jerusalem's Bar-Illan street on the Sabbath each week. As in the case of the elevator, many religious Jews consider driving on the Sabbath a desecration of God's day of rest (as is using the telephone).

The legal precedent for closing down streets in areas populated by ultra-Orthodox had been set decades before, but it had always been limited to areas where the secular rarely appeared anyway, like the overwhelmingly ultra-Orthodox Tel Aviv suburb of Bnei Brak. Bar-Illan street, on the other hand, was a main Jerusalem thoroughfare that had once been secular-populated. Closing it down would make traversing Jerusalem much less convenient.

Reacting to the Supreme Court decision, thousands of ultra-Orthodox traveled in from around the country to demonstrate on the street for several successive Saturdays, throwing dirty baby diapers at police and stoning cars that dared drive by. After two months of tumult, both sides agreed to establish a commission made up of religious and secular representatives to study the matter. Several months later it ruled that the street be closed during part of the Sabbath, but also recommended the secular population be compensated with the right to public transportation — previously unavailable on the Sabbath — in some other areas of the city.

Orthodox politicians, meanwhile, threatened to prepare legislation to change the appointment procedure for Supreme Court justices to require them to be approved by the Knesset. They pointed to the fact that this was the way Supreme Court appointments are handled in respectable democracies, like the United States. But secular activists knew that such legislation would be a disaster for their cause, because without a proper constitution to protect individual rights, the Israeli Supreme Court is often the only line of defense against gross abuses and against efforts in the Knesset to legislate morality in a way that pleases religious coalition partners. The religious have long opposed any effort to enact an Israeli constitution, viewing the Bible as their sole code of law. Meanwhile, rantings in the ultra-Orthodox press against the liberal and unusually activist chief justice, Aharon Barak, became so extreme that he was assigned government bodyguards.

And the assault went much further than attacking the Supreme Court only, seeming to endanger the judicial system as a whole. Shas spiritual leader Ovadia Yosef, to the horror of intellectuals who admired him for his pro-peace positions, declared Israel's courts not only to be "worse than the courts of the *goyim*"—the derogatory word for the non-Jewish—but even, in a sort of world record, "worse than the courts of Syria." Yosef and other rabbis declared that Jews must not honor these civilian courts, instead turning only to religious tribunals.

In 1998, that question itself rose to the Supreme Court in the case of a woman who had filed for divorce from her husband in civil court while he had filed in a rabbinical court. The latter issued its ruling first — in favor of the husband. The Supreme Court ruled that the decision of the civil court, however, which in this instance favored the wife, had to be obeyed by the husband, despite the rabbinical court ruling. This prompted more fuming at the Supreme Court by religious Knesset members.

In December 1996, the Orthodox took on the overwhelmingly secular population of Tel Aviv. About 10,000 ultra-Orthodox descended upon a Tel Aviv auditorium to protest against the opening of businesses and restaurants on the Sabbath in the city. Again Yosef was the star, declaring that according to Jewish law anyone desecrating the Sabbath "would be put to death." Later Yosef's handlers explained that he was not actually calling for capital punishment for Sabbath-breakers, and that he believed strongly that only God himself was qualified to rule in such matters.

Within days Labor Minister Eli Yishai, of Shas, began dispatching squads (whose members were Arabs to avoid Jewish Sabbath desecration) to find Tel Aviv businesses open on the day of rest and enforce stiff fines. Cafe owners on Sheinkin Street, the main drag of the city's bohemia, also reported visits by ultra-Orthodox thugs recommending that they consider the will of God in a more urgent fashion.

Thus, despite the protests and assurances of the liberal mayor, Roni Milo, fewer and fewer businesses opened on the Sabbath in Tel Aviv, too.

The trouble, for the secular, is that while they abhor what is happening, they are by nature much less inclined to fight about it. Their live-and-let-live philosophy urges tolerance and their laid-back approach makes them self-conscious about aggressively beating back the ultra-Orthodox challenge. Furthermore, as a political grouping they are weakened by their individualism. Few secular Israelis will follow any other secular Israelis into the breach for any cause (except fighting the Arabs, I guess), while their ultra-Orthodox counterparts fall in line quickly and strictly adhere to established channels of authority. As a group the secular are non-aligned, nebulous, and uninterested in committing themselves to a long-term political engagement.

The weakness of the secular was evident in several confrontations in December 1996. The first occurred when a young comedian named Gil Kopatch began satirizing Torah study during his skits on a weekly variety program shown on state-run Channel One TV. He discussed the private parts of various biblical figures, referred to Eve as "the first sex bombshell," and drew unflattering parallels between biblical heroes and the anti-heroes of modern Israeli public life. Since the channel's funding is authorized by the Knesset, the religious were able to summon Kopatch to justify himself before the Knesset Education Committee.

The encounter turned into a debate between the rattled Kopatch, wearing a baseball cap, and Shas legislator Shlomo Benizri, who termed the young man "an evil clown." The ultra-Orthodox sat stone-faced as a video of Kopatch's act was broadcast and then launched an attack on the youth. I have seen Kopatch on stage, where he has a quick and acid tongue, to say the least. But in this Knesset forum, he turned out to be the wrong guy for defending free speech or explaining the nature of satire to self-righteous politicians. Instead, he stammered about how he had been misunderstood and about how his weekly spot was a modern effort to bring Israelis closer to the Bible.

But the secular have a much deeper problem. They want to go on being Jewish somehow. Yet to be secular and spiritually Jewish means either that a definition of Jewishness must be refined beyond religion, or that a new, uniquely Jewish spiritual ethos be isolated that is compelling enough to fight on equal terms with Orthodoxy.

The latter is what Yosef Dan advocates. "Today, to be a secular Israeli means to be deliberately ignorant of Jewish thought. Anything associated with Judaism is rejected," he postulates. "Secular Israelis see more and more areas of life are being defined as Jewish; and if Jewish, then ultra-Orthodox; and if ultra-Orthodox, then we hate them."

But it was not always this way, he argues. "The utopia of Israeli culture is not in some future time — it was here! In the '50s and '60s!

"Forty years ago, in the Department of Jewish Studies [at Hebrew University], many of the professors were secular. But no one doubted that what that meant was to be open and knowledgeable about Jewish thought, philosophy, music, and at the same time open and knowledgeable about Western thought, philosophy, and music. ... No one saw a contradiction. ... Everybody had his own *Halacha*—his own Jewish law—but there was no conflict."

Dan knows that the change took place with the arrival of the biblical lands in the '67 war and the emergence of messianic Judaism. But he refuses to exonerate the secular. "The ultra-Orthodox [divided Israeli society], but they could not have done it without the spiritual and financial support of the secular for all those years," he states.

If anything shows how unlikely it is that secular Israel is suddenly to embrace any form of Judaism at all, it is definitely in their ambivalence, if not apathy, to the battle of American Jewry to have Reform and Conservative streams of Judaism fully recognized in Israel, dislodging the Orthodox monopoly over a whole array of issues, especially conversions.

Riding high in 1997, the Orthodox parties once again introduced into the Knesset a law that, if passed, would formally deny recognition of non-Orthodox conversions in Israel. This would mean that conversions performed by rabbis of the Conservative, Reform, or Reconstructionist branches of Judaism would not be valid as a basis for Israeli citizenship.

Even though the law only makes formal what is already the case in practice, the proposed law triggered a titanic reaction from the leadership and members of those three branches of Judaism, primarily in North America. While they have mounted serious and noisy campaigns against the proposed law, threatening a cut-off or reduction in charitable giving by American and Canadian Jews to Israeli institutions, there has been comparatively little response from Israeli Jews themselves. The main fear is that the ultra–Orthodox campaign will undermine Israel's support among American Jews, which is still the largest community in the world and where the Conservative and Reform branches are dominant.

The conversion law, if it is passed, would block the path to resolving one of the country's ticking time bombs: thousands of immigrants to Israel from the former Soviet Union. Up to a third of them, according to some estimates, are non–Jews or part Jews who do not fulfill the Orthodox requirement for a maternal line of descent. Many of them would like to "join" the Jewish people in order to simplify their process of becoming Israeli. Most of these people could never undergo a religiously rigorous and (in their case) hypocritical Orthodox conversion. Unless simpler conversions are made available and legitimate in Israel, a new type of "non–Jew" will be perpetuated, and a new kind of bitterness will be born.

So why is mainstream Israel not rising as one against the ultra–Orthodox campaign? The reason is simple: almost no native Israelis and few residents of Israel are adherents of non–Orthodox synagogues.

In the nineteenth century, when Judaism was undergoing its most dramatic changes in the modern era, the Conservative and Reform movements sprang up in Europe as more liberal, adaptable alternatives to Orthodoxy. Although the movements remained fairly small in Europe, they blossomed with the emigration of huge numbers of Jews to North America beginning in the middle of the century. Reconstructionism came along in their wake. Meanwhile, it was the Orthodox branch that stayed behind in Europe and, in the wake of the Holocaust, made a belated migration itself — mainly to Israel.

So most Israelis, especially the native-born, have little personal experience with the non–Orthodox branches of Judaism and cannot muster much sympathy for their outrage over the conversion law debate. One secular man, quoted in the *New York Times* as representative of the breed, said, "Orthodox Judaism is the only kind I know about. It's what we grew up with here. The others just don't seem like real Judaism to me."

They do, of course, represent true Judaism to millions of Jews outside of Israel. They see the conversion law as not only another sign of the divisive role of Orthodoxy within Israel, but as a wedge separating Israel from the rest of the world's Jews.

Naomi Hazan, a Knesset member representing the liberal Meretz Party, put it this way: "No one can deny that a basic feature of Jewish history has been the constant creation and reshaping of different streams of tradition and practice. ... Refusal to recognize the different interpretations [of Judaism] that exist today, in the very country dedicated to respecting and honoring the lives of all Jews, is to reject the basic tenet of Jewish tradition."

Yet, it seems as if a part of Israel — secular people too — wants the debate to be over, to establish once and for all time what Judaism is, to hedge the bets of a Westernizing nation with a tip of the hat to God.

Because Hebrew is such an old language, old words applied in new circumstances sometimes go in funny directions. The Hebrew word *aliyah*, for example, literally means "an ascent," but in contemporary usage it means immigration to Israel. Emigration from Israel to another country is called *yerida*, a lowly descent. Similarly, the religious have their own Hebrew phrase for the adoption of the religious lifestyle by a secular Jew: *hazara be-tshuva*, or "a return to the answer."

The first well-publicized wave of *hazara be-tshuva* came in the mid-1970s, when a series of well-known public figures adopted the religious lifestyle to the surprise and dismay of their fans. Chief among them was Uri Zohar, a gifted comedian and filmmaker who concluded in his early forties that his life lacked spiritual values. Zohar had been particularly famous for a TV skit ravaging religion and for movies celebrating a hedonistic lifestyle and the wanton pursuit of women. His most famous movie was *Metzitzim*—"Peeping Toms"—about a boorish, hard-drinking lifeguard (played by Zohar) and his youthful hangers-on who pass their days peering into the women's showers at the beach.

So it was a shock to Zohar's fans when he began appearing on television with prayer braids hanging from his shirt and delivering religious sermons on his radio talk show. His conversion, however, came to symbolize the wave of *hazara be-tshuva* that had its roots, once again, in Israel's 1967 military victory. The Six Day War had turned frightened little Israel into an overconfident regional bully and had ended an era of frugality and humility on all fronts. In a society weaned on socialist ethics, it had become ever more fashionable to show off wealth, power, and individual achievements. Zohar had symbolized the brash new Israeli. His customary punchline during on-stage performances was "Well—am I handsome?" Many older Israelis, who were sickened by what was happening, thought not.

The disastrous 1973 war was thus seen as punishment. The personal penance for Zohar, the man who symbolized the hubris and vapidity of the times, was *hazara be-tshuva*.

A parallel set of circumstances unfolded in the 1990s. The peace process made Israelis overconfident, sure that the good times had come. The prosperity of the peace process fed a crass materialism that sometimes made Israel seem like a caricature of the most superficial aspects of America.

And then came the comeuppance: the wave of horrific suicide bombings in early 1996. The terrorist attacks made clear to Israelis how vulnerable they remained and brought down the peace government of Shimon Peres. The result, in addition to a rollback of the diplomatic and economic gains, was another wave of religion, this one perhaps deeper and broader than before.

In many secular households in Israel, the possibility of children becoming religious is a keenly felt, constant fear of secular parents. "My father told me that the worst thing that could possibly happen was if I did *hazara be-tshuva*," says Limor Shmuel, a struggling journalist working for a small paper. "He made it clear that if I became religious he would consider it to be as if I had died. I wouldn't exist anymore for him. I was told this throughout my childhood. Some kids are programmed to become doctors or lawyers. With me, it's ingrained in my mind: Must not be religious."

The number of Israeli Jews defining themselves as totally secular varies depending on how the question is phrased. It's a complicated self-definition. It does not necessarily mean that the individual who identifies as secular does not believe in God, or that the individual does not adhere to some of the practices of traditional Judaism. On the contrary, most do sometimes take part in Jewish ritual, although more as an expression of cultural memory or respect of family tradition than of religious faith in all the particulars. The vast majority succumb to tradition and convenience and undergo religious weddings (rather than go to Cyprus, or elsewhere, for a civil wedding that would then be recognized by Israel's Interior Ministry). Many go to synagogue at least once a year, generally for Yom Kippur, the Day of Atonement. Almost all have a traditional seder meal on Passover, and the majority observe religious holidays like Rosh Hashana, Hanukkah, and Shavuot, which have become national holidays.

Despite all this, the definition does signify that secular Jews do not wish to be bound by Orthodox rules or other shackles. They claim Jewishness without fully succumbing to religious doctrine. And, as individuals, they determine which aspects of Judaism and the Jewish experience they choose to live by.

Not surprisingly, the strongly secular population is mostly Ashkenazi, including recent immigrants from Western Europe, America, and the English-speaking world. These are the groups within the larger Israeli population that are most adapted to Western culture and values, particularly the Western emphasis on individualism.

Amos Oz, who is probably the chief oracle of secular Israel, says it's not religion that defines Jewishness. For him, there's something more meaningful to the Jewish cultural tradition of argument, disagreement, and debate.

"There is a certain latent anarchism which I identify as Jewish. It exists in many nations. It's a gene, I think ... a gene that perhaps traveled [with] the Jews. A certain sense of relativism. A certain self-biting sense of humor. A certain rejection of authority. A certain disquiet.

"I don't think it's religion [that] defines the Jews. [In the Bible, the Jews] are defined very often not by their love affair with God but by their arguments with God — which is a standing part of the Jewish heritage. It's very difficult to define — this quality of argumentativeness I am talking about — and it's even more difficult to convince an Orthodox Jew that in this sense I am more of a traditional Jew than he is! But who cares?"

On a voluntary social level the religious and secular rarely mix. When they do meet, discussion often turns quickly to the thing that most clearly divides and distinguishes them. But the discussion often amounts to just contradicting monologues. Neither side really understands the other's point of view.

So it was when my brother Ron, a young advertising executive, struck up conversation in Jerusalem's raucous Underground Pub with David, who had attracted Ron's attention by walking through the door wearing a *kippa*. After a few minutes of curiously observing, Ron went over and spoke to David, who engaged him willingly.

"So you're truly religious?" said Ron.

"Absolutely," David answered. "Totally religious."

"What I mean is, do you take everything the Bible says literally?"

"Every word," said David. "If you don't believe it all, why believe any of it?"

Ron pressed a bit harder. "What about carbon dating? The world is older than the Bible says."

"The rabbis explain it all. Carbon dating is based on molecular structure. God put those bones in the earth with the ancient-seeming molecular structure prearranged in order to test our belief."

Ron rolled his eyes: "I see. And how do the rabbis feel about you drinking beer with the infidels at the Underground Pub at four in the morning?"

"If the rabbis knew I would be severely chastised," David responded. "But apparently, God doesn't want them to know."

Ron viewed this exchange with humor. But for more and more people, there is nothing funny about the chasm.

"I guess one of the meanings that I attach to the label 'secular' is that it means I am one of the givers, not one of the takers," said one young woman I met at a Tel Aviv party. "The ultra–Orthodox don't give; they take. They don't help; they hurt. The secular do so much more: they earn money and pay taxes; they serve in the army; they play important civic roles like police and doctors, and teachers, and firefighters. But the religious do nothing for the country. They only take. The state is too young to already have people who are doing nothing."

Her counterpart in the argument might be someone like Yehezkel Farbstein, an ultra–Orthodox Jew who studies at a yeshiva in Jerusalem. In his late twenties when I met him, Farbstein could barely support his wife and two children. He studied religion up to 15 hours a day, survived on a meager state handout, and did without much recreation. But he loved his life.

"I would give anything for secular Israelis to all be like me," he says. "I'd rather convince people to do it voluntarily, but if we can make the country more religious by imposing it, I don't mind imposing."

Farbstein is considered quite educated in his circles, but he knows next to nothing about secular world history or about science and math. This does not concern him, because he feels it is part of God's plan, a plan in which his community has the noblest role of all: to carry the torch of the Chosen People. For the secular he has contempt: "They lead utterly empty lives. Look at secular TV. All you see is little girls undressing. So I've been told."

His brother Simha is more radical. The secular "are not even Jews," he declares.

The degree of the rift over religion became stunningly clear to me one day when I met Bentzi Cain during a trip to an air force base. I spent the hour-long bus ride listening to Bentzi's fascinating story. He was in his forties, a successful manager of a large catering company, when he decided to study law. He found himself in the same class as his son, who routinely got better grades and helped his father graduate. Now he was working on a book about the global legal implications of the Internet.

Later, as we toured the base, Bentzi mentioned to me that his youngest son was in the army and hoped to become the "first religious chief of staff."

Until then I hadn't noticed that Bentzi was religious, but now I snuck a peek at the back of his head and noticed a small knitted *kippa* hiding in the shock of his full gray hair. Bentzi was therefore a member of the National Religious movement — not to be confused with the ultra-Orthodox *haredim* who make religion the absolute center of their lives. Bentzi, in the eyes of secular Israelis, was still "normal." I told him so.

He laughed ruefully. "I wish that were true. But sometimes the secular make me feel closer to the *haredim* than to them." It was clear he had no fondness for either group.

He told me what happened to his son one day. Walking down the street in Jerusalem, he was accosted by a man who claimed to represent a modeling agency. "My son's very tall, with broad shoulders, and very handsome," Bentzi explained.

The man and his son talked, an offer for an audition was soon extended, along with a business card, and the two parted.

"Then, as my son was walking away, he heard the guy shout back at him. The guy had just seen the *kippa* on the back of his head. 'I didn't realize you're religious,' the guy told my son. 'Don't bother auditioning.' He wouldn't have gone anyway — but can you imagine the insult?"

Things got worse after Rabin was assassinated by the National Religious Yigal Amir, Bentzi continued. "You can feel the hatred of some of the secular when they see the *kippa*."

One day another son was boarding a bus, and the driver became abusive when he noticed the telltale *kippa*. Bentzi seethed as he recounted the story. "This driver told my son that he wouldn't have let him on to the bus if he wasn't required by law to do so! I told him that if such a thing ever happened again, he should slug the driver, and I would personally defend him in court."

Up until this point Bentzi and I were getting along fantastically, so I figured I could be straightforward, and I suggested to him that the National Religious had stoked some of the acrimony by allowing their community to become totally identified with the Jewish settler movement in the West Bank, a highly controversial enterprise that many Israelis believe is endangering the future and the security of the state. Second, I said, the National Religious too rarely disassociate themselves from the violent fanatics their community seems to occasionally spawn. "And it seems to be pretty much a one-way street," I added. "I don't remember hearing about a single Meretz supporter grabbing a gun and mowing down his political opponents."

Bentzi didn't like this at all. He said the problem was entirely different: too many secular Israeli Jews didn't understand that they simply must accept what may appear as inconvenient religious restrictions and impositions in order to make it possible for them to live together with their religious fellow Jews. For example, on the topic of observance of the Sabbath, Bentzi favored the total abolition of entertainment, business, transport, etc. on the day of rest.

"I don't expect you to want this," he said. "You must accept it, though, to live with me."

Our camaraderie was fading fast.

I said I feared there was no end to compromising with the religious parties' attempt to use the state as a tool of domination and coercion. Accept a state-imposed Sabbath, and next there will be calls to forbid "immodest" dress. I told him I cringe at the notion that women these days are sometimes not allowed to sing at official ceremonies when there are religious politicians present out of respect for the view that a woman must not sing in public because her voice is too erotic for men to hear and still maintain decorum. I also told him I don't approve of the *haredim* trying to banish immodest women from billboards.

"I am a little tired of hearing about the restrictions I need to tolerate in order to 'respect the feelings' of the religious," I said. "No one seems to consider 'the feelings' of the secular. I am truly insulted by the constant assault on freedom of speech, and behavior, in the name of religion. It honestly hurts my feelings, and they matter no less than those of the religious."

At this Bentzi seemed completely appalled, and his judgment was immediate and severe: "If that's how you feel, then there is really no possibility for us to live together. We have to agree it just won't work, divide the country into two, say a polite good-bye to each other and live apart."

Back at the air force base, with F-16s screaming overhead, a bitter truth dawned: despite our initial camaraderie, Bentzi cannot be my friend.

One religious Israeli who is my friend, however, is David Landau, one of Israel's leading journalists and my one-time boss when I was a young reporter at the *Jerusalem Post*. David — who wears a black knitted *kippa* — is an expert on the religious issues in Israel and has written an excellent book on the ultra-Orthodox. I heard him observe once that, for the Jewish people, Israel is a mixture of "home with the holy." It is a holy place for Jews, even many non-Orthodox, but it must also serve as home for them. He noted that it is difficult to make your home in a holy place — it creates an inherent inner tension.

It was a brilliantly sunny February day in Tsfat, a small town situated high in the northern mountains. I was there for a press conference at an army base nearby, and, enjoying the winter sun, I decided to stroll down the town's hillside alleys through a maze of ancient dwellings.

Tsfat is one of the few places in Israel that has hosted a Jewish population more or less continuously over the last 1,000 years. A historic center of Jewish mysticism, it attracted a steady flow of religious scholars and other devotees one generation after another. Isolated in the hills, it was sufficiently remote that the conquering armies that claimed Jerusalem, some ninety miles to the south, never paid much attention to it, and the town thrived through the centuries as a religious center and gathering spot for exiled prophets and sages. When Jerusalem was re-conquered by Jews in two stages in 1948 and 1967, and its glory as the capital of Judaism was fully restored, Tsfat might have lost some of its spiritual appeal. But as the sages of Orthodox Judaism converged in Jerusalem, Tsfat became an outpost for a more eclectic mix of free thinkers. Today, its winding stone passages are home to a blend of artists, philosophers, and spiritual seekers. It was past their doors, most of them open, that I strolled.

From a particularly pleasant little plaza, by the meeting of two walks, came the soft sound of a guitar being played, accompanied by the steady singing of a man's voice. In this environment one might expect rhythmic chanting in Hebrew, but instead came English words, and songs of a different time and place: "Blowin' in the Wind." Then, "Yesterday," followed by a Cat Stevens song.

The bearded singer occupied a second-floor balcony. He was wearing a *kippa* and a black prayer shawl, like an Orthodox rabbi, and strumming an old guitar held comfortably across his lap, like a veteran folk singer. He appeared to be in his forties, but he had the tanned, weather-beaten look of a drifter that made identifying his age difficult.

What was an Orthodox Jew like this doing in Tsfat, strumming the Beatles on his guitar?

"I am just a quiet, singular man," he said.

His name is Daniel Yedidya. Born in Morocco, he spent 20 years in Quebec as a young man, and emigrated to Israel in 1995, after a religious awakening. Now he lives in Tsfat, alone, and spends his days praying, studying religious texts, and performing a mixture of odd jobs for his neighbors.

This was a time in Israel when everyone was talking about politics, a military pullout from Hebron, the fortunes of Netanyahu — an exceptionally beleaguered prime minister even by Israeli standards — and the antics of his religious coalition partners.

Yedidya was not so interested in politics, however. Orthodox and ultra-Orthodox Jews had voted almost to a man in the 1996 election for their candidates, but Yedidya said he hadn't voted at all.

"I don't want to be put in a box. People always want to put you in a box, and once you get there it is very hard to get out.

"Parties are a game," he continued. "Politics are a game. My rabbi told me who to vote for, but I only smiled and kept quiet until the vote was over. I did not want to play."

Everything that he uttered emerged, convincingly, as if from a reservoir of total peace, and although he never mentioned God, he repeatedly spoke of "the spirit." He said that he loved Israel; that he felt proud and inspired by the "daring people who choose to live here." He spoke with quiet satisfaction about his own life as an Israeli and as a religious person.

Had he any advice for his fellow Israelis — about religion, about peace, about nationhood?

"Look," he said placidly, "Israel is a beautiful country. It is a spiritual country. I wish peace for Israel. But other people must decide for themselves; they must decide about spirituality each one alone. For me, I want to wake up in the morning and smell the fresh air, and I want to let others do the same."

Here, quite possibly, was one of the few spiritually contented persons in Israel. Not simply a person content with his religion, but one whose entire spirit, whose whole existence as an Israeli, was unconflicted, at peace.

He achieved this by making a choice that very few Israelis make. He chose to confine his reverence to the spiritual domain alone, keeping it out of politics and forswearing any role for himself in determining the future of the state.

His brand of religion conjures up no difficulties. Without or within.

Beyond

Nothing holy in sight: The Tel Aviv beach (photograph by Herman Chananya).

For almost five decades, Israel was led by its founders: men and women who were present at the beginning; who gathered in a small, echoing auditorium in Tel Aviv and declared the state of Israel; who led tank brigades to the gates of Jerusalem; who built the defenses of the nation. With the moral authority and special aura that attached itself naturally to their deeds, they led Israel forward — widely trusted to see the nation safely through the perils of war and the sacrifices of peace.

They have appeared in this book like characters in a novel: the utopian Herzl, the determined Ben-Gurion, the unsung Eshkol and the oversung Dayan, the enigmatic Begin. Rabin, who watched the rising sun of peace from afar, and his impossible partner Peres, who got close enough to touch it and was burned, were the last.

But, as with any country in its sixth decade, Israel is a nation whose founding generation is nearly gone. With the passing of those founders, and of the legion of Holocaust survivors that accompanied them, a young Jewish nation now faces its future unbound by the vision of Israel that they represented. Now, a different generation of Israelis faces a changed world — both outside of Israel and within it.

The conflict between Jews and Arabs has dominated Middle East politics since Israel's inception. For much of that time, the Arabs fought with the hope that the Jewish state was only a temporary thing — that with enough resistance it would collapse like a sand castle under a rising tide. But Israel's sheer determination, and the gradual tiring on both sides, created a willingness to find out if peace could bring the accommodation that war could not. For Rabin and Arafat, it seemed to be workable. For extremist factions in both the Arab and Jewish camps, it did not.

And yet, as the year 2000 dawns, the peace process seems perhaps perturbable, but not reversible. Even Benjamin Netanyahu, whose rise to power was built on a lifelong belief in a "Greater Israel" and a hard line toward the Palestinians, could not ultimately renounce the half-finished land-for-peace process he inherited.

Over the years Netanyahu had been a brilliant defender of Likud's policy of holding on to the West Bank, emphasizing a seemingly pragmatic security argument instead of the historical and religious claims that had been less convincing with swing voters in Israel and with world opinion. But unlike Shamir, for example, Netanyahu had other goals. In particular, he wanted spectacular prosperity for Israel. In that sense, he did not appear willing to pay an unlimited economic, political and security price to hold onto the West Bank.

Because of these cross purposes, Netanyahu neither abrogated the Oslo accords — as many of his supporters had hoped and expected — nor adopted their spirit, which would have required him to treat the Palestinians as equals, even friends, and accept the unwritten terminus of a Palestinian state in the West Bank and Gaza. Netanyahu tried to find some indeterminate middle ground.

After tormenting itself for its first eight months in office, the Netanyahu government agreed to withdraw from part of Hebron in early 1997, as the Oslo II Accord negotiated by Rabin and Peres had promised. Then, to placate the right wing on which his coalition depended, Netanyahu proceeded to expand West Bank settlements, haggle interminably over the implementation of the rest of Oslo II (two more pullbacks in the West Bank) and generally project distrust and hostility toward the Palestinians. His unilateral decision to open a new archeological tunnel under the Temple Mount in Jerusalem led to violent Palestinian riots, and a botched attempt to assassinate a Hamas leader in Amman, Jordan, a year later deeply damaged Israel's relationship with King Hussein. Both episodes took place within Netanyahu's first 15 months in office, bringing international condemnation upon the state for the first time since the start of the peace process and setting the tone for Netanyahu's devil-may-care governance.

As Netanyahu dodged and parried, refusing to move Israel in any clear direction, the entire country seemed to fall into a trance. The economy slumped into recession, unemployment grew, national unions went on a seemingly endless series of strikes, and in the spring of 1998 the fiftieth anniversary came and went with subdued celebrations and a certain amount of rancor over the distribution and use of celebration funds.

While the nation went about its daily business as though everything was fine, a kind of malaise was perceptible, as if everyone, like Netanyahu, was talking around the big issues, knowing all the while that things could not go on forever as they were and that the other shoe could drop at any moment. A sense of stagnation and unfulfilled expectations seeped into media coverage of just about everything: peace, the stock market, Israel's involvement in Lebanon, the future of the nation.

Quietly, imperceptibly, frustration was building over the incomplete peace process and the political and economic limbo in which it left Israel, and Netanyahu began sounding a little desperate in his justifications for further stalling.

In October 1998, about to lose the centrists within his delicate coalition, Netanyahu finally traveled to the United States and signed the Wye River Accord with Arafat. Israel agreed to President Clinton's proposal to withdraw from another 13 percent of the West Bank to complete the implementation of Oslo II, and Arafat agreed to once again abrogate the anti–Israel sections of the PLO charter and (once again, with gusto) promised to fight terrorism. But before the ink had dried Netanyahu was badmouthing the accord to placate the right; after carrying out a tiny fraction of the promised pullback he froze the accord amid accusations, contradicted by the Americans, that Arafat had not done his part.

So magnificently confusing, so artfully deceptive was Netanyahu that no one could say for sure what if anything he was trying to achieve. Perhaps he was simply trying to put off the Palestinian issue, leaving it for his eventual successors to deal with as they saw fit. Alternately, he may have been hoping to kill the peace process in as subtle a way as he could, confusing the issue of blame and reducing the certain backlash. Or maybe he had secretly adopted Labor's general goals and was just trying to drive a hard bargain while easing his rightist constituency onto the peace train.

At various times he hinted at all three. But whatever his intentions, the last option appears to be what he achieved. By meeting with Arafat and later condemning him, by constantly swearing fealty to peace while pursuing policies of confrontation, by withdrawing a little here and seizing a little there — in essence, by transforming his opposition to Oslo into a relative thing rather than an absolute — Netanyahu weakened the objections of his fellow right-wing Israelis to territorial compromise. His get-tough slogan regarding the Palestinians was not something obviously rejectionist — like "Hell no to Oslo"— but almost acquiescing. "They have to *give* to *get*," he would bellow. It sounded like a war cry in tone; in substance, however, it was acceptance of the principle of land for peace.

With the benefit of hindsight, the supremely confident Netanyahu cuts a somewhat tragic figure a little reminiscent of Peres. He injected believable passion into a vision that even many of his political opponents shared, one that seduced American backers but was sadly beyond his reach: an Israel friendly to investment and business, a prospering high-tech powerhouse, an intellectual and entrepreneurial Garden of Eden. But such a vision could not be achieved while scuffling with the Arabs, angering world leaders, and running a chaotic, crisis-plagued government dependent on the extreme right and religious parties for its existence.

Thus, within two months of signing and then abandoning the Wye accords, Netanyahu's government collapsed under the weight of its own contradictions. The Knesset, whose factions had been aligning and realigning for months in a threat to dissolve, finally voted in December 1998 to do so in favor of new elections, setting them for May — a year and a half early.

If, in the 1996 elections, the new, deeply splintered character of Israeli society had emerged for the first time, the 1999 campaign made it all the more obvious that the nation was ready to finish the peace process and move on to other issues. A record 33 parties registered to compete, representing everything from religious fundamentalism to the legalization of marijuana to the rights of retirees and the protection of the environment. There were at least seven parties representing various ethnic groups. The nightly broadcast of campaign ads on TV, running one after another for thirty minutes straight every evening at 8:30, provided a kaleidoscopic peek at a society bursting with things to talk about and axes to grind. Truly, new national agendas had emerged.

The key match-up for prime minister, pitting Netanyahu against Labor Party leader Ehud Barak, was, as usual, as much about the past as it was the future. Barak, Israel's most decorated soldier and head of the army under Rabin, leaned heavily on his military credentials during the campaign. His involvement in the freeing of a hijacked Sabena airliner near Tel Aviv in 1972 was featured heavily in the campaign ads. In a black and white photograph that appeared over and over, commando leader Barak, disguised in workman's overalls, is seen stepping over a dead Palestinian hijacker on the wing of the plane — playing directly to the military machismo that is a central element in Israeli culture. The ads did not mention the extraordinary fact that one of Barak's team members in that famous rescue was Netanyahu.

Barak also wisely played down his tired, if grand, old party and cobbled together a bloc he called "One Israel." Trying to bridge the nation's emerging ethnic and religious divides, he brought in the Sephardic party of David Levy, who had quit as Netanyahu's foreign minister, as well as the moderate religious group Meimad. On top of that there was a new Barak-allied centrist party led by Yitzhak Mordechai and Dan Meridor, who had earlier resigned as Netanyahu's defense and finance ministers, respectively. Along with other Likud defectors, they paraded around the country denouncing Netanyahu as everything from a liar to an incompetent to an egomaniac.

Netanyahu seemed out of touch, rattled, and virtually alone. He trumpeted his achievements in lowering inflation and terrorism — only three major suicide bombings during his tenure. He also tried to revive the tactic that had been so successful against Peres: accusing Labor of being soft on the Arabs. But that didn't stick too well to the former military chief.

Meanwhile, Netanyahu was pilloried by the media and the academic and cultural "elites" whom he frequently blamed for society's ills (but obviously belonged to anyway). He was silently opposed by government professionals, business leaders, and top army brass. As the election approached he was abandoned by key Likud allies, who in impressive numbers allied themselves with Barak. Even the religious parties that had been the backbone of his administration, including Shas, were slow to endorse the incumbent prime minister, carefully trying to avoid locking themselves out of the next governing coalition should Netanyahu lose.

By May 1999, a substantial majority of Jewish Israelis were resigned to a Palestinian state and growing tired of the ever-maneuvering Netanyahu. Remaining disagreements over the exact nature of the final agreements with the Palestinians were not enough to prevent a voter flight to Barak, who promised to pull the army out of Lebanon, revive the economy, and run a less chaotic government.

On Monday, May 17, in balloting in which 78 percent of the electorate cast votes, Barak ousted the incumbent by a margin of more than 12 percentage points — an enormous landslide in Israeli terms. Twenty-eight minutes after the first exit polls were broadcast, Netanyahu gracefully conceded defeat and, with tears in his eyes, announced his resignation from the leadership of the Likud party.

By midnight, just two hours after the polls had closed, a raucous, ecstatic crowd of more than 100,000 people was dancing and partying in Rabin Square in Tel Aviv. Barak showed up at 2:30 A.M. and gave his victory speech before a crowd that by then was tired, a little tipsy, and perhaps a bit bewildered by the sight of him upon that particular plaza, embracing that particular widow, Leah Rabin, and shaking hands with that particular anachronism, Peres, who himself was showered with a sustained, almost forgiving applause. He stood before it unsmiling, erect and dignified — as a man of his generation would.

The results of the Knesset vote were no less fascinating. Barak's "One Israel" came in first, with 26 seats, although that represented a loss from 1996, when Labor pulled in 34. Some of the lost seats probably went to the new Center Party, which got 6 seats, and the revived, now anti-religious group Shinui, which also got 6. Labor's first and best ally, Meretz, got 10 seats.

Meanwhile, the vast majority of Russian immigrants voted for two Russian parties, which together received 10 seats. Shas got a huge vote from the Sephardic public, giving it a whopping 17 — almost as much as the sadly diminished Likud, at 19. In fact, Likud's precipitous fall from 32 seats almost certainly provided for the boost in Shas's fortunes. Virtually all Israeli Arabs voted for Arab parties, giving them a record 10 seats. The Orthodox and ultra-Orthodox parties of the Ashkenazim together hauled in 10 seats, and an ultra-right settler party got 4 seats.

The total number of parties that won seats, 15, broke the record of the 1996 elections by 2. More tellingly, the seats were spread around more evenly. Thus the new Knesset fully reflected the people's interest in issues beyond the peace process; more than ever in 50 years, their votes did not ultimately turn on the Arab-Israeli conflict or peace. Instead it was citizenship, ethnicity, and religion.

In short, the future of the nation.

Indeed, whatever Barak or future leaders do, I think a certain kind of peace will come. It's just unlikely to be the idealistic peace of wildflowers and brotherhood that Peres touted.

To be sure, any combination of Israelis and Arabs in a given room can take a stab at forgiveness, and often they might succeed. Any combination of regional leaders, or leaderships, can do this too. But the problem is that there is absolutely no way that everyone on the Arab side — especially among the Palestinians, who have such a legitimate gripe against Israel — can be mollified in the foreseeable future.

There's nothing Israel can do to satisfy extremist Palestinians other than rolling up the Zionist project and leaving on the next boat. Those Palestinians — a small but extremely potent minority — are willing to carry out horrific acts of violence against Israel, given the chance. So a peace of open borders means a continued threat of violence and terrorism, regardless of what Israel concedes to its more moderate Palestinian partners in the peace process.

As illustrated in the closing years of the 1990s, terrorism can do significant damage to the peace process because it inflames anti-peace sentiment. It reinforces and appears to confirm the stereotype in Israel that "Arabs" can't be trusted; that "Arabs" don't want peace; that "Arabs" hate Israel; that there is no one to do business with.

Put simply, if terrorism can't be controlled, there will never be peace.

Therefore, sadly, Israel and the Palestinians will probably conclude that in their case, good fences are the only thing that will make good neighbors. Barak certainly understands this, and he espouses the less-than-brotherly concept of "separation." This probably means that once the borders are set they will be fenced, patrolled and otherwise made difficult to cross. "Israeli Arabs" may have difficulty visiting "Palestinian" relatives a few miles away. Cross-border cooperation would be heavily regulated.

This is not the stuff of Nobel peace prizes. It's much more alluring to talk about cooperation, and economics prevailing over politics, and a new world without borders. But that kind of ambitious agenda in the past has led to exploding buses, and the sad fact for Israel is that even among Arabs who are ready for a truce, there are many who do not fully accept the Jewish state, who are still potential enemies, who have still not forgiven the fact that the Jews showed up and took a central part of the region away. This is particularly striking in the case of Arab intellectuals and professionals in Egypt, Jordan and elsewhere, whose frequent anti–Israel stand is much at odds with the overwhelming mobilization of their Israeli counterparts for the peace camp. (The interesting exception appears to be among Palestinians, where intellectuals are generally pro-peace). All this stands in the way of the perfect peace envisioned by Peres.

Yet an imperfect peace seems possible. It will probably not be a peace of friendship, or even true acceptance. Not for a very long while. But it will bring to a close the Arab-Israeli conflict as we have known it, and end Israel's long struggle with the occupied territories of 1967.

Such a deal is on the table, actually. It was reached in secret talks between Labor's Yossi Beilin and Mahmoud Abbas (Abu Mazen) just five days before Rabin's assassination. Two years later, sitting in the small Tel Aviv office where this non-binding agreement was concluded, Beilin laid out the plan's parameters:

•žA Palestinian state would be established in most of the West Bank and Gaza.

•žIsrael would annex small parts of the West Bank, mostly along the Israel–West Bank border, where the vast majority of the settlers live, and along the Jordan Valley, as a protection against incursion from the east; the remote settlements would either be dismantled or their residents could choose to become — however improbably — Palestinian citizens.

•žThe Palestinians would have their capital on the outskirts of Jerusalem, but Israel would also give them control over Muslim holy sites and in particular the Al-Aqsa Mosque on the Temple Mount.

This plan was too daring for Peres to embrace before the 1996 election. Beilin predicted that had Peres been elected it would have been implemented within a few months. It was in deep freeze under Netanyahu. With Labor now back at the helm, it might return to favor. In any case it's difficult to imagine that if a peace settlement is reached one day, it would be very different from this plan.

"This solution is ... a fair compromise which does not humiliate any side, which meets their vital needs," the intellectual, soft-spoken Beilin said sadly. "The question in my eyes is only when, and what the price and the death toll will come to until we achieve something like it."

When the peace process is finally complete, then — and only then — will Israelis be free at last to turn to the burning question of what kind of society they want theirs to be. Herzl had his ideas, of course, as did the founding generation of leaders. But Zionism has left much undecided about who the true Israeli should be.

In 1956, trying to defuse the conflict with the Arabs and resolve the question of who is an Israeli, a group of intellectuals published *The Hebrew Manifesto*. In the words of one of its authors, journalist and pacifist Uri Avneri, "Zionism was a tremendous revolution, but after the establishment of the state it became an impediment, imposing on the country myths whose time has passed."

The *Manifesto*, therefore, sought to establish real equality for the Israeli Arabs and build peaceful ties with the region. It favored a Palestinian state alongside Israel and supported other post-colonial nationalist movements in the Arab world. It called for separation of religion and state and accused the nascent Israeli government of fostering not the freedoms and liberal values promised in the Proclamation of Independence but rather "Jewish separatism [and] nationalist mystique." It said the state was suppressing individual rights in favor of "lifeless conformist norms."

This was the first attempt to look beyond the vision of the founders who, still being very much around, gave it no consideration whatever, sweeping it under the rug instead. There the *Manifesto* remained for three decades before reemerging in a new stream of thought called "post-Zionism."

Post-Zionism grew out of the work of so-called "new historians" like Benny Morris who, in the late 1980s, exposed the fact that many of the Arabs who were always believed to have fled Israel in 1948-49 had actually been expelled. Post-Zionist historian Ilan Pappe argued that the supposedly outnumbered Israelis were actually stronger than all the invading Arab armies in the 1948-49 war. The new historians revealed that Ben-Gurion had refused several peace overtures by the Arabs because he did not want to give up the spoils of that war, chief among them sole control over the Sea of Galilee.

Then came political scientists like Baruch Kimerling, asking difficult questions about Israel's democracy. Did it suffer from built-in racism and elements of theocracy? Did it suppress the individual?

Kimerling argued in 1996 in *Ha'aretz* that because Israel had not yet completed its nation-building phase, and because its nation-building was based partly on religion, Israel's democracy was sadly lacking. Beyond the oppression of the Palestinians in the West Bank and Gaza and the second-class status of Israeli Arabs, he argued that even the supposedly preferred group — the Jews of Israel proper — were living in a twisted, coercive environment. He asserted that the secular majority were, by dint of Israeli history and its imperfect institutions, regularly subjected to an array of unwanted religious impositions.

"The Land of Israel was not chosen [by the Zionists] for its land, its cheap workforce or its markets but out of religious ideological motivation," Kimerling wrote. "This fact made Zionism [an] essentially religious enterprise ... dependent on religious symbols, ideas, and scriptures even when ... its prophets, priests, builders and fighters saw themselves as utterly secular."

In its fullest manifestation, post–Zionism would wipe out all the elements of official Israel that are geared toward drawing in the world's Jews and maintaining them as a separate unit from the non–Jews of the country. Gone would be the Law of Return that stipulates that anyone even barely Jewish can come, while Palestinians one generation removed are locked out. In its place would be the kind of restrictive, regular naturalization laws that most countries have. Gone would be "Hatikva," the national anthem one million non–Jewish citizens can't relate to at all. And gone would be the kid gloves with which society tolerates the ultra–Orthodox agenda of turning Israel into a theocracy. Post–Zionism would enact a modern, egalitarian constitution without hesitation. It would abolish the religious monopoly over marriage and other personal status issues as well as the state-sanctioned monopoly of Orthodoxy in Jewish religious affairs.

The social engineering that invades every part of life here would be over, too. No longer would there be a national effort (run by an entire government ministry!) to "absorb" immigrants into the Israeli way. No longer would the Western orientation receive preference: Israel could just as easily join the Arab League as the European Union (and most likely neither). No longer would the "Jewish" character of the state be officially paramount. The state would have whatever character its people naturally created.

Some of post–Zionism's views have already gained favor in recent years, perhaps another reflection of the gradual fading of the founding generation. The fact that a majority of Israelis grudgingly accept that they must divide the land between themselves and the Palestinians reflects the first step forward.

There are also subtler undercurrents, such as the 1995 decision by the government to no longer require its representatives abroad to adopt Hebrew names in an effort at enforced Israeliness. Ben-Gurion (born "Green") had set the heavy-handed tone by personally overseeing name changes like that of his protégé Peres. Premiers Golda Meir ("illuminating") and Yitzhak Shamir ("dill"), born Meyerson and Yzernitzky, respectively, set an example followed by legions of Israelis and imposed on diplomats and top army officers. But after decades this policy was finally deemed a violation of basic rights and discarded.

One promising young officer, Amnon Lipkin, changed his name to Shahak ("grind to powder"). In 1994 he became the military chief of staff, bearing a name that was perfect for the job. However, needing to impress no one any further, he quietly let it be known that he rather liked his original name, and the media dutifully — and without explanation to a confused public — revived "Amnon Lipkin" and in addition created a new name, "Amnon Lipkin-Shahak."

Post-Zionism is also evident in the way other sacred cows are being challenged. The Shin Bet secret service agency is now under constant scrutiny for the way it treats detainees. The fabled Mossad intelligence agency became the subject of a campy TV soap opera, and the once untouchable army is constantly fielding complaints about everything from how it spends its money to whether recruits are allowed to use mobile phones to order pizza.

Post-Zionism, some say, is also evident in the ambivalent fate of the kibbutzim, the communal farms that once produced the cream of Israel's army, politicians, and thinkers. The kibbutzim were admired for their Spartan, dedicated lifestyle: equality was strict, everyone did manual labor, and even child-rearing was shared. The kibbutzim were not only part of the world's grand socialist experiment, they were seen as a core success of Zionism.

Today they are slowly declining. The entire kibbutz movement survived on the strength of a huge government bailout in the mid-1990s. Some have shut down anyway. Some pay salaries and import foreign workers to plow their fields. Some are selling their land to speculators, and many have turned to industry over agriculture.

Kibbutz Shfayim, just north of Tel Aviv, is one of the most successful. It uses its land off the coastal highway to attract legions of shoppers to a strip mall featuring Toys-R-Us and Office Depot. There is also a water park for kids and a sort of motel. Shfayim's ability to change with the times has been hugely profitable. The community's income is about $40 million a year: $80,000 for each of the 500 members.

I drove there one evening to meet Benny Katznelson, one of the veterans. His last name was familiar to me: when I was a kid we lived just off Katznelson Street, named after Benny's uncle Berl, one of the great thinkers of early Labor Zionism.

A kibbutznik jogging around the community's well-tended track directed me efficiently toward Benny's little house, never breaking his stride. As I approached, I saw him through the window, an elderly man with a full head of white hair and a mustache. The door was open, and I walked in.

Benny, who has lived on the kibbutz all of his 65 years, welcomed me into his study, a pleasant room whose walls are lined with hundreds of books on topics ranging from impressionist art to world history to Judaism. He sat next to a personal computer and reminisced about his childhood visits to Uncle Berl's apartment in Tel Aviv.

"It's the bananas I remember," Benny said, eyes twinkling. "He would put these big plates full of bananas on the dining room table. I remember thinking, 'How rich they must be here in Tel Aviv, to have so many bananas.' We couldn't dream of such luxury on the kibbutz!"

Today, Benny has no trouble at all filling his refrigerator with bananas. But he seems to take little joy in the kibbutz's prosperity. He had been proud, he said, of the life of labor in the past, despite the deprivations. And he recognized that everything must evolve, even the kibbutz. But, he sighed, "We might be changing too fast."

Benny has a thesis, which he bases on the traditional saying *Col Yisrael arevim ze le-ze*, or "All the people of Israel are each other's guarantors."

"There really *is* such a thing as Jewish togetherness. It's the reason why Jewish fundraising in America is so effective. It's the reason we survived a 2,000-year Diaspora. We need it. And the kibbutz, with its old ways, was the manifestation of this in the secular side of Israel. There were always relatively few kibbutzniks, but they represented this great Jewish communal ethic, and in this sense they made the whole Zionist effort worthwhile. If the kibbutz abandons its ways, what will we have to compete with the religious community's brand of Jewish togetherness? Nothing."

Benny's face hardened. Without the values represented by the kibbutz, without the Jewish communal ethic, he said, "All we are is an uninteresting, unimportant suburb of New York."

I hear this a lot: if Israel isn't something truly remarkable, if it doesn't stand for a lofty ideal or redefine the meaning of human existence, why bother? Just being a country like all the others is not good enough, it seems.

This is especially true of secular Israelis. "Why are we in Israel?" they are constantly asking themselves. The obvious answer — Jewish nationalism of Herzl's variety — is uncomfortable to them because nationalism has discredited itself so badly in the twentieth century and, in its worst manifestation, focused its evil on the Jews so unforgettably.

So to feel their Israeliness is justified, they look for some higher meaning in it, tying themselves up in a thousand knots. Ambition, pride, megalomania, and, ultimately, self-flagellation are all there, all part of the complicated national psyche.

Viewed without ideology, Israel is doing quite well for a small former colony with practically no natural resources and a mountain of challenges. The standard of living it has afforded its citizens is by far the highest in the region and is fast approaching that of the most advanced countries in the West. This is astonishing considering that the country bears a colossal defense burden and has been building an economy for little more than a few decades. It's safe to say that Israel is vastly richer than the countries of Eastern Europe and the Middle East from which most of its people emigrated.

Israel also has a tremendous concentration of engineers, scientists, and doctors, in large part due to immigration from the former Soviet Union. Its population is one of the world's quickest in adopting new technologies, with cable TV in 90 percent of homes, personal computers in 40 percent, and more mobile phones per capita than anywhere in the world except Hong Kong. Indeed, for the uninitiated, the omnipresence of the chirping contraptions in grocery stores, sidewalk cafes, and cars, where every passenger seems to have one, can be unsettling.

But Israel's penchant for technology extends beyond the consumer. It is a world leader in agricultural technology — its famous drip-irrigation system is what makes the desert bloom — as well as military technology, computers, and communications. Israeli companies, which in 1996 were second only to Canada in listings on American stock exchanges, play a disproportionate role in dynamic new fields like Internet-related software.

But none of this is anywhere near good enough for most Israelis. Because from the beginning, the Zionist movement was afflicted with megalomania.

Continuing a tradition that saw the Jews as God's "chosen people," Theodor Herzl advised his people that they were "too fine" to assimilate into their host nations. Should they set up an independent state, he crowed, "The world will be freed by our liberty, enriched by our wealth, magnified by our greatness." The man who carried out his vision, David Ben-Gurion, invoked the phrase "a light unto the nations" to describe Israel.

Reality, of course, has not quite lived up to all this. Though successful in their enterprise of building a state, it is not altogether clear just how sturdy an edifice Israel's founders created. And the "light unto the nations" ideal is a little weak considering that much of the world associates Israel more closely with the brutality and injustice it has dealt the Palestinians than with being a guiding light in human affairs.

Neither has Israel turned out to be a perfect home for the Jews themselves. Because of its inability to resolve its conflict with the Arabs, more Jews have been killed in Israel, in absolute and relative terms, than anywhere else since its establishment. Jews living here face more dangers than do their counterparts in any Western country taken as a whole. And for all the country's recent economic advances, Israel still offers its citizens less economic opportunity than does the United States, where most of the rest of the world's Jewish population has located itself.

Nonetheless, the "higher purpose" so many Israelis believe they are serving explains to me why the Jews—who in the United States produced Lenny Bruce, Woody Allen, Mel Brooks, Groucho Marx, George Burns, and Jerry Seinfeld, to name just a few comedians and entertainers—are so serious all the time in Israel.

This quality was particularly striking to me after I returned to Israel from my stint in Romania in 1993. I had spent three years in a situation I can best describe as mirthful. Partly, it had to do with the euphoria in that country at the collapse of communism, even though their own form of capitalism kept most people mired in poverty. But regardless of the actions of bumbling governments, Romanians preserved their joie de vivre. They knew how to have a great time. They knew how to laugh at themselves. They maintained a light perspective on life.

One of Romania's favorite phrases is *nu e locul, e dobitocul*, which, very loosely translated, means, "It doesn't matter where you are, it matters who you are."

Israelis often seem to think the opposite. Society here is geared to the idea that the be-all and end-all of life is one's presence in Israel. Even the Hebrew words used to describe immigration to Israel, and emigration from it, convey a value judgment: *aliyah*, ascension; *yerida*, descent. On Rosh Hashana, the Jewish New Year, the Central Bureau of Statistics ceremoniously releases population figures for the year just ended. Every major paper publishes these in front-page headlines that read like the winning score of a football game. Being here and being counted is serious business in Israel.

Despite a few recent TV satires that have sprouted up, Israelis are overpoweringly serious about their country. Foreigners who spend any time here are amazed at their stamina in braving hours upon hours of political debate. If two Israelis met at a bathhouse in Bombay, the chances are good that they would soon be sitting in a corner of the sauna debating which West Bank settlements should be annexed as part of the final status deal with the Palestinians, and whether Labor or Likud would negotiate the better deal.

This self-seriousness is fed by the intense and unique overexposure Israel receives in the world media. The situation is extreme: Israel/Palestine is a problem directly affecting a population of less than 9 million people. But over the past half century it has received far more attention in the Western press than, say, the progress and setbacks of India, which affect a population 100 times greater. Other small nations have temporarily seized center stage — like Bosnia during its 1992–95 civil war — but none with the staying power and intensity of Israel. Not even close.

Some Israelis who believe their country is getting a bum rap complain about *what* is being exposed and claim the coverage is superficial or distorted to their disadvantage. Many Arabs argue the opposite point. But one thing is clear: the glare of the spotlight has endowed Israeli society with an actor's vanity and ego. It seems to prove to Israelis that the Jews were indeed chosen — although it's not always clear if they were chosen by God or Ted Turner.

The tension between the absurdly high expectations and reality has made Israeli society manic-depressive. On one hand, there is a strong instinct for self-aggrandizement. When Israeli prime ministers addressed the U.S. Congress with record-breaking frequency — such as occurred in 1994–96, with three such appearances — this was no big deal; Israel was obviously just getting its due as a major world power. When the American movie *Independence Day* momentarily depicted Israeli jets taking part in the global battle to defeat alien invaders, there was not a secret smile of pride but a feeling that Israel's military had received the recognition it was due.

But on the other hand, Israel occasionally wilts under its people's merciless self-flagellation. Tell many Israelis that their nation is a backward and impoverished backwater and they will sadly agree, adding nonsensical explanations as to why it is so.

In part, this is because the country is a kaleidoscope of shattered national aspirations. None of its people's various dreams of what Israel should be like can ever be fully realized.

Amos Oz put it to me this way: "There are those who hoped to create here a Marxist paradise. There are those who opted for the re-creation of the Kingdom of David and Solomon. There are those who wanted to create a replica of pre–World War I Austria-Hungary with very good manners.... Now many want America."

Israel is a little of all of these, with a strong dose of North Africa thrown in. But it can never fully duplicate any single model, and its people cannot agree on an entirely new model either. The result is a national zero-sum game. With each step taken in the direction of one model or another, some people rejoice while many others groan.

In their angst, many Israelis have developed a fatalistic tendency to sum themselves up in unflattering generalizations and stereotypes, even though the nation's people emigrated from every continent and exhibit qualities imported from all these diverse places.

The old Zionist effort to create a "new Israeli" did yield some things: Israelis tend to be more brash than Europeans, more improvisational than Japanese, less formal than practically anyone. But the bottom line is that even today about half the Jewish population is foreign-born and consequently foreign-seeming. My parents from Romania and Adisso Masalla, the Ethiopian lawmaker, are both Israelis to the same degree. Yet what traits do they share as Israelis? Not many.

In 1984, while spending a college semester in Israel, I met a young woman named Iris Be'er, the daughter of some old friends of my parents. Sitting in her parents' apartment on the evening we met, I explained to her that I was thinking of returning to Israel after graduation. She struck me as the kind of girl who was looking for a relationship with a future, and I figured this approach, which for once contained more than a grain of truth, would be the most effective.

She looked at me like I was an idiot.

"Are you having social problems in America?" she asked. "Is there something wrong?"

Iris had it all in Israel. She worked, as part of her mandatory two-year army stint, for the head of military intelligence. She was blonde and attractive, had many friends and, it seemed, a comfortable life ahead. When I asked her what she lacked, she could think of nothing. But she found it incomprehensible that I would wish to return.

Yet I did, and eventually we married. Eleven years after we first met, we were together in Tel Aviv singing the "Song to Peace" with Yitzhak Rabin, just moments before the shots rang out.

After the Rabin assassination, there was much hand-wringing in the media about the supposed aberration of "Jew killing Jew." But Jewish internecine conflict existed long before. Twice already it had led to the Jews' undoing as a free people in their homeland.

For all the drama of their return from exile in Egypt (celebrated today in the feast of Passover) and their conquest of the land God had promised Abraham, the Jewish people spent centuries as a bunch of disunited tribes until the united Kingdom of the Israelites was established in 1028 B.C.

This kingdom existed for a century under the Hebrew kings Saul, David (the well-publicized slayer of Goliath), and Solomon. It built the first Holy Temple in Jerusalem and enjoyed prosperity. But after Solomon's death, the kingdom split following a rebellion by the northern tribes. Judea, with its capital in

Jerusalem, remained dependent on alliances with foreign powers; the Kingdom of Israel ruled the north. In 586 B.C. both were overrun by Babylonians, and many Jews were carted off into Babylonian exile.

Fifty years later, the Babylonians were defeated by Persians, and the Jews, under leaders Ezra and Nehemiah, were allowed to return to Jerusalem, build the Second Temple, and establish a new Judea. The festival of Hanukkah celebrates the victory of the Jewish "Maccabee" militia over Greco-Syrians in 165 B.C., which made Judea a fully independent kingdom again.

The century-long rule of the Maccabees (immortalized today through a fine Israeli beer) was bedeviled by civil strife that, according to the Jewish Roman historian Josephus, cost 50,000 Jewish lives. Fanatics called *sikarii* roamed the hills, killing Jews considered insufficiently patriotic. Similar Jewish zealots eventually gained fame for a mass suicide in the Masada fortress just as the Romans were about to overrun it. The Talmud, the great book of Jewish learning, concludes that the Roman victory, the destruction of the Second Temple, and the scattering of the Jews to the winds were all the result of "baseless hatred" among the people.

The Jews survived two millennia of Diaspora, and the modern state of Israel is often referred to as the "Third Temple." Yet, like its predecessors, the Third Temple today is being riven by a new kind of intra–Jewish hatred — and this time it may not be baseless.

The issue of religion in Israel has placed much about the country that was once taken for granted into question. Is a secular Jew a Jew at all? Can a Jewish state be a democracy? Can Israel have any place in this world without ultimately becoming a theocracy?

The secular founders of Israel — whatever their compromises to religion might have been — succeeded in launching a new society based largely on Western values and thought. You may like their handiwork, you may not. But it's what Israel is and, short of all-out civil war, it's what Israel is likely to remain.

Not that the next 50 years will be easy for Israel and its people. The very idea that a democratic state deliberately cultivates contradictory visions of itself through competing branches of its school system is not good for harmony. In the ultra–Orthodox schools, increasing numbers of children go through years of study learning only the most minimal math, science, or history.

"We won't be the ones producing engineers. So what? We'll produce the rabbis," says Shlomo Benizri, the outspoken and quite charming Knesset member from Shas, justifying his party's schools.

"Isn't your goal to expand until everyone is like you?" I ask.

"Of course," he confirms.

"And then where would we get engineers?"

"Maybe we can import them from Japan the way we import workers from Thailand and Romania," Benizri offers.

"But if we're all studying the Torah all day, where would we get money to pay these Japanese engineers?" I ask.

Benizri laughs and gives in. "Look, having an advanced economy is very nice, but I'll take having good Jewish culture over it any day."

It is a friendly enough conversation, but the civility is a veneer.

The religious are staging an assault on the nation's "elites," a euphemism for the establishment and its functioning civil democracy. The ultimate goals are to replace civil courts with rabbinical courts (which presently exist and can be turned to voluntarily in many cases), to supplant universities with seminaries for Torah study, and to scrap the Knesset in favor of councils of Torah sages.

The religious offensive violates an unspoken contract that has existed in Israel ever since its founding: that the country will be essentially a liberal democracy, but one that tips its hat to Jewish tradition. The religious have unbalanced this equation so badly that many among the country's secular majority are starting to equate religion itself with fundamentalist militancy, driving both sides to an increasingly angry and entrenched intolerance of the other.

Many of my secular friends used to fast on Yom Kippur, the annual Day of Atonement, as is traditional. It was a pleasing reminder of the traditions that unified the Jews for generations. But fewer and fewer respect this traditional fast. These days, avoiding the fast is a statement, one of the small ways in which one can register displeasure at the religious camp's effort to transform the country.

Given everything that's at stake, it's difficult to simply say "live and let live" — the two visions of what kind of country Israel should be are just too incompatible. And for the secular, there is an added concern: the prodigious birthrate of the ultra-Orthodox camp, where families of 10 and 12 children are not uncommon. Most people tiptoe around this delicate issue, but I know few informed secular people who are not worried about it.

Professor Menachem Friedman, an expert on the religious at Bar-Illan University, believes the demographic dynamic will change because the ultra-Orthodox already can't support themselves, and secular society's willingness to subsidize them will reach a limit. Their lack of family planning and their mass reliance on state subsidies are relatively new phenomena for the ultra-Orthodox, and they will have to end, Friedman says.

But if he's wrong, the ultra-Orthodox could grow from a small minority to about a third of the population in two generations, and eventually become a majority. That would obliterate the Israel that exists today. It would make a mockery of Herzl's vision. I can see myself as a bent old man walking by synagogues that used to be my favorite bars, record stores, and bookshops, encountering segregation of the sexes at every turn, being ruled by rabbis.

Many secular Israelis prefer to point to the country's Westernization, to the gains of secular culture over the years. They have a point. However vocal the current religious assault can be, and despite the demographic issue, the fact is that 30 years ago much of Israel was shut down on the Sabbath and today this is no longer the case. Whereas Israel was once depressingly insular, today it is completely connected to the global village. "In the end, really, we're winning the war," they claim.

Maybe so—but it's a costly war that casts a shadow over the land. It is energy wasted, opportunities lost, children condemned to poverty. The burden for Israel will be large, and around the corner may lie a serious clash betwen supporters of these conflicting world views.

But before this issue can be tackled, one precondition must first be satisfied: reaching peace with the Arabs, first and foremost with the Palestinians. This is the issue that divides the Israeli left and right into antagonistic camps, each desperate to prevail. This is what makes the leaders of both sides court the religious with hypocritical deference and truckloads of state funding. And this is what has created an appetite among the religious to actively pursue their otherwise unattainable dream of a Jewish theocracy.

Only with the main problem — war and peace with the Arabs — out of the way, will Israel be able to turn to the question of religion. And then Netanyahu and Barak — and their supporters — will find themselves on the same side.

Thus it's not certain, but it is possible, that the end of the Arab-Israeli conflict will remove the wall that divides the people now comprising the Israeli right and the left, and the majority of them will unite against the fundamentalists. This need not necessarily create conflict with the religious. With the loss of their power could well come a diminishing of their appetite and, critically, of their mutually destructive economic dependence on the state as well.

I am reminded again of Thomas Jefferson. In his first draft of the Declaration of Independence in 1776 he included a passage that would have freed America's slaves. In a heated debate in the Continental Congress in Philadelphia, southern delegates declared that if the clause remained they would vote against independence. Despite his grave misgivings, Jefferson was ultimately persuaded to relent. The clause was stricken.

It took more than 80 years for America to produce Abraham Lincoln, a president capable of doing what the founders had left undone. It took still another century for real civil rights laws to be established, and the process of reconstituting American society is still incomplete two centuries after its founding.

Israel's struggle with religion is analogous. Finding a way to somehow heal this destructive societal rift is the greatest challenge facing the nation.

I grew up in King of Prussia, Pennsylvania, a patch of green flatland with a huge shopping center, a sprinkling of split-story homes, and a few apartment blocks such as the one where my family lived—all connected to Philadelphia by 18 miles of ramshackle expressway that my father was always said to be redesigning.

It was not a glamorous place. When the high school football team played neighboring Norristown, it was big news. If they won, that was history in the making.

It was there that I got my first taste of journalism. I started as a photographer for the weekly *King of Prussia Courier*, then gradually started writing. It was not demanding work; the town was quiet and uneventful, for the most part. But I loved what I was doing, and to my parents' chagrin, I chose journalism as my eventual career.

In media terms, Israel is the polar opposite of King of Prussia. Scandal and uproar are the norm. Periods of stability and repose are few and far between. It's an exciting situation, but it's also a powerful grind. I can never relax by the TV and watch reports of the latest terrorist attack or assassination. I must be out there myself, fighting through police to get at the facts, or at my computer late into the night, constantly updating copy. So after work I need, more than most, to really enjoy what's left of the day. That is why, whenever I live in Israel, it absolutely has to be in Tel Aviv.

Tel Aviv, founded in 1909 on coastal sand dunes north of the ancient port of Jaffa, was known as "the first Hebrew city," the first real city that was entirely the invention of Zionism. It's not the prettiest place in the world. Most of it was thrown up in the 1940s and 1950s to accommodate the flood of immigrants, and it still looks like a bunch of Lego pieces blown around a room. But the important thing is that more than anyplace else in Israel it lives up to what Herzl really wanted: a place for the Jews to become, as he saw it, normal.

I sometimes work in Jerusalem, too, but it's an entirely different feeling. I sense tension building in me as I drive up the winding highway through the hills.

The city of stone has a special beauty. The downtown shopping districts show some European flair and much residue of the faded glory of the Ottoman Empire. There is a concerted and generally successful effort to make modern additions to the city aesthetically pleasing. Abutting the downtown of Jewish West Jerusalem is the Old City, a square kilometer surrounded by Ottoman-built stone walls that make it look like a huge fortress. Within those walls is what American journalist P. J. O'Rourke referred to as "God's monkey house."

Here you find ultra-Orthodox Jews praying by the holiest spot in Judaism, the Western Wall, the last remnant of the Second Temple. The wall forms one side of the Temple Mount, where the temple was long ago replaced by the Al-Aqsa Mosque and the golden Dome of the Rock, a complex that is considered the holiest spot on Earth for Muslims, after Mecca and Medina. Many thousands of Palestinians converge there for Friday prayers, and when times are tense the area is crawling with police. Sometimes Muslims try to throw rocks at the ultra-Orthodox Jews gathered on the plaza below.

Sometimes these same ultra-Orthodox Jews scuffle with other Jews, such as the time in July 1997 when they threw diapers full of excrement at their arch-enemies: Reform Jews — American immigrants, mostly — who were minding their own business in a distant corner of the plaza.

A short walk away is the Via Dolorosa, the narrow cobbled street where Christ is believed to have borne the cross, and the Church of the Holy Sepulcher, where he is believed to have been buried and resurrected.

Several thousand Jews now live in the modern "Jewish Quarter" of the Old

City, outnumbered on all sides by the Palestinians who live and work in the teeming alleyways and hovels of the Christian, Muslim, and Armenian quarters.

To the east of the Old City sits a conglomeration of Arab villages surrounded by imposing, recently built Jewish neighborhoods. This is East Jerusalem.

What an unstable cocktail is this beautiful city, the city to which Jews throughout the ages have set their sights, the city that has been transformed from a hilltop village into a magical symbol of their loftiest aspirations. They spoke of "Jerusalem of the heavens" as a spiritual entity, as a higher plane of existence. And the very name of the movement comes from "Zion," a synonym for Jerusalem.

Yet what do we really have here? About 150,000 ultra-Orthodox Jews who live in tense coexistence with twice as many secular Jews, most of whom are blue-collar Sephardim. It is the poorest major city in Israel and the most nationalistic. Within it also reside more than 160,000 discontented East Jerusalem Arabs, most of whom have declined Israel's offer of citizenship.

The Palestinians say East Jerusalem must be their capital. Israel says all the city will remain united under its sovereignty forever. Given the new Jewish neighborhoods that surround much of East Jerusalem, trying to divide the city as it was before the 1967 war would be a nightmare. In any case, giving the Palestinians part of Jerusalem would make it impossible to have a border between Israel and a future Palestine — short of erecting a serpentine wall through the city. Both sides promise to avoid this, saying that Jerusalem will "never be divided" again.

Truly, men have tied a knot that only God can untangle.

The complication of Jerusalem in one way or another touches most of the news that I deal with. But I do this from my office in Tel Aviv, and when I go home, I hardly think of Jerusalem at all. This is true of most of the people who live here. As the problems with Israel compound, they retreat more and more into Tel Aviv. Some consider Jerusalem virtually a foreign country.

There is even fanciful talk of renewing the biblical split between Judea and Israel.

Author Ze'ev Chafets brought it up in 1996 in the *Jerusalem Report* magazine. He noted that many of Orthodoxy's most prominent rabbis are "for profound and sincere reasons, bitterly opposed to Israel's pluralistic form of government, secularist popular culture, and Western civic values" and consider "Western-style democracy, with its civil rights and constitution, to be inherently opposed to God's law and the Torah."

Consequently, Chafets wrote, secular Israelis "fear and dislike the *haredim* more than they do the Arabs." He concluded that "unity slogans notwithstanding, we are not one, but two, with the fault line running between those who want to be ruled by the Torah and those who want to live in a democracy. The difference is so profound that in fact we have become two separate peoples with a common history but no real connection or shared fate."

Chafets sees Jerusalem as the capital of "Judea," where Torah study is the highest value and the government is a ruling council of Orthodox Jewish sages whose courts ensure the media reflects wholesome Jewish values. On Sabbath everything is shut; all restaurants are kosher.

Tel Aviv, meanwhile, would be the capital of Israel, a model democracy with separation of religion and state and a constitution including a full bill of rights. Nonsectarian schools are expected to promote "Israeli culture and values such as democracy, patriotism, tolerance, intellectual curiosity and the scientific spirit."

The borders would be complicated, and some population movement and complex division of property might be needed, but in the final analysis this divorce "is the alternative to Jewish civil war," he wrote. The division would permit today's quarreling Israelis "to live in the Land of Israel as they wish to live, free of political coercion, Kulturkampf, and violent sectarian hatred."

Is separation really necessary? Is civil war possible?

I remember in Yugoslavia most people thought it wasn't. A few years later, hundreds of thousands of them were casualties of war.

The potential for conflict, ironically, comes from something I have thought of with affection all my life: that Israel is a nation of people who mind each other's business. The ultra-Orthodox, the kibbutzniks, the survivors, and everyone else all see Israel as a personal project.

Israelis still constantly intervene in one another's daily affairs. They engage in sidewalk lecturing and debate—not as strangers, with a fit of moral indignation or self-righteous defensiveness, as occurs now in America, but as members of the same big family. This is part of that sense of being part of a larger project, of having a stake in the overall management of the country, that I remember from my childhood.

So I am strangely pleased when I take the trash to the shed outside my apartment building and hear voices of instruction. I look up. An elderly couple is standing in the living room of their ground floor apartment, looking out at me. "Make sure the cardboard boxes are placed separately, not in the main containers," they say. I assure them I will follow these rules.

I am not annoyed with their petty intrusion because in it I see the essence of Israel's fading generation of founders. How much longer will their values—common purpose, common decency—survive the modern era? When they are gone, will the new tenants of that apartment guide me in my ritual of emptying the trash?

The old couple is framed in the middle of a large picture window, lit dimly in the gray tones of the alley, the interior of their home even darker and less distinct behind them. They have a vague European accent. Where were they during the Holocaust? In Romania, perhaps? Did they meet there, a product of tragedy, or did they find each other here, as young people living in a new country? Whatever the case, I want to give them pleasure in their final days, even if simply through a proper handling of the trash.

They are old and bent and do not move or say anything else, they just watch as I finish my task and walk back inside the building.

Out of the corner of my eye they look like a painting: *Israeli Gothic*.

Like the leaders who founded the nation, their generation is dying. With it will go a significant connection to the larger Jewish world, for it was primarily the Holocaust and the survivor generation that, in their ability to move the heart and mind, held Israel and the world's Jews together in the decades that followed Israel's coming out in the 1960s.

When the State of Israel was founded, Jews felt an urgent physical and psychological need for it. The idea of a haven, a place where they would never again be at the mercy of non–Jews, was overpowering. It was what brought many Jews here in the beginning, and what still holds many here today.

Fifty years later, with the passing of the Holocaust generation and the end of the last great wave of immigration from the former Soviet Union, that urgent physical need seems much diminished. But the emotional need for the state lives on, among all the world's Jews. This need is harder to define, less obvious, less immediate than the postwar need for a haven. But Israel is unique among nations in the role it plays in the lives of the Jews, in the maintenance of their very identities.

Israel, as a project, has been the one thing that the world's Jews could get behind and feel part of. This was driven by their need for a vessel of hope and achievement in the wake of the Holocaust. But it was also driven by the underdog odds faced by the new state, and the decades of isolation and warfare it weathered. Through the years it wasn't just Israel that survived, it was the common spirit of world Jewry.

But Israel today is a nation that will increasingly turn to domestic issues in its search for its own path, bringing to center stage issues that Diaspora Jews may not understand, relate to, or even be aware of. They are issues pertaining to everyday life within the state and to relations among its citizens. In these areas, where a certain history has amassed over 50 years, the meddling or involvement of Jews from overseas will probably be less and less welcome. Israelis and Diaspora Jews could increasingly grow apart. Israel beyond fifty will be a nation defined more by its own citizens, less by the world's Jews.

One Saturday I was thinking of the future as I bounced around town with my daughter, Maya, who had just turned two. What kind of country do I want her to live in? What sort of values would I want to define her life? Do I want her to live in a pure democracy, or a country with a strong Jewish feel? How do I want the legacy of Jewishness, which is her birthright, transmitted to her, and to her children? It was a balmy early spring day, and we strolled on the beachfront promenade.

On the beach I met my friend Lenny, who had immigrated recently from Canada and had a high-flying job as an assistant to an Israeli industrial tycoon. We threw a football back and forth over Maya's head as she worked on filling the pockets of my discarded leather jacket with sand. Trance music wafted over from a nearby cafe.

Lenny is an extremely purposeful character at most times. But on this day he was having trouble concentrating on the football. He was thinking of his upcoming blind date. "God, there are a lot of beautiful women here," Lenny sighed, as one walked by.

"Do you think there's an equal degree of physical and spiritual beauty in the world?" I asked. "Is there some cosmic factor that keeps them at the same level? Are they related?"

We looked at the people passing by, the leering musclemen and the beautiful, coquettish women, chewing gum with determination.

"No way," Lenny said. "They're not the slightest bit related."

We discussed what Lenny might do with his date. They could go to a movie. There are about 30, mostly first-run American films, to choose from. Or maybe to the nearby Camelot bar to hear live blues, played Israeli-style. To me, his ability to do this, in a way, was sacrosanct. The reassuring normalcy of bookstores, bars, and record shops, the urban clamor, the vibrant economy and culture — are these not the foundations of a creed?

I think the religious who criticize secular Israelis for lacking spirituality may not understand the spiritual value of "life, liberty, and the pursuit of happiness." They also may not understand the intensity of the modern Israeli culture that has sprung up in the century of Zionism.

It was powerful enough, I now understand, to draw me back to Israel after graduate school.

I remember the song that was a smash hit in Israel when my family left. The singer was Arik Einstein, a beloved pop star of towering national stature who is considered the father of Israeli rock. It was a beautiful, soulful ballad called "Ima Adama" — "Mother Earth." The song etched itself into my soul as profoundly as any prayer. And no matter how American I became, I would still find myself walking my university campus like a zombie and humming it, occasionally wiping away a secret tear and feeling like a fool.

Today Arik Einstein's Israel is under attack. So in July 1997, when his latest album came out, I automatically rushed to buy it on the first day. I had no intention of listening to it before shelling out the money, as I usually do. First, because a sort of religious faith told me it would be fantastic. And second, because I was not only buying an album but making a statement. I was not the only one who felt this way, in that year of growing discontent: I got the last copy at the record store.

I see now that there is a kind of nationalism most people cannot escape. It has to do with not only understanding, but *feeling* the culture of your nation. It is a form of love on a national scale.

Lenny's date was blonde and pretty, her legs wrapped in fashionable black stockings. She looked at Maya. Maya eyed her back unhappily and dragged me away. That was OK with Lenny.

Outside the Opera Tower, Maya spotted a vendor selling balloons in all shapes and colors and demanded one. By her accent, the teenage girl selling the balloons was a recent immigrant from Russia. She recommended a heart-shaped balloon with Minnie Mouse on a silver background. Maya grabbed at the string, indicating approval.

"The sea!" Maya demanded, looking at me with big, questioning eyes, and pointing west. She said it in Hebrew, and my heart swelled. "Sit?"

We sat down on the concrete embankment separating the promenade from the sands of the Tel Aviv beachfront and faced the setting sun. Slowly it turned from orange to purple, dipping beneath a line of clouds and finally descending beneath the waterline. Light came now from the city behind us, from a million light bulbs in the row of tall hotels lined up like dominoes along the beach.

There's nothing holy about these hotels — or is there?

Two barking dogs came over, drawn by the balloon. The owner, a young woman, soon followed, apologizing. "What's his name?" she asked, pointing to Maya.

"Her name," I corrected.

Maya smiled at the dogs and at the woman, who moved on.

"Home!" Maya announced. We got up and headed toward the car.

There are certainly worse places for her to grow up, I thought to myself, than Tel Aviv. It is a friendly, living city whose people are not zealots but are proud to be Israelis because they are comfortable with the Israel their city represents.

Tel Aviv has an ultra-Orthodox minority. With a few exceptions, it has made little effort to change the nature of civic life. It's as if they accept that Tel Aviv is not part of the religious tug-of-war that applies elsewhere in Israel, and first and foremost in Jerusalem. I see them walking around Sheinkin Street, which is an area shared by ultra-Orthodox and the most bohemian of secular Israelis. A place of a few synagogues, many funky fashion outlets, deteriorating buildings. The ultra-Orthodox here appear happier and calmer than their counterparts in embattled Jerusalem, who seem to wear a constant frown.

As Israel searches for its true self, it may have to choose between the earth and the heavens. It may have to undergo a humbling transformation of the spirit.

The next day the air raid sirens wailed over Tel Aviv once more. It was a haunting siren, the kind that sears into your soul and gives you pause. It was a siren very much like the one I had heard 30 years before. It was, it turned out, a siren in memory of the men who had died fighting to protect Israel during the Six Day War, and others.

Memorial Day, for Israel's fallen, is part of secular Israel's special spiritual geometry, coming exactly one week after Holocaust Remembrance Day, when the country remembers the 6 million lost to the Nazis, and one day before the festival of Independence Day, when it celebrates the freedom that rose from the ashes of the inferno.

On the evening of Memorial Day, as Independence Day celebrations were about to commence, Iris and I made plans to watch the spectacular fireworks finale over Rabin Square. Not far from where I spent my early childhood, a few blocks from where Maya was born, at the square where I watched peace crescendo and a great man fall, I would join tens of thousands of my neighbors and fellow Jews as Israel entered its fiftieth year.

We made plans to meet friends at a cafe between our homes, then stroll to a good viewing location together. As the sky exploded in a blaze of noise and colors, I was jarred suddenly by the memory of the last time I had been to that cafe. It had been just a few months before, when I ran breathlessly under the urgent echo of a different kind of explosion. That day, Cafe Apropos had been the site of a terrorist attack that killed three young women, and I ran from my house into a barrage of screaming people, ambulances, police barricades, and chaos.

On this day we walked pleasantly, warmly, my wife's hand in mine, as fireworks lit the night sky, punctuating a pleasant Mediterranean breeze. We stood outside the cleaned-up Cafe Apropos, looking up. I felt a powerful surge of expectation.

This was a new Israel — a nation that had survived, but whose quest for permanence was only just beginning.

My eyes were held upward, entranced by the streaks of light across the ancient sky.

Bibliography

Arian, Asher. *The Second Israeli Republic.* Haifa: University of Haifa, 1997.
_____, and Michael Shamir. *The Elections in Israel 1992.* Albany: State University of New York Press, 1995.
Collins, Larry, and Dominique LaPierre. *O, Jerusalem!* New York: Simon & Schuster, 1972.
Grossman, David. *Sleeping on a Wire.* Trans. Haim Watzman. London: Jonathan Cape, 1993.
_____. *The Yellow Wind.* Trans. Haim Watzman. New York: Farrar, Straus and Giroux, 1988.
Herzl, Theodor. *The Jewish State (Der Judenstaat).* New York: Dover, 1998 (orig. pub. Vienna, 1886).
Herzog, Chaim. *The Arab-Israeli Wars.* New York: Random House, 1982.
Jabotinsky, Zeev. *The Hebrew State.* Tel Aviv: T. Kopp Press, 1937.
Landau, David. *Piety and Power.* London: Secker Warburg, 1993.
Laquer, Walter, and Barry Rubin, eds. *The Israel-Arab Reader.* New York: Penguin, 1984.
Meir, Golda. *My Life.* New York: Dell, 1975.
Melman, Yossi. *The New Israelis.* Tel Aviv: Schocken, 1993.
Netanyahu, Benjamin. *A Place Among the Nations.* Tel Aviv: Yediot Aharonot, 1995.
Pedatzur, Reuven. *The Triumph of Embarrassment.* Tel Aviv: Bitan, 1996.
Peres, Shimon, and David Landau, eds. *Battling for Peace.* London: Weidenfeld and Nicholson, 1995.
Rolef, Susan Hattis, ed. *Political Dictionary of the State of Israel.* Jerusalem: Jerusalem Publishing House, 1987, 1993.
Rubinstein, Amnon. *From Herzl to Rabin and Beyond.* Tel Aviv: Schocken, 1997.
Sachar, Howard M. *A History of Israel: From the Rise of Zionism to Our Time.* New York: Alfred A. Knopf, 1993.
Segev, Tom. *1949: The First Israelis.* Jerusalem: Domino Press, 1984.

Index

Abas, Josef 105
Abbas, Mahmoud 63, 184
Abdullah, King of Jordan 67
Abu Shaab, Bilal 130
Abulafiya, Hamis 128–129
Adam, Yekutiel 47
Adams, John 4
Aharonson, Malka 146
Al Fatah 44
Allen, Woody 190
Aloni, Miri 87
Amir, Hagai 91
Amir, Yigal 87–88, 90–91, 100, 106, 175
Amital, Yehuda 181
Arafat, Yasser 44–45, 53–54, 62–64, 66–67, 79, 83, 99–101, 103, 106, 181
Aref, Abd Al-Salaam 18
Argov, Shlomo 47
Arian, Asher 144
Ariel 34–36
Artzi, Shlomo 120
Asfour, Yousef 130
Assad, Hefez 84, 106
Association of Civil Rights in Israel 126–127
Ayyash, Yehiya 99–100

Baker, James 58–59
Balfour, Alfred 138
Balfour Declaration 138 139
Banai, Ehud 146
Barabash, Gabi 90
Barak, Aharon 168

Barak, Ehud 145, 182–184, 195
Basel Congress 10
Batsheva Dance Co. 4
Begin, Menachem 22, 28–31, 44–45, 47, 49–50, 52, 54–55, 82, 140, 144–145
Beilin, Yossi 154, 165–166
Beirut 42–49, 52, 84
Ben-Eliezer, Benjamin 84
Ben-Gurion, David 12, 18, 25, 31, 80, 95–96, 122–124, 139, 141, 160–161, 180, 186–187, 190
Ben-Porat, Miriam 158
Ben-Yehuda, Eliezer 159
Benizri, Shlomo 169, 193–194
Bernstein, Carl 30
Betar Youth Movement 31
Black Panthers 143
Black September 44
Bradlee, Ben 30–31
Bronstein, Ofer 138
Brooks, Mel 190
Bruce, Lenny 190
Bucharest 58–59, 68
Burns, George 190
Bush, George 162

Cain, Bentzi 175–176
Carter, Jimmy 45
Caspi, Arye 85
Chafetz, Ze'ev 197–198
Chamoun, Camille 43
Chamoun, Danny 43
Chamoun, Walid 43, 48

Ciobotaru, Virgil 58
Clinton, Bill 64, 103, 181
Cohen, Nir 89
Cohen, Raz 34–36, 61
Collins, Larry 123
Conservative Jewry 170–171

Damti, Menachem 88
Dan, Yosef 162, 170
Dankner, Amnon 152
David, King 192
Dayan, Moshe 19, 22, 27, 61
Democratic Movement for Change 28
Deri, Aryeh 150–152
Devash, Yitzhak 47–50, 53
Diaspora 8, 159
Dreyfus, Alfred 8
Dromi, Uri 94

Eshkol, Levi 18, 21–22, 47, 95

Farbstein, Simha 175
Farbstein, Yehezkel 174–175
Federman, Elisheva 39
Federman, Noam 39
Feiglin, Moshe 73–74, 83
Finkelstein, Arthur 106
Fisch, Asher 3
Franklin, Benjamin 7
Friedman, Menachem 194

Galili, Lily 165
Geffen, Aviv 88
Gelblum, Aryeh 140–141, 152
Genesis 24–25
Gilon, Carmi 84
Gold, Shalom 80
Goldstein, Baruch 65
Gore, Al 4
Gush Emunim 28

Ha'aretz 52, 85, 140, 152, 165, 186
Habad 109, 162
Haber, Eytan 90
Hadad, Saad 45, 47
Hagana 31
Halaby, Jamal 70–71
Hamas 64, 98–99, 100–101
Hananel, Moshe 69
Harel Brigade 60
Harnik, Nati 69
Hazan, Naomi 171

Hebron 24, 39, 46, 65–66, 77
Hecht, Abraham 80
Herut Party 140
Herzl, Theodor 7–10, 12, 25, 47, 121, 145, 159–160, 164, 190
Herzliya 78
Hess, Moshe 8
Hezbollah 52, 165
Hod, Motti 18
Hovevei Zion 8
Hussein, King of Jordan 44, 66–69, 83, 181
Hussein, Saddam 90

Intifada 53–55
Irgun Zva'i Leumi 29
Islamic Jihad 65

Jaber, Abdullah 69
Jabotinsky, Vladimir 121–122, 149
Jackson, Andrew 5
Jaffa 127–130
Jefferson, Thomas 41, 195
Jemayel, Amir 50
Jemayel, Bashir 49–50
Jerusalem Post 53, 176
Josephus 193
Judea, Kingdom of 192–193
Der Judenstaat 8–10, 122, 145

Kadish, Alon 168
Kadoori, Yitzhak 109, 151
Kalifa, Mohammed 68
Kalischer, Hirsch 8
Katznelson, Benny 188–189
Kawash, Yousef 71
Kennedy, John 103
Kfar Tappuah 36–37
Khartoum Conference 61
Khrushchev, Nikita 16
Kimerling, Baruch 186
Kiryat Arba 25, 80
Kopatch, Gil 169

Labor Party 28–29, 59–60, 72, 96, 113, 119, 131, 144–145, 161–162
Landau, David 176
Lapid, Miriam 75
Lapid, Mordechai 66
LaPierre, Dominique 123
Lass, Yoram 90
Law of Return 153

Lebanon War 46–52
Leibowitz, Yehoshua 21
Levinger, Moshe 24, 26, 38, 40, 80
Levy, David 97, 183
Levy, Yair 150
Likud Party 28, 59–60, 65, 72, 96, 113, 131, 144, 153, 162, 184
Lilienblum, Moses Leib 121
Lincoln, Abraham 195

Maariv 152
Manowitz, Zeev 52
Marx, Groucho 190
Masada suicide 193
Masalla, Adisso 136, 154
Meimad Party 161, 183
Meir, Golda 27, 47, 86, 123, 143, 187
Meretz Party 171, 184
Meridor, Dan 183
Milo, Roni 169
Monroe, James 5
Mordechai, Yitzhak 152, 183
Morris, Benny 186
Mossad 24, 27, 188
Mubarak, Hosni 83
Mula, Shula 154

Naphtali, Motti 90–91
Nasser, Gamal Abdel 17–18
National Religious Party 25, 80, 175
National Water Carrier 16
Netanyahu, Benjamin 60, 82, 84, 97–101, 106–113, 151, 180–183, 195
Netanyahu, Benzion 97
Nixon, Richard 27
Nordau, Max 159

One Israel 183–184
Operation Magic Carpet 131
Operation Moses 154
Operation Solomon 154
O'Rourke, P.J. 196
Osirak reactor bombing 46
Oslo Agreement 62–66
Oz, Amos 51, 166–167, 113, 191

Palestine Liberation Organization (PLO) 44–47, 49, 53, 59, 62–64
Pappe, Ilan 186
Peres, Shimon 12, 28, 45, 62–64, 71, 79, 83, 87, 94–108, 118, 131–132, 145, 180, 183–184

Peretz, Yitzhak 151, 153
Pinsker, Leo 8
Poliker, Yehuda 146
Porush, Meir 158
Post-Zionism 187–188

Qureia, Ahmed 62

Rabin, Leah 88, 90, 112
Rabin, Yitzhak 12, 17, 19, 31, 54, 61–68, 79–91, 94, 96, 98, 106, 118, 120, 144, 147, 180
Rabinovoch, Nachum 80
Rafael, Yitzhak 141
Ramati, David 26, 39–40
Ramon, Haim 60, 106
Ravitzky, Avi 161
Reagan, Ronald 103
Reform Jewry 170–171
Rubin, Yoram 88–89

Sadat, Anwar 27, 30, 45
Saul, King 192
Savir, Uri 62, 98
Schneerson, Menachem 109
Schwartzenegger, Arnold 147
Seinfeld, Jerry 190
Shahak, Amnon 187
Shalom Aleichem 163
Shamir, Michal 144
Shamir, Yitzhak 52–55, 58–60, 96–97, 153, 162, 180, 187
Sharabi, Boaz 146
Sharansky, Natan 113
Sharon, Ariel 46, 49–50, 130
Shas 109, 113, 150–152, 168, 183
Shifren, Nahum 36–37
Shifren, Rivka 36–38
Shinui Party 184
Shiran, Vicky 147
Shoval, Zalman 3
Sinai 17, 27, 29, 45
Six Day War 17–22, 172
Solomon, King 192
Suissa, Yamin 153

Taibe 119, 131–133
Tibi, Mohammed Amin 119–121, 125–126, 131–133
Tomb of Patriarchs 66
Topaz, Dudu 145
Tsaban, Yair 154

Turk, Rifat 131
Turner, Ted 191

United Nations 9, 19

Weizmann, Chaim 138
Weizmann Institute 16
Woodward, Bob 30
Wye River Agreement 181

Yavin, Haim 59–60, 64–65, 73
Yedidya, Daniel 177–178

Yediot Aharnoth 20
Yishai, Eli 169
Yom Kippur War 27–28, 162
Yosef, David 151
Yosef, Ovadia 151, 168, 169
Young, Andrew 119

Zionism 8, 22, 25, 29, 51, 138, 149, 159, 186–188, 196
Zohar, Uri 152
Zu Artzeinu 73–75, 83, 91

www.ingramcontent.com/pod-product-compliance
Ingram Content Group UK Ltd.
Pitfield, Milton Keynes, MK11 3LW, UK
UKHW042001140426
5217IPUK00015B/913